THE ISLAMIC REPUBLIC AND THE WORLD

The Islamic Republic and the World

Global Dimensions of the Iranian Revolution

Maryam Panah

Pluto Press
London • Ann Arbor, MI

First published 2007 by Pluto Press
345 Archway Road, London N6 5AA
and 839 Greene Street, Ann Arbor, MI 48106

www.plutobooks.com

British Library Cataloguing in Publication Data
A catalogue record for this book is available from the British Library

Hardback
ISBN-13 978 0 7453 2622 1
ISBN-10 0 7453 2622 6

Library of Congress Cataloging in Publication Data applied for

10 9 8 7 6 5 4 3 2 1

Designed and produced for Pluto Press by
Curran Publishing Services, Norwich
Printed and bound in India.

Dedicated to my children, Leyla and Kilian.

Contents

Chronology of key events since the Second World War

1941   Occupation of Iran by Britain and Russia. Deposition of Reza Shah in favour of his son, Mohammad Reza. Iranian Communist Party founded.

1943   Deployment of US missions in Iran.

1951   Mohammad Mosaddeq becomes Prime Minister. Parliament votes to nationalise British-dominated Anglo-Iranian Oil Company.

1953   Mosaddeq overthrown in coup engineered by US and British intelligence. Shah assumes autocratic control.

1957   SAVAK secret police agency established.

1959   Signature of bilateral defence agreement between United States and Iran.

1960   Confederation of Iranian Students in Europe established.

1963   Launch of shah's 'White revolution' – programme of land reform and socio-economic modernisation.

1964   Khomeini's historic speech against granting of capitulatory rights to United States leads to his later exile.

1965   *Mojahedin-e-Khalq* (MKO) guerrilla organisation established.

1978   Riots, strikes and mass demonstrations against shah escalate.

1979   Shah exiled (January); Khomeini returns to Iran (February); Islamic Republic of Iran proclaimed following referendum (April); 52 Americans taken hostage in US embassy.

1980   New government established and launches nationalisation programme. Invasion of Iran by neighbouring Iraq (September).

1981   Dismissal of first Iranian president, Bani Sadr, repression of MKO and other leftist organisations.

1983   Communist Party of Iran (Tudeh) banned.

1988   Shooting down of Iran Air passenger plane by *USS Vincennes*. Iran accepts ceasefire to end eight-year war with Iraq.

1989   Khomeini dies and is succeeded by Khamenei. Rafsanjani becomes president.

1996	New trade and investment sanctions imposed by United States on Iran.
1997	Khatami becomes president following landslide election victory.
1999	Pro-democracy student demonstrations crushed by regime.
2000	Reformists gain majority in parliament. Judiciary imposes tighter limits on freedom of press.
2001	Khatami re-elected president for second term.
2002	US President Bush describes Iran as part of the 'axis of evil'. Work commences by Russia on construction of Iranian nuclear reactor in Bushehr.
2003	Demonstrations against regime repressed.
2004	Conservatives regain control of parliament. Iran comes under pressure from IAEA to suspend uranium enrichment.
2005	Conservative Mayor of Tehran, Ahmadinejad, elected president. Stand off between Iran and US on nuclear issue.

Acknowledgements

I am first and foremost indebted to Fred Halliday, my PhD supervisor, for inspiring me to study revolutions – and the Iranian case in particular – in an international context. The ideas behind the book developed further through numerous discussions with graduate participants of the modernity and historical materialism seminars at the Department for International Relations, LSE. The manuscript benefited from the insights of Nikki Keddie during my brief stay at UCLA and the comments of my examiners Sami Zubaida and Hazel Smith. It goes without saying that weaknesses and deficiencies in the text remain mine alone.

I am grateful to the Pluto editorial and production teams, and in particular to my editor Chris Carr at Curran Publishing Services, for their speed and efficiency in the race to ensure the manuscript was completed before the arrival of our son in April 2007!

Finally, special thanks go to my mother for her help and support over the years and, of course, to Benno for his comments from the very start and his persistent encouragement and motivation to return to and complete this project.

Maryam Panah
May 2007

Introduction

Over a quarter of a century after the Revolution of 1979, the Islamic Republic of Iran continues to challenge policymakers and scholars alike. The outbreak of the Revolution attracted the attention of state leaders, policy analysts, commentators and social activists globally. The Islamic turn of this ostensibly modern revolution confounded almost all. Its 'anti-imperialist' proclamations, its anti-Western slogans, the pictures of burning US flags and the taking of hostages were cause for consternation, while the Islamic Republic's policy of 'exporting revolution' stimulated a range of hostile responses from policy makers in the region and beyond.

The recent escalation of tension throughout the Middle East has again thrust Iran into the centre-stage in a pivotal role. Domestically, meanwhile, the election in 2005 of Mahmoud Ahmadinejad, the previously little-known hardliner and conservative presidential candidate, took the world by surprise. Here was a new Iranian president who, in contrast to his reformist predecessor, ratcheted up the revolutionary rhetoric against US imperialism, who called for Israel to be 'wiped off the map', and who vehemently asserted Iran's right to the development of nuclear capabilities in the face of international condemnation. The election ended a long period which some had seen as an Iranian 'Thermidor', the onset of which had come with the end of the Iran–Iraq war of the 1980s and with the death of Ayatollah Khomeini in 1989. It signalled the end of the precarious reform and reconciliation attempted by the Khatami governments since 1997. Shortly after his election, Ahmadinejad pronounced that Iran remained not just a regional force to be reckoned with, but also an Islamic revolutionary state which continued to challenge the prevailing international order.

How and why did this resurgent revolutionary populism emerge in 2005? Why is it that after almost three decades, Iran has not, as many expected, consolidated the reform process initiated in the 1990s, but has reasserted the militancy and rhetoric of its early revolutionary years? The key to understanding the 'Ahmadinejad phenomenon' lies in the history of the Iranian Revolution and the early formation of the Islamic Republic. It lies particularly in the early post-revolutionary period – the decade of the 1980s – and the revolutionary rhetoric of the Ayatollah Khomeini in which Ahmadinejad and his generation were schooled. It was also during this period that the institutional structures of the post-revolutionary state were established. Thus, not only does Ahmadinejad's language mirror the nationalist, anti-imperialist and Islamic universalist populism of Khomeini in the 1980s, but the origins of the current state apparatus on which he relies, with all its contradictions and peculiarities, can be found in the 1980s and, in particular, in the war years. It was during that decade that the *Pasdaran* (Islamic Revolutionary Guards), and the *basij* (mobilisation militia) forces – of which not coincidentally Ahmadinejad was an active member – were formed. It was in the early 1980s when the first Revolutionary Guards were dispatched to Lebanon to form the Hezbollah. It was during the same decade that the Islamic Republic's state and para-statal institutions were consolidated in the hands of a religious minority who remain in control of the means of distribution, production and coercion and who are able to wield power and obstruct attempts at true reform. To see Ahmadinejad merely as a face of 'Islamic fundamentalism' in the region is crude and simplistic. He is, rather, to be situated in a contradictory process of post-revolutionary state building and ideology formation in Iran.

To explain Iran's current political order, we must understand not only the revolutionary movement of 1979 – its social bases, discourse and rhetoric – but importantly also the formation of the post-revolutionary state during the 1980s, a period marked more than any event by the long Iran–Iraq war. The Islamic Republic is, in this sense, not just a post-revolutionary state. It is a state formed both by revolution and by war, and the resurgence of militancy since the 2005 election is a manifestation of a 25-year-long contradictory process of post-revolutionary and post-war state formation.

This book deals primarily with the emergence of an Islamic state subsequent to the outbreak of the Iranian Revolution of 1979, its consequences for the global order and the consequences of global responses to it. Chapter 1 sets out a brief theoretical context on states and revolutions, and the framework for the narrative analysis of the subsequent chapters. Chapter 2 provides an account of how international developments and the policies of foreign powers shaped Iranian politics in the decades before the Revolution. It considers the impact of socioeconomic changes during the pre-revolutionary period on various social groups, and the consequent impact on the formation of a revolutionary coalition. In this sense, this chapter shows that the Iranian Revolution was very much a *modern* social revolution. However, the Iranian revolutionary movement also displayed its own specificity and it is at the nexus of the more general impact of global social processes and the particular and specific conditions of the Iranian social formation that we should seek the emergence of the Revolution.

Chapter 3 then develops the theme of specificity as it pertains to the evolution of the rhetoric and ideology of the Revolution. It explains the transformation from modern social revolution to Islamic state by analysing the emergence of 'Khomeinism' – Ayatollah Khomeini's populist politics – in the context of the specific local and global conjuncture and the implications for the internal and external relations of the Islamic Republic of Iran. The chapter brings out the international roots of the hostility of the post-revolutionary state to the prevailing international system and the implications of its populist politics for both domestic politics and external relations.

Chapter 4 focuses on the international responses to the Islamic Republic and the strategies for its containment formulated by a range of international actors. It deals with the concrete policies implemented by a variety of political actors, ranging from leaders of neighbouring countries to governments of leading capitalist states. The main focus of the chapter is how, due to a threat to their social and political interests, regimes of the status quo acted to counter and limit the impact of the Iranian Revolution and Islamic Republic. The main backdrop to this chapter is the Iran–Iraq war, which continued for eight years after the Iraqi invasion of its revolutionary neighbour in September 1980.

Chapter 5 explores the impact of conflict at the international level on the internal relations of the post-revolutionary state. Here the main focus is on the concentration of the means of coercion, production and distribution in the post-revolutionary state, and the contribution of international pressures, specifically war, to this evolution. This process is key to the explanation of the entrenchment of revolutionary institutions which led to the contradictory processes of reform and reaction in the following decades.

In Chapter 6 we investigate the impact of combined international and domestic pressures on the post-revolutionary state and how internal and external pressure together instigate a crisis of the state, leading to the development of the important concept of *maslehat* devised by Khomeini, which gave the state primacy over revolution.

Chapters 7 and 8 together consider the tension between reform and revolution which beset the Islamic Republic in its second and third decades up to the election in 2005 – a resolution, albeit an interim one, of this continual tension. Chapter 7 explains the apparent course of reform taken by first the Rafsanjani and then, more intensively from 1997, the Khatami government, and uncovers the reasons for the ultimate failure of this course and the success of the recent conservative backlash. Chapter 8 discusses the tensions at the international level due to the continued revolutionary foreign policy of the Islamic Republic and the particularly difficult and hostile relationship with the United States. We conclude with a few general remarks which show how the received notion of 'socialisation' of revolutionary states is challenged by the evidence of the post-revolutionary history of Iran.

1 The Iranian Revolution in international context: a theoretical perspective

For some commentators the Islamic militancy of the Iranian regime is merely an expression of the confrontation of an 'Islamic monolith' with the West.[1] Common references to the recent 'Islamic resurgence', of which the Iranian Revolution is regarded as a component, tend to assume that Islamic movements may all be understood as part of a single process explained in terms of a common culture or civilisation.[2] For Bernard Lewis, for instance, contemporary Islamic activism is the continuation of 'the struggle between these rival systems [i.e. Islam and Christendom]' which has 'now lasted for some 14 centuries. It began with the advent of Islam, in the seventh century, and has continued virtually to the present day.' This for Lewis is 'no less than a clash of civilisations— the perhaps irrational but surely historic reaction of an ancient rival against our Judeo-Christian heritage, our secular present, and the world-wide expansion of both'. For Samuel Huntington, similarly, the 'Islamic resurgence' is the 'latest phase in the adjustment of Islamic civilisation to the West, an effort to find the "solution" not in Western ideologies but in Islam.'[3] The West's problems, according to Huntington, are not with violent extremists but with Islam.

> The relations between Islam and Christianity, both Orthodox and Western, have often been stormy. Each has been the other's Other. ... Across the centuries the fortunes of the two religions have risen and fallen in a sequence of momentous surges, pauses and countersurges.

Many have tended to see the event of an 'Islamic Revolution' in Iran and the subsequent establishment of an Islamic state as definitive markers of Islamic resurgence on the global scene. The Islamic Republic of Iran is posed as the model par excellence of Islamic fundamentalism in power. The Iranian Revolution has come to be seen as a trigger for the most recent phase of a trans-historical, centuries-long civilisational battle. 'Given the prevailing perceptions Muslims and Westerners have of each other plus the rise of Islamist extremism,' Huntington argues, 'it is hardly surprising that following the 1979 Iranian Revolution, an intercivilisational quasi war developed between Islam and the West.'[4]

[4]

In contrast, historically sensitive scholarship has pointed to the differences between various Islamist movements and focused attention on the particular conditions that have given rise to the phenomenon of 'political Islam' in each case.[5] While recognising that Islam has in recent decades emerged as a potent political force on a global scale, these scholars emphasise that the form the Islamic revival has taken has varied almost infinitely from one country to another.[6] Analyses of specificity and variation between Islamist movements have successfully challenged the idea of a uniform and homogenous Islam as an actor in international politics.

The argument of this book also is that these movements can only be analysed with reference to context-specific socio-economic and political processes. This book is a case study of the Iranian Revolution of 1979 and the post-revolutionary development embedded in a theoretical framework based on the wider context of capitalist development and its implications for revolution and social upheaval. The analysis is firmly rooted in the belief that the Iranian case – as all such social and political events – is to be studied not through essentialised categories of culture or religion, but with recourse to universally applicable social scientific analysis and, in particular, social processes that have international dimensions.

Social revolutions dotted the history of the twentieth century and there has been an international dimension to both causes and consequences of these revolutions. As Fred Halliday puts it, revolutions are international events.[7] But if revolution has been a favourite subject for historians and sociologists, particularly in the field of comparative study, international relations (IR) scholars have at best approached the subject only tangentially.[8] The result has been a lack of adequate theorisation for the study of international aspects of revolution. Sociological and historical approaches have tended to remain insular while IR has largely ignored revolutions and revolutionary states.[9] Thus, a number of vital questions regarding the emergence and evolution of revolutions and revolutionary states within the international system remain unanswered by orthodox theories: the role of international processes in the emergence of revolutions is largely neglected; revolutionary states are labelled 'rogue' or 'renegade' without explaining why they tend to contest the prevailing international order and exhibit foreign policy goals that differ from those of status quo states; and, finally, there is little adequate explanation of why, how and when revolutionary foreign policy is rescinded through a process of 'socialisation'.

The analysis of the Iranian case presented here is based on the assumption that the emergence of revolutionary crises and social revolution in the modern world are rooted in global social processes. In the modern international system, the mode of social organisation dominant at the global level is capitalism, and social change cannot be considered without taking account of its dynamic. The expansion of capitalism – in the geographic or spatial sense as well as in the intensification and development of the process of capitalist production – has a far-reaching impact in continuously bringing new areas of social life under its logic. However, this expansion does not occur of its own accord as a mechanical and automatic process, but is driven by political actors and institutions operating at the international level. In this schema, revolutions – broadly defined as rapid transformations in the social and political structure – are the outcome of social crises emerging in response to global developments mediated by the activities of these political actors.

The common universalising tendency of revolutionaries, the common rhetoric against the prevailing international status quo, and the common attempt to create qualitatively different societies and global orders are all indicative of the common causes of revolutionary change. It is the similar international origins of disruptive social change that best explains the tendency for all revolutionary leaderships to pursue 'anti-systemic' objectives and to direct their rhetoric against the international status quo. Furthermore, international responses to revolutionary change and revolutionary states ought to be analysed within the context of the existing social order and the attendant vested interests in preserving that order. Under the contemporary international system, capitalist interests have often driven political intervention and counter-revolutionary activity aimed at preventing changes that would hamper the mechanisms of surplus extraction in revolutionary states and other areas where the impact of the revolution could be felt. Such counter-revolutionary activities have usually translated into military intervention on the part of status quo actors and ensuing inter-state conflict. The impact on postrevolutionary states – both on their external relations and on internal development and the balance of social forces – is then considerable.

A theoretical framework: causes and consequences

Capitalism is a mode of social organisation with an expansive drive.[10] The copious literature on 'globalisation', though diverging in the analysis of its dynamics, attests to the reality of this expansion and intensification. One crucial aspect of the expansion and establishment of capitalism is the disruptive manner in which it proceeds, overturning old ways of life and giving cause to potential social upheaval. This is the result of the tendency to bring prevailing social relations under the logic of capitalist market relations though the dispossession of pre-existing direct producers by turning them into wage labourers forced to sell their labour on the capitalist market.

Capitalism has developed unevenly across the globe, resulting in the relatively greater or lesser development of capitalist social relations in various states and localities. The rate of this development is, however, not uniform as more and less capitalistically developed regions coexist contemporaneously, often resulting in pressures on the less developed to compete with and 'catch up' with the more advanced.[11] Crucially, the changes and 'modernisation' entailed in the 'catching up' process has more often than not been led and implemented through political institutions and by state leaders. This is of great significance in explaining social revolutionary change.

As various parts of the globe have come to be subsumed under the logic of capitalism, the tendency has been to invest the social power to extract surplus in the 'international market'. The major implication for the international system has been that 'aspects of social life which are mediated by relations of exchange in principle no longer receive a political definition'.[12] In other words, where social power is exercised in the international market place, it appears to have little to do with political relations and everything to do with purely 'economic' considerations. But power at the international level has two aspects. The first is public/state: the management of the state-system and inter-state relations. The second is private/market: the exploitation of resources and extraction of surpluses. These two 'spheres' are internally connected as social forms of a unified mode of social organisation.

Nowhere is the internal connection of these aspects clearer than in the emergence of social upheaval and revolutions in the modern world. The global expansion of the capitalist market has universally had a disruptive impact on social life. Under conditions of uneven global capitalist development, the prime movers of this expansion have, as we noted before, more often than not been states – both local ones and external imperial or colonial ones. The state has directly and *visibly* been involved in the socio-economic transformation and upheavals of various societies. Often those in control of the state have carried out these changes at the behest of foreign powers or collaborated with international actors, and the latter have assumed a direct or indirect role in the exploitative process. The 'expansion' of capitalism, in other words, has been mediated by the geopolitical institutions of the international system.[13]

These processes all disrupt societies by uprooting old modes of social existence, altering prevailing social structures, and resulting in the rise and fall of various social classes. Examples are the separation of peasants from land, creating massive urban migration, the rise not only of a modern working class but also of large unemployed populations who then join the ranks of 'urban marginals', and so on. All these give rise to grievances, which may then be traced to the role of the local state and its international collaborators as the source of change and dislocation. Social struggles against the effect of the expanding capitalist market have repeatedly led to contest and ultimate overthrow of 'modernising' states. Where the impact of the social power of capital to extract surpluses has been borne by domestic social classes, this has emerged as a political contest that has revealed the inner connection of 'political' and 'economic' social forms. Where this connection has been more visible and obvious – in other words where political institutions have taken a more active part in altering the mode of social organisation – the occurrence of revolution aimed at overthrowing those institutions has been all the more imminent.

This is clearly the case where exploitation is not merely mediated but actually carried out directly by the state – the fusion of social and political power – but also where a local or external (colonial, imperial) juridical power intervenes to create the conditions for the exercise of social power within the market. Thus, potential revolutionary coalitions have emerged as anti-colonial struggles and revolutions on the periphery of global capitalism, where the object of revolutionary overthrow has not merely been the state apparatus, but also imperialist powers, which have intervened to create the conditions for the extraction of surplus by forcing open 'free markets' and thereby acting in the capacity of the state-backers of international capital.

Thus the Russian Revolution of 1917, for instance, was preceded by social structural changes resulting from rapid state-led industrialisation using foreign capital and technology. The role of foreign or imperial powers in altering the social matrix of many colonies or semi-colonial areas laid the ground for anti-colonial and radical nationalist movements, of which the Vietnamese, Egyptian, Cuban and Nicaraguan are examples. In the Iranian case, as we shall see in the next chapter, these processes were combined. Socio-economic changes consequent upon the state-led development of capitalism combined with a history of imperialist intervention to create the conditions for the formation of a successful revolutionary movement.

Of course, these social processes cannot be sufficiently explained in abstract terms, but depend on the particular historical circumstances of the particular social formation concerned. This is meant in two senses. Firstly, the very unevenness in the development of capitalism results in differences in socio-economic circumstances, variations in the form of the state and balance of social classes. Secondly, revolution is not the necessary outcome of a particular balance of forces, but also requires the formation of a 'collective will'. The subjective positions of social classes clearly display numerous variations in which cultural and 'national-popular' elements play a crucial part.[14] Ideologies inform the structure of institutions, the nature of social co-operation and conflict, and the attitudes and predisposition of the population. These ideologies however may be conceived of as a 'mix' made up of the fusion of 'popular' elements and global ideological structures that are articulated in particular ways and may give rise to revolutionary discourses that mobilise the aggrieved populations.[15] We shall see in Chapters 2 and 3 how this ideological battle was played out in post-revolutionary Iran.

Where social revolutions have succeeded, they have then disrupted the social and political relations which underpinned the pre-existing mode of exploitation and extraction of resources. Revolutions may overthrow states that previously acted to guarantee the conditions for extraction of surplus by the dominant classes. Of course, under revolutionary conditions, the sphere of indeterminacy is widened as previous social relations are disrupted and new ones are yet to be established. It is then in the dynamic between the activities of the social actors participating in the revolution and the responses to the revolution by those whose interests are affected that its consequences are to be determined.

In this theoretical light, we can address the shortcomings of accounts that assert the 'rogue' behaviour of post-revolutionary regimes. A number of related developments need to be accounted for. Firstly, the pattern of hostility of modern social revolutions towards the international status quo and the corresponding drive to 'export revolution' must be explained. Secondly, the responses of status quo states to their revolutionary counterparts – often in the form of aggression or 'containment' of the post-revolutionary state – and the consequences for the revolutionary regime need to be considered. Finally, we need to explain how revolutions have had an impact on the broader regional and global order, and what the longer-run implications of the occurrence of revolutions are for the international system.

If as we have suggested, social revolutionary movements emerge in response to social changes rooted in global processes, it should come as no surprise that revolutionaries often consider the international system and its corresponding socio-economic and political structures to be the 'root of all evil' and the source of their social problems, although this disposition may be expressed in a variety of forms of rhetoric – the evils of international capitalism, Yankee imperialism, Westernisation, global arrogance and so on – and may take different trajectories, depending on the local and global conjunctural circumstances. As the impact of the international expansion of capitalism is felt by populations and is seen as the source of exploitative processes, post-revolutionary regimes have often sought to withdraw from the realm of the capitalist market and follow an alternative trajectory of socio-economic development in an effort to establish a qualitatively different type of society.

The significance of the impact of revolutionary states on the global order has been debated and disputed by various schools of thought. Adherents of the realist school of international relations consider the internal upheaval within states to be of little consequence for the international order.[16] From an ostensibly radically different perspective, proponents of World Systems Theory seem to reach similar conclusions. For the latter, the dominance of a capitalist world economy means that the presence of states following alternative developmental trajectories makes no dent in the world system.[17] According to this view even if every nation in the world adopted such a strategy, the world system would still be a capitalist system.[18] According to these theorists, existence in a capitalist world economy defines a capitalist state. But this is not only to elide the variations in production relations amongst different states, it also ignores the actual attempt by some states to withdraw from the realm of the capitalist market. More importantly for us here, how do we explain the continued hostility of the dominant capitalist states towards revolutionary regimes if they ultimately have little influence on the system?

The pursuit of alternative courses of development can, in fact, seriously affect international capitalism. In a predominantly capitalist world order, there is an imperative to counter and contain radical revolutionary movements through the agency of the dominant powers. As we have already noted above, under capitalist social relations, social power is exercised through the extraction of surpluses in the 'free market'. However, the state is the guarantor of the institutions through which the exercise of this 'private' power is mediated. Revolutions may, by overthrowing existing states, threaten the power of capital in the sphere of the market. As a result of the activities of subordinated classes, the state may no longer act to serve the interests of the capitalist class. The potential withdrawal by revolutionary regimes of their societies from the realm of the capitalist market, in effect, constitutes a move to cut the political power invested in that realm. Robbed of the 'hidden' mechanism of exploitation, the only means to restore that power is to use the visibly coercive instruments of force. This then is where the public political aspect of international power – which appears as the management of the international system – is most explicitly manifested giving a twist to the story of the 'socialisation' of 'rogue', 'renegade' or revolutionary states. In the context of a dominant capitalist order, 'socialisation' can now be conceived of as the imposition or restoration of the mechanisms for the exercise of the social power of extraction. The hostile relations between status quo and revolutionary states may have at their root the obstacles posed by the revolutionary regime to the exercise of a more incisive form of social power.

These processes are best exemplified by the policies of the United States, as the leading capitalist power and hegemon through most of the twentieth century. A threat to US interests was posed by the potential of anti-capitalist social revolution to alter prevailing property relations. The danger of revolutions for capitalist interests entailed the potential limits on the domain of the 'free market' where surplus would be extracted, and the overthrow of states which guaranteed the existence of the market and through which the exercise of this social power was mediated. It in fact mattered little whether this came in the form of a communist movement or a radical nationalist one; where anti-capitalist outcomes loomed social revolutions had to be confronted. The interests of global capital dictated the firm integration of these states into the capitalist world market. Since the middle of the twentieth century, the United States has been committed to containing antisystemic revolution wherever it developed across the globe.

These are the forces underlying counter-revolutionary strategies: the drive to intervene in the internal processes and evolution of the revolutionary regimes, and the pressure to 'contain' the revolution and prevent its spread to other areas. As we noted, revolutionary regimes have often seen the prevailing international system as an exploitative one. This predisposition and the claim to a different alternative model for society have translated into a policy of international promotion of revolution and its 'export'. The internationalist drive of the Iranian Revolution, which called for 'Islamic universalism', will be elaborated later in the book. Regimes of the status quo have in turn not failed to respond to these impulses with severe measures. Conventional accounts offer only vague analyses of the responses of international actors to revolutionary regimes which tend to be limited to structural models. The hostility of status quo states to their revolutionary counterparts is explained only in terms of the 'rogue' status of the latter, and no adequate account of the mechanisms of the alleged process of 'socialisation' has been given. We may now be better placed to explain the international pressures on revolutionary states and the policies of 'containment' with respect to the new post-revolutionary regimes.

It is the drive of revolutionary regimes to export revolution and change the configuration of the international system that threatens the vital interests of those who wield social and political power. Elites in control of other states face threats to their political authority and countenance destabilisation of their regimes in face of the spread of revolutionary fervour. These ruling elites then take action ranging from accommodation, containment or 'critical dialogue' to economic and political sanctions or outright counter-revolutionary invasion and war. A clear example of international reaction, as we shall see later in Chapter 4, was the Iraqi invasion of post-revolutionary Iran, at least partly due to the threat of revolution in Iraq and the subsequent assistance to the Iraqi regime from other regional and global actors.

The hostility of external powers towards the revolutionary regime, which is expressed in a variety of ways including the imposition of sanctions, withdrawal of capital, providing aid to opposition groups, and even war, takes its toll on the revolutionary regime and serves decisively to affect the internal constitution and political formation of the post-revolutionary regime. These actions also help to explain the pressure on post-revolutionary states to submit to the dictates of the domestic and international capitalist class. The increasing concentration of the means of production, administration and coercion in a new 'state-class' may be a feature of post-revolutionary regimes. However, the dependence of state managers on a certain level of economic activity limits the strategies available to them. State managers are not completely autonomous.[19] As we shall see in the later chapters of this book, in Iran, their strategies were often tied to and dependent on class interests – in particular that of merchant capital – in the post-revolutionary years.

The impact of the response and reaction to revolutions has bolstered the conviction of most revolutionary leaders that the revolution needs to be spread internationally in the search for a greater base of allies and support. In Iran, Khomeini repeatedly insisted that the 'Islamic Revolution' needed to extend beyond the borders of the Iranian state to survive the hostility of external powers. The drive to universalise and 'export' revolution is on the one hand powered by ideology, but on the other it is also motivated by the need for allies in the context of a hostile international environment. Thus, revolutionary regimes engage in a variety of means of international organisation, from the declaration and formation of 'internationals' to the extension of material and moral support to other potential revolutionary coalitions regionally and globally.

These activities counter further international resistance as powers of the status quo strive to contain the impact of the revolution, resulting in an interactive dynamic of challenge and response between the revolution and the status quo. However, while various forces, including the coercion of status quo powers, stand in the way of the internationalist drive of revolutionaries, revolutions may nonetheless carry significant consequences for the regional and global order both in the immediate term and in the longer run. Firstly, and more immediately, the adversarial dynamic between revolutionary and status quo states may escalate into military conflicts, which then have an impact not only on the internal structure of the societies concerned, but also on the regional and global order and politics.

Furthermore, the impact of revolutions transcends the immediate consequences of military engagements, internationally supported civil wars and the like. Revolutions on the one hand become models for action by masses that are dissatisfied with the status quo. On the other hand, they prompt regimes of the status quo to pre-empt and prevent revolutionary mobilisations through a variety of strategies, from direct intervention and 'counter-insurgency' policies to pre-emptive reforms and limited social change. A global dynamic is set in motion that surpasses the immediate effects of the original revolution.

Despite the efforts of status quo regimes to forestall revolution, however, there remain both a 'push factor' and a 'pull factor' which encourage the repercussion of revolutions globally. The 'push factor' stems, as we have argued, from the incessant global drive of capitalism. This is a continuously disruptive process and leads to the dislocation of societies through changes to their previous modes of life. Under such circumstances of constant crisis and upheaval, the ideological rhetoric and material support of revolutionary regimes, the 'pull factor', may have considerable appeal to various social groups across the globe. This is not to corroborate the idea of a domino-like spread of revolution, but to suggest that successful revolutions serve as models of action for other potential coalitions of social classes.

Revolutions and revolutionary states thus contribute to the development of the international system by becoming part of its history, with effects which are unpredictable. These effects may diverge from the original intentions of those who participate in the revolution, as their ideas are appropriated by others and transformed in numerous ways – an impact which eludes theories which stop at the foreign policy of the state when considering the external effects of revolutionary states. These repercussions may be observed across the globe and long after the original crisis and revolutionary outbreak. Social revolutions within particular states change the international system not just by triggering pre-emptive measures by actors wishing to preserve the status quo, but also by contributing to the uneven historical development of that system by simply existing within it.

Revolution and the Islamic Republic: an analysis

The emergence of an 'Islamic state' subsequent to the successful outbreak of the Iranian Revolution of 1979 seemed to turn on its head the widely-held view that revolutions herald progress and modernisation. The modern phenomenon of revolution had occurred in a seemingly strong and semi-developed state as a result of participation of the masses in popular demonstrations and strikes leading to the overthrow of the 'old regime'. In place of the latter, however, a state was established led by Islamic clerics apparently claiming legitimacy from the seventh-century rule of the Prophet Mohammed and proposing a return to tradition.

Did this vindicate those who perceived the Iranian revolutionary movement as primarily religious or cultural? Did this mean that the rise of the revolutionary movement, the actual success of the Revolution in overthrowing the monarchy, the establishment and survival of an Islamic state in Iran, and finally the subsequent international repercussions are all explained by cultural or religious factors?

Explanations in terms of the peculiar features of culture and religion, or even the allegedly uniquely revolutionary features of Shi'i Islam, are contravened by the historical account.[20] The quietism, and therefore acquiescence to the status quo, of the religious leadership through long periods of the modern history of Iran refutes this. Although the religious leadership does have some history of political activity in Iran, this by no means extended to the whole religious body or to a permanent role in history. The quietist stance of Ayatollah Boroujerdi, the Grand Ayatollah of the pre-1960s period, while the active opposition was led by secular nationalists attests to this. Furthermore, the motives for the participation of religious figures in various movements remain palpably ambivalent, as is evident from statements by the foremost religious elite in Iran with respect to a variety of social issues, and their severe admonition of the 'radical Islam' of lay religious intellectuals until very shortly before the Revolution.[21]

The popular form of the Iranian Revolution and the participation of modern social forces with secular demands as well as the modern discourse of the movement – including modern concepts from revolution to anti-imperialism, national independence and socialism – pointed to the need for greater elaboration of the emergence of a heterogeneous coalition of forces with the state as the target of their collective actions.[22] Socio-economic development, made possible by state revenue obtained through oil sales, took place both in the countryside and in developing urban industries, while a parallel change in the political system was prevented by the old regime, which was maintained by coercive measures of the military establishment, intelligence and security organisations, court patronage, a one-party state and extended bureaucracy, all of which were made possible by the plentiful oil revenue. In other words, revolution was consequent upon *uneven* development.[23] The focus on state breakdown has in fact been characteristic of an area of scholarship of the Iranian Revolution influenced by the state-centred neo-Weberian school of sociology.[24]

Despite the advances of the sociological and structural accounts of the Iranian revolution, a number of areas of analysis have remained wanting. Firstly, there is a neglect of the historical role of international agency in the pre-revolutionary state-building process. By screening out this historical legacy, the nationalist and anti-imperialist discourse of the Revolution is either reduced to particular classes or explained in terms of cultural factors and 'xenophobia'. Secondly, the development of the pre-revolutionary state within the context of an uneven global economy and heterogeneous international system needs elaboration. While, some scholars have made references to notions of 'uneven development', this has usually been in the context of the alleged unevenness of economic and political development. The claim is that while economic development takes place, political institutions remain archaic. However, a historical account of the process would consider the characteristics of such development under conditions of unevenness at a global level. The role of the state in socio-economic development can thus be seen as taking place under conditions of international competition where external exigencies force the state to become the initiator of technological change that affects the internal social structure. A more complete discussion of the creation of the structural conditions for revolution would give greater consideration to the subjective factor of backwardness under conditions of uneven development at an international level. Two issues must then be addressed. First, under what conditions does backwardness become a social and political problem and under what conditions may it be seen as the motive force of revolution? Second, comparison with the more technologically advanced countries may drive the impetus for a catching-up process, setting in motion a process of reforms not due to an inherent interest in reforms but because they are necessary for the catching-up process.

This, however, raises the third question of what particular set of circumstances enables the evolution of a successful revolutionary movement. Why is it that only certain states are vulnerable to revolutionary overthrow and others which have faced similar pressures have managed to escape the same fate? Many analyses concentrate on the specific characteristics of states and their internal organisation. But the role of ideology in the making of revolutions is also of crucial relevance, and paying adequate attention to 'ideological structures' necessarily entails an examination of the international historical context of ideas. This requires an understanding of ideology not as a programmatic set of actions, but as a prominent 'world view' which is at the same time constantly regenerated and erupts in different guises as the social context of world historical time changes. It is only with such a perspective that we can begin to discuss the rise to power of the religious leadership in Iran and the post-revolutionary outcome of a clerical-led state.

2 The Iranian Revolution: internal and external causes

In this chapter we consider how the old regime, the Pahlavi state under the shah, was shaped by and evolved under international influences, particularly of the United States. This historical legacy is central to the making of the Iranian Revolution in two senses. On the one hand it created a national-popular culture with a memory of external intervention in the affairs of the country that played a vital role in the formation of revolutionary ideology. On the other hand, foreign pressure and influence affected the social structural changes in Iranian pre-revolutionary society. While prior to the era of American influence in Iran capitalist social relations hardly existed, through this period external pressures encouraged a process of state-led capitalist development with tangible consequences for the fabric of Iranian society.

External interests and influence in Iran need to be conceived within the broader picture of international developments and the world historical conjuncture. Thus, assessment of the policy of foreign powers from the Second World War and its impact on Iranian social and political development can only be undertaken in the context of the historically situated structure of global capitalism, the onset and consolidation of the cold war, and the rise of movements of national liberation and self-determination across the globe. Against this background, the interests and activities of the major capitalist powers, at the head of which stood the United States, took novel forms and features which would play a decisive role in the internal development of countries of the periphery, including Iran. The post-war period saw the rise of US power on a global scale and the establishment of US hegemony within the international capitalist order. US influence in Iran forms a part of the broader global strategies of this power.

Historical legacy of foreign influence in Iran

In the first half of the twentieth century Persia (later Iran) was for both strategic and commercial reasons the scene of incessant great power rivalry and the object of influence and even occupation. Prior to and during the Second World War, Reza Shah, Iran's dictatorial monarch attempted to play off classical Russian and British rivalry by harbouring relations with Nazi Germany, leading to the occupation of Iran by the two allied powers and the forced abdication of the monarch in 1941. The succession to the throne of his son, Mohammad Reza, thereby coincided with the securing of geo-strategic advantages for the Allies. Economic interests revolved around the oil industry, which remained an enclave with almost no linkages to the domestic economy and was controlled by the British-owned Anglo-Iranian Oil Company (AIOC). While the terms of the British concession had been re-negotiated they nevertheless provided very favourable terms for AIOC. However, during the early part of the 1940s both the Soviet Union and the United States began to exert pressure on the Iranian government for the negotiation of new oil concessions.[1]

Most accounts of US policy in Iran, tracing orthodox histories of the cold war as a political rivalry between two blocs, have focused on US concerns regarding a communist takeover in various states across the globe, either through Soviet expansionism or infiltration and insurgency of the Soviet-dependent Communist Party. The 'revisionist' critiques of US foreign policy thus centred on the misinterpretation by scholars and state leaders of 'indigenous nationalist forces' as agents of communism. This, however, is a false debate that fails to take account of the underlying interest of the United States, as the leading capitalist power. The kernel of US concern was not mere domination by the Soviet Union, but the potential of *any* anti-capitalist movement to adversely affect the prospects of global capital accumulation. Soviet influence was, of course, one such potential, but other radical nationalist movements could have made a similar impact. The US policy of establishing greater influence in Iran and the history of intervention in the social and political development of Iran in the post-war period need to the regarded within this broader context of global interests.

On the one hand, the communist challenge posed a consistent dilemma, reinforced by Iran's proximity to the USSR. On the other hand, contemporaneous global developments such as the revolutions in China, Vietnam and other instances of anti-capitalist revolt bolstered the conviction that these movements had to be managed and contained. The Soviet Union not only aimed to obtain a commercial foothold in Iran by pressing for an oil concession in the North, but also sought political advantage by supporting radical movements which emerged during the 1940s in Iranian Azerbaijan and Kurdistan. Soviet forces continued to occupy northern Iran after the end of the war as an autonomous government was announced by the left-wing leader Pishevari in summer 1945, and a counterpart was announced in Kurdistan in early 1946. The United States adopted an uncompromising opposition to the Soviet occupation, leading to what was arguably the first crisis of the cold war between the superpowers in 1946 as the United States became directly involved in demanding the withdrawal of the Soviet forces and played an active part in crushing the two radical movements. Furthermore, US strategic interests in Iran were demonstrated by the establishment of a number of diplomatic, financial and military missions in the country. In 1943 six major US missions were already located in Iran. Involvement was subsequently increased with the establishment of the US army mission (ARMISH) and the Military Assistance Advisory Group (MAAG) in 1950.

The immediate post-war years formed a period of domestic socio-political developments in Iran making for a situation of increased political activity that threatened capitalist interests and led ultimately to imperialist intervention to protect these concerns. The war had given rise to a series of economic difficulties. Despite a period of modernisation instigated by Reza Shah prior to the Second World War, largely relating to infrastructural development of transport and communications, Iran remained a largely agricultural society where pre-capitalist social relations predominated. Rural areas in which the majority of Iranians lived were the domain of extreme poverty.[2] In the cities, the traditional *bazaar* merchants suffered from the post-war decline in demand, and shortages – including food scarcity – became widespread. Meanwhile, educational reforms and the previous limited modernisation led to changes in popular expectations and rising demands, with the emergence of a new politically active intelligentsia. Many radical intellectuals were released from prison as the inter-regnum following Reza Shah's abdication spelt a period of relative political freedom. Political parties and publications proliferated and numerous incidents of urban unrest emerged in this period.

The communist Tudeh Party, formed in 1941, played a significant role in the revival of trade union activism that had been repressed under Reza Shah, leading to the formation of the Central Council of Federated Trade Unions in May 1944 and the support of a general oil strike in 1946. In fact, spring and summer of 1946 marked a peak of Tudeh influence as 1 May was celebrated with huge demonstrations.[3]

A nationalist movement also emerged focused on the question of the control of Iranian oil. In the broader international context of the rise of anti-colonial movements, demands for greater sovereignty and control over the natural resources of the country, resentment against the AIOC and foreign oil concessions grew, providing the impetus for the rise of this anti-imperialist nationalist movement which called for Iranian ownership of oil. This then formed the backdrop to the rise of the National Front movement, whose core demand at the time was the nationalisation of the oil industry that was finally pushed through during Mohammad Mosaddeq's pivotal rise through the Iranian parliament (*majles*) to the premiership in 1951.

The centrality of Iranian oil to British imperialist interests had already been indicated by the dispatch of naval reinforcements to the Abadan area during the strike of 1946.[4] Nationalisation of oil in 1951 thus clearly dealt a blow to the immediate interests of the AIOC and the British state which benefited from the taxes levied on the company. However, the movement posed a broader threat to the interests of the capitalist world order which better explains the US involvement in Iran. Firstly, the nationalisation movement threatened to limit the extraction of surpluses and profits not only of the AIOC but also future potential US interests, indicated by the eagerness already displayed by Vacuum Oil (later Mobil) and other US oil companies in obtaining a share in Iran. Secondly, the movement could potentially have led to the complete withdrawal of Iran from the capitalist market either by leading Iran into the 'Soviet bloc' or the prevalence of a radical nationalist government that would have made such demands. Thirdly, the potential global impact of Iranian nationalisation could damage capitalist interests elsewhere as the Iranian movement could serve as a model for other governments. Certainly, the concern that if Iranians carried out their plans countries such as Venezuela and Saudi Arabia, on whose supplies the United States depended, might follow suit loomed on the minds of US policy makers.[5]

These strategic interests dictated the active engagement of the US government in protecting immediate and future property relations by opposing the nationalisation movement. The United States supported the British boycott of Iranian oil after 1951 not only directly but also by preventing Japanese, Italian and other interested customers from purchasing Iranian oil by threatening the withdrawal of much-needed US aid. With the inauguration of the Eisenhower administration in Washington, a political environment of greater willingness to intervene directly prevailed. Involvement of the Central Intelligence Agency in the subsequent *coup d'etat* of 1953 engineered jointly with British Intelligence, which overthrew the Mosaddeq government and reinstated the shah as dictatorial monarch, was a crucial turning point and the beginning of an enduring close relationship between various administrations in Washington and the Pahlavi regime which was to last almost three decades until the 1979 Revolution.

The role of respective administrations in Washington in establishing and helping to maintain a dictatorial monarchy in Iran not only tied the fate of US influence in the country with that of the *ancien regime*, but also had implications for the direction of internal social developments in Iran that contributed to the structural prerequisites of the Revolution and were decisive in the formation and emergence of the revolutionary movement. The advent of the Revolution of 1979 and the legacy of US influence and intervention in Iran are closely bound by this history. In the aftermath of the 1953 coup, the Iranian regime became visibly and explicitly dependent on the political support of the United States while serving the latter through guaranteeing the tight integration of Iran into the capitalist market and the military and security system of the Western world. If the coup itself, criticised and reprimanded across the political spectrum in Iran, left a 'running wound that bled for 25 years', subsequent developments and relations between the regime and the United States further implicated Washington in the undertakings and policies of the Pahlavi state and the socio-political evolution of Iran.[6]

A subsequent agreement between Iran and a consortium of foreign oil companies, while raising the royalties paid to Iran to a 50–50 basis, left control of production and marketing decisions in the hands of the companies. A 40 per cent stake was now held by US corporations, thus putting an end to the British monopoly. However, the interests of the capitalist world in general and the United States as the paramount and unrivalled beneficiary within it were principally served by the integration of Iran into the capitalist market. The 1955 Law for the Attraction and Promotion of Foreign Investments confirmed this situation by providing a variety of benefits and incentives for international capital, including tax breaks, exemption from duties and the legal repatriation of profits, while licenses were limited to a few companies in each field so that monopoly profits were guaranteed.[7]

The tightening integration of Iran into the capitalist bloc was sustained by a stream of US support and assistance. The Eisenhower Doctrine, which guaranteed the granting of US military and economic assistance to regimes 'threatened by communism' either through armed invasion or internal insurgency, provided the ideological justification for the widespread US aid to Iran in ensuing years. The $45 million emergency loan which immediately followed the coup began a period of readily forthcoming US aid such that between 1953 and 1960 the United States granted $567 million in economic and $450 million in military aid to Iran.[8] The United States also became involved in the establishment and training of the international security apparatus. US advisors formed a permanent secret mission supporting the SAVAK (*sazman-e ettela'at va amniyyat-e keshvar*) set up in 1957, which engaged in espionage and counter-espionage and domestic repression such that by 1975 Amnesty International proclaimed Iran as the state with the worst human rights record in the world.[9]

In 1955 the United States supported the formation of the Baghdad Pact — a formal defence agreement between Turkey, Pakistan, Iran and Iraq tying these states firmly to the Western military alliance and steering them away from the course of 'non-alignment' that could again have led to a withdrawal from the capitalist sphere. Iran remained a member of the Central Treaty Organisation (CENTO), which replaced the Baghdad Pact after the withdrawal of Iraq in 1958 subsequent to the overthrow of the monarchy. Furthermore, following the Iraqi revolution, the US military commitment to Iran was reinforced with the signing in March 1959 of the Bilateral Defence Agreement which stated that the United States would undertake 'such appropriate action including the use of armed forces in order to assist the government of Iran at its request in the case of aggression against Iran'.[10] The shah's Iran thus remained firmly integrated into the US-led strategic alliance and served the geopolitical interests of the West in a number of ways, including the consistent support of the state of Israel, defence of the US engagement in Vietnam and adoption of a security role in the Persian Gulf after the British withdrawal, and involvement in local conflicts such as those in Oman and the Horn of Africa.

Iran's demands for military aid, later replaced by sales — thus forming an outlet for US arms manufacturers — were therefore consistently met. Military sales increased dramatically from $0.2 million in 1964 to $12.9 million in the following year, increasing steadily to $127 million in 1970.[11] In the wake of the Vietnam War, the United States adopted the 'Nixon Doctrine' of arming Third World clients to fight regional 'proxy wars'. As US Undersecretary of State Richardson explained with regard to the Persian Gulf area in 1970, 'the Nixon Doctrine regards that in order to realise the objectives of peace and security the US should focus all attention on the states of the region, in particular Iran.'[12] In May 1972 the Nixon administration made an unprecedented promise to the shah to provide any conventional weapons ordered by him.[13] In the ensuing years up to 1977 the regional interests of the two countries were increasingly fused — a trend that was compounded by close personal contacts maintained between the shah and influential figures in the US administration or corporate realm, including Kermit Roosevelt, Richard Nixon and David Rockefeller.

In sum, the Pahlavi state under the shah came into existence with the influence and assistance of external powers, and continued to be supported by the United States in a bid to ensure the strategic interests of the capitalist world. The internal implication of this external source of support was to allow the state a certain degree of autonomy from domestic social forces. However, its corollary was that the United States was implicated in subsequent social processes in the eyes of the Iranian population. Before we elaborate on the implications of this subjective association and the role it played in the emergence of the Revolution, we shall consider the socio-economic development of Iranian society in the pre-revolutionary decades which led to substantial changes in the social configuration of the country. As we shall see, this process was not without notable and international influences that had significant consequences.

Socio-economic development and structural change

Though there is considerable debate over the nature of socio-economic development in Iran in the decades preceding the Revolution of 1979, and specifically on the extent of capitalist development, there is little doubt that by 1979 old social relations, including former peasant–landlord arrangements, had been irrevocably changed and that some capitalist development had taken place.[14] The development of capitalism took place not through 'indigenous development' of a domestic bourgeoisie in Iran, but by the imitation of and often coercive importation from more advanced countries. Moreover as Maxine Rodinson noted of Muslim countries – and as may be said of most states of the periphery more generally – the state played a significant role in assisting capitalist development as 'the attitudes of modern capitalism have not developed spontaneously ... and because it was in fact a question of importing, by conscious decision from above, structures that were foreign to these countries.'[15]

Capitalist development in Iran was influenced by external or international forces in two senses which are, nonetheless, not unique to the Iranian case. Firstly, international actors, more specifically the United States under the Kennedy administration, encouraged social structural changes in Iran which inaugurated the spread of capitalist social relations. The promotion of this development by the Pahlavi state was thus launched at the behest of and with the support of Washington. Secondly, however, industrial development was undertaken by the regime in imitation of more advanced forms and by adoption of techniques prevailing in the industrially advanced countries. Thus, the specific world historical conjuncture and structural conditions of the global economy made a decisive impact on the shape of this evolution in Iran, though mediated through the state.

In the 1960s a series of social reforms, the central feature of which was a programme of land redistribution, was instigated by the regime and labelled the shah's 'white revolution'. The details of the land reform programme, initiated by the Amini government in January 1961 and declared complete in 1971, have been extensively studied elsewhere and need not detain us here.[16] Of greater relevance is the role of international pressure in the instigation of these reforms, and the centrality of the state – backed by external forces – in this process and the peculiar development of capitalism in Iran.

International pressure played a significant part in the initiation of the changes which took place in Iran in the 1960s. Land reform, the centrepiece of the social reform process, was the means by which the state encouraged the capitalist transformation of rural areas.[17] However, the rationale behind the reform process went beyond an economic one. A political motive of pre-empting revolutionary change in Iran formed the backdrop to pressure from the United States on the shah's regime to instigate limited agrarian reform.

The Cuban Revolution of 1959 had revealed the potential revolutionary threat posed to Third World dictatorships devoid of a popular base.
United States policy makers were also deeply concerned by Soviet insistence on the inevitability of revolutionary change in these societies. This
prompted the Kennedy administration to formulate policies designed to
forestall revolution from below by encouraging reform from above. The
strategy was most explicit in the formation of the Alliance for Progress
programme announced in March 1961 for Latin American states, which
aimed at effecting limited and controlled social change largely through
the instigation of a series of land reforms.[18]

A strategy similar to that of the Alliance for Progress was adopted
with respect to Iran, and was also designed to stop at limited reforms.
It was designed to circumvent peasant unrest by creating a rural class
of property owners loyal to the prevailing regime. Thus reforms were
widely seen as a 'substitute for revolution in the countryside'.[19]

In the early 1960s, concerns regarding the political stability of Iran
multiplied as the potential threat of communism communicated both
by presidential advisors within the administration and the shah
himself coincided with the very real manifestation of internal unrest
within the country. In 1960 protests against rigged elections and a dete-
riorating economic situation led to demonstrations in Tehran led by the
National Front. In May 1961 violence erupted in Iranian cities as
teachers demonstrated against low wages and bad conditions. These
and other demonstrations of social discontent were suppressed, often
with brute force, by the regime. Against this backdrop of international
and domestic events, recommendations for change emanated from
policy circles in Washington. US policy shifted towards making aid
and support conditional on the pursuit of a programme of reforms.
The United States administration was increasingly of the view that it
might be important to US strategic and economic interests in the area
to have an Iranian government with a broader internal base. US loans
and grants decreased and the shah was urged to support a reform
programme.

The US policy recommendations encompassed three aspects. Firstly,
the instigation of a series of social reforms centred on the redistribution
of land was advocated aimed at undermining the power of rural dominant classes and circumventing peasant rebellions. This would create a
broader base for the regime by cutting landlord power and creating a
wider class of peasant owners with the effect also of establishing capitalist social relations in Iran making for the development of capitalism.
Secondly, public and ostentatious gestures by the shah towards
proclaiming his independence from the West and profession of greater
respect for nationalists and nationalism were advised. Thirdly, in order
to prevent popular upheavals, counter-insurgency activities and state

repression through the use of coercive instruments were ultimately also supported. As far as the Kennedy administration was concerned, 'if reform failed then friendly elites were to employ military force to smother popular uprisings'.[20]

The ensuing changes to the socio-economic structure of the country as a result of these reforms were immense. On the one hand, land reform led to a reduction of former landlord power. On the other hand, though the traditional land-owning elites were weakened, this did not initially have a major impact on the ability of the members of this class to reproduce themselves. Rather, the programme helped to shift the capital of landlords into industry while most former landowners diversified their holdings also to include urban land, real estate or even foreign securities.[21] The major impact of the reforms for the rural areas was the establishment of capitalist social relations and the corresponding creation of a rural bourgeoisie and a class of rural wage labourers. As we shall see below, this process, together with state strategies for rapid industrialisation had a major impact on Iranian class structure which formed the backdrop to the 1979 revolution.

The land reform in Iran, as carried out by the state, had a 'bourgeois-capitalist bias'.[22] But land reform, designed to create a capitalist agricultural sector, inscribed only one side of the coin. The other was imprinted with a state-led programme of industrialisation aimed at advancing Iran towards the more developed capitalist countries and creating an indigenous capitalist class. Although some industrialisation had taken place both before the Second World War and also in the course of subsequent development plans, the agricultural sector continued to predominate in the pre-land reform period such that more than half of the labour force was engaged in agricultural pursuits as late as 1961.[23] Government economic strategy in this period became the transformation of the economy from a backward oil dependent one to a mature industrial structure. The state's role in the industrial development of Iran included direct investment in industries, provision of funds and credits for the private sector and protectionist policies geared towards a programme of import substitution industrialisation.[24]

The shah was himself quite explicit about the necessity to 'catch up' with the West and the central role of the state in this process with the ultimate aims of nurturing a full blown advanced capitalist industrial society by adopting and adapting advanced technology:

> Today we have far to go to catch up. ... It requires lively insight and imagination to transplant Western technology effectively to a country like Persia. As I have said much adaptation is necessary. ... In modernising a nation, just as in conducting a military campaign, you need a plan of action. ... I have described how,

chiefly through government initiative, my father expanded Iranian industry. Because of the shortage of technicians and managers and because private investors were timid about entering the industrial field, the government had to do much of the pioneering. This was true of my father's time, and in some fields it is still the case today. For example, only the government can launch Iran's new steel industry. ... It is our policy gradually to hand over the government's existing factories to private concerns. ... We are [also] taking vigorous steps to encourage domestic and foreign capital to establish new industrial and commercial enterprises.[25]

The regime's economic strategy was to develop large capitalist enterprises by relying as much as possible on modern technology. Thus using the more industrially advanced countries as a model of development and by importing vast quantities of high technology and employing foreign experts, the shah embarked on a 'hot-house' programme of rapid industrialisation and technological development.[26] By 1967–68 the public sector accounted for 49 per cent of all investments compared to 34 per cent in 1963–64. During the 1960s the state took an active role in the development of heavy industries of which the Isfahan Steel Mill, the Ahvaz Rolling Mill and large-scale petrochemical projects under the auspices of the state-owned National Petrochemical Company are examples.

This strategy of state-led capital formation in the absence of agricultural surpluses was possible in pre-revolutionary Iran due to the oil income of the state. Revenue obtained from the oil sector allowed the state to finance industrialisation whether by providing ample credit and tax incentives for private production or by engaging in the productive process itself. The availability of oil revenues meant that industrialisation projects could be pursued independently of agriculture. This independent source of revenue thus allowed the state to nurture industrial projects. The income for the government's Plan Organisation which concentrated on industrial development was drawn from an 80 per cent share of oil revenues. The public sector became responsible for 58 per cent of investment expenditure and 'government policy was specifically designed to underpin the industrialisation policy through the creation of a base level of heavy industry and large-scale capital-intensive plants held predominantly by state controlled organisations.

In the Fifth Five-Year Economic Plan of 1973–78, emphasis was above all placed on the further expansion of high technology industries and iron and steel production capacity. In light of the 1973 oil price rises, all the measures of this plan were revised upwards. The government strategy seemed to be to take advantage of the oil wealth to import and acquire technology and assets from the more advanced countries. Amongst advanced capitalist states, although the United States had the greatest presence, other countries were also encouraged to participate in industrial development projects. Economic agreements were signed in particular with Japan in the Petrochemicals industry, Britain and Germany in the Automobile industry, Germany in heavy industries such as steel and cement and France and Italy in other areas.

Notably, due both to its oil income and strategic location, the Iranian regime was able to employ the resources not only of the advanced capitalist countries, but also of the Soviet Union and Eastern Europe for these purposes.[27] In the context of the limited superpower *détente* and the shah's attempts to demonstrate relative autonomy from the United States, government industries were set up not only with the support of the capitalist countries but also through economic and technological co-operation with the Soviet Union and Comecon states. Russian experts were employed in major joint ventures including the Isfahan Steel Mill. The Soviet Union became a major trading partner in the 1970s, with a five-year trade agreement being signed in 1976.[28]

The state in Iran thus took the lead in economic planning designed to encourage the development of a modern capitalist economy. It is important to stress this latter point, for the state's initiative in planning should not be taken as a sign of 'autonomy'. As we have already noted, externally this policy was implemented with the encouragement of the United States. Internally, we also need to consider how the policy was supported by particular classes which benefited from its outcomes.

The policy of the state, as we have elaborated above, was to guarantee the conditions for the reproduction and expansion of capitalism and the participation of capitalist enterprise – domestic and foreign – in the economy. It is in this sense that the Iranian state in this period may be considered capitalist.[29] However, by dint of its extensive participation in the economy, the state itself acted not only as part of the capitalist class, but increasingly as its more dominant section. In other words, the dominant class in Iranian society actually included part of the state apparatus.[30]

State policy favoured capitalist industrialisation with the participation of both foreign and domestic capital. It protected the interests of foreign capital by placing few restrictions on it and, by law, allowing the free repatriation of profits. The emerging domestic rural and urban bourgeoisie, however, remained reliant upon the state. While private investment took place in the service sector, the state dominated agricultural and industrial production by pouring oil rents into these sectors in a way that often caused the evolution of inefficient industries whose profits rested upon state subsidies. This led to the evolution of a form of capitalism dependent on the state and its oil revenues and lacking the competitive pressures which drive the capitalist process.

In the rural areas, as peasant ownership failed to provide subsistence incomes let alone the anticipated agricultural surpluses, due to a combination of inadequacies in the land reform process and natural shortages, the state moved to effectively dispossess the new peasant owners by the creation of large farm corporations and agri-businesses. Peasants were forcibly encouraged to hand over their recently acquired land in return for membership of corporations with share-holding rights. These corporations were then managed by state institutions and run by appointees of the Ministry of Co-operatives and Rural Affairs. By March 1973 these farm corporations numbered 43.[31] Alternatively, large-scale agri-businesses owned by the state in joint venture with foreign companies were often set up by clearing peasants off the most fertile lands. Both the farm corporations and the agri-businesses were heavily mechanised and capital intensive, incorporating both foreign capital and foreign expertise.

The state further dominated the economy through public sector investments, financing the capital requirements of the banking system, and high levels of public consumption. The existence of finance capital made available through the various commercial banks set up by the regime was not the result of a fusion of industrial and banking capital. The banks existed, rather, to make state oil revenues available for the financing of various agricultural and industrial projects.[32] Assisted by the availability of oil revenue, the state played the dominant role in the economy in order to realise a programme of rapid development in a bid to catch up on the international playing field of advanced industrial countries.

The dominant position of the state in such a case does not detract from the capitalist character of the economy. It simply means that the state bureaucracy needs to be regarded as one section of the increasingly dominant capitalist class. State policy served to protect the interests not only of foreign and domestic capitalist enterprise, but also the 'bureaucratic bourgeoisie' – the upper strata of the state bureaucracy at the top of whom stood the shah himself and who increasingly encroached upon the other sectors of the dominant capitalist class. The success of capitalist enterprises depended more and more on maintaining contacts with the higher echelons of the state bureaucracy. This dependence of the newly emerging industrial capitalist class, however, further bolstered the growing pre-eminence of the state section of the dominant class as people with high positions within the state, and especially the shah personally, were offered shares in enterprises in return for political support.[33]

The socio-economic changes instigated by the Pahlavi state gave birth to the revolutionary coalition of classes that eventually overthrew the regime. The irredeemable upheaval of the Iranian social structure and the disruption to the previous mode of life of the major part of the population gave impetus to the emergence of a revolutionary heterogeneous coalition with diverging grievances, but united by the common thread of state policies. By playing a direct role in economic processes the Iranian state was the self-evident source of social ills and the natural object of censure and incrimination. The revolutionary coalition was composed of different social classes, including the rural and urban working class, an increasing population of urban migrants, and the middle class or petty bourgeoisie, stratified into modern and traditional sectors, both rural and urban.

We shall discuss the formation of revolutionary ideology in Iran and the subjective positions of various social groups in due course. First, however, we give an outline of the stratification of different classes that participated in the revolutionary coalition.

The revolutionary coalition

The consequence of the state's land reform programme initiated in the 1960s and declared complete in the following decade was to establish capitalist social relations in the countryside. This led to the creation of a class of small-scale landowners. However, many of these farmers held plots which proved inadequate for subsistence and often had to engage in wage labour. Many others were forced to hand over their land in return for shares in large farm corporations. Furthermore, areas of traditional agriculture that were not immediately brought within the scope of the large-scale corporation or agri-business programmes nevertheless still suffered the heavy hand of the government bureaucratic intervention, eroding the confidence of small farmers who stood in fear of losing their property in state-led takeovers. Thus, while a class of small property owners had been created, this did not guarantee its loyalty to the regime.

The land reform further resulted in the creation of a rural proletariat composed both of the 40 per cent of peasants who had enjoyed no cultivation rights and therefore were not eligible for proprietorship of land under the programme, and of the peasants who did receive land but who were led to engage in wage labour because either their plots were insufficient for subsistence or they were forced off the land by the state, which came to replace the old landlords as the most powerful rural force. Wages of agricultural workers employed by the large agribusinesses or farm corporations were kept down partly due to the capital-intensive nature of these enterprises that reduced the demand for labour. The rural proletariat which was employed by the agri-business companies suffered poor living conditions and was accommodated in resettlement centres which came to resemble shanty towns due to lack of provisions, while rural unemployment also increased. These conditions led to an ever-increasing flow of migrants to the cities in search of employment and better living conditions.

Migrants streaming to the main urban centres constituted a 'surplus rural labour force' which largely joined the increasing mass of poor urban unemployed.[34] In Iran, as in many other relatively backward states which attempt to 'catch-up' by importing technologies from more advanced countries, demand for labour decreased due to capital-intensive industrialisation resulting in the creation of a small urban proletariat and a large class of what has variably been referred to as a 'marginal population' or a 'sub-proletariat' that suffers high levels of unemployment or engages in low-paid temporary jobs such as street-trading and peddling. The technology bias in new industries in the urban centres also resulted in an increasing urban unemployment problem. Where the migrants managed to gain employment, therefore, was not in stable wage-earning positions in urban industries, but in low-paid and temporary jobs in the service and construction sectors. Only around a third of this population had regular work and more than half remained unskilled.[35] Thus, rather than forming part of an organised working class, rural migrants more often joined the poor urban unemployed living in squalid conditions at the outskirts of cities and margins of urban life. By the mid-1970s Tehran contained around 50 slums and squatter communities, and by 1979 an estimated total of almost 1.5 million lived under such conditions. These communities then came face to face with the coercive arm of the state as authorities attempted to displace them both through legislation – such as the 1966 Provision 100 of the Municipality Law, which designated these areas as 'unlawful constructions' – and subsequent attempts at demolition.[36] During the 1970s, confrontations between the population living on the outskirts of cities and the municipal authorities were frequent.[37] Organised participation in the revolutionary movement by these communities did not occur until a few months before the success of the Revolution. However, the struggles of this sector are evidence of antagonism with state authorities. The significant numbers of 'underclass youth' were to become the Revolution's critical 'mass on the stage' (*mardum-i dar sahneh*).[38]

The urban working class in Iran also suffered from oppressive conditions although there was significant disparity amongst different sectors of this class in terms both of material benefits and of political consciousness and organisation.[39] While the living standards of sections of the working class improved during the oil-boom years in the 1970s, many less-skilled workers did not see similar significant rises. Moreover, increasing inflation and, in particular, the rise in housing prices put considerable material pressure on the majority of the working class. In addition, this class suffered not only from adverse economic conditions, but also from oppressive practices in the work-place on the one hand, and limitations imposed by the regime on political organisation on the other.

The adverse conditions of the working class in the workplace were characteristic of an organisational structure and labour rela-tions in the backward periphery where capitalist development is grafted onto the pre-existing social relations that include various forms of domination. Rapid industrialisation in Iran led to the creation and expansion of a labour force with specific features and peculiarities.[40] The urban proletariat remained largely of rural back-ground and origin due to the concomitant state policies of land reform and urban industrialisation, and was highly differentiated due to the survival of traditional manufacture alongside the new industries. The personalisation of the capital–labour relation in tradi-tional manufacture persisted, but so also did the survival of such relations in the management structure and practices of the new industries. Physical punishment and imprisonment were rife. Condi-tions of work deteriorated and the rate of industrial accidents increased dramatically between 1968 and 1975.

Large factory units, on the other hand, were dominated politically by the state as independent unions were banned after 1953 and the Labour Law of 1959 allowed only state-run unions. Strikes and polit-ical activities were thus forbidden as acts of violence against the state. Repressive measures were employed to control workers and factories were infiltrated by the SAVAK. The coercive arm of the state was thus apparent in the factories and where a hierarchical system of manage-ment prevailed, layers of authority were often perceived by workers as agents of the security services. Nevertheless, in some industries, most significantly the oil industry, a history of political movements and working-class political culture formed the grounds for collective action and opposition.[41] As the potential of worker unrest loomed in the 1970s, the state also attempted to complement coercion with consent by instilling a corporatist ideology of nationalism to encourage class collaboration symbolised in the creation of the Organisation of Iranian Workers in 1976 and the schemes for workers benefits such as shares and bonuses. However, such legislation, limited as it was, encountered opposition from owners of enterprises who were antagonised by the infringement of their freedom and profits.

Meanwhile the traditional urban middle class, which was largely concentrated in the *bazaar* and engaged in artisanal or trading activities, had different cause for grievance. The state's industrialisation policies served the interests of modern industrial and financial capital at the expense of the small commodity producers and traders of the traditional *bazaar*. The attempts to expand the national banking system, the favouring of large industries in the distribution of state credits, direct interference by the state in the importation of goods that was the traditional domain of the *bazaar*, attempts to tax traditional merchants and extend labour relations to the *bazaar* all had a negative impact on the *bazaar* merchants.[42] Moreover, the regime pursued policies aimed at reducing the political and social influence of the *bazaar*. With increases in industrial unrest and popular demands in the 1970s, the government began an anti-corruption and anti-profiteering campaign largely aimed at the *bazaar*. State authorities were established for the purpose of controlling prices, leading to the unwelcome presence of inspectors and the arrest of large numbers of traditional *bazaar* merchants. The *bazaaris* thus harboured grievances against the state and the new industrial elite whose interests state policies benefited.

The clergy as a social group cannot be considered as a social class. Variations and differences were rife, so that it would not be possible to consider all religious figures as belonging to one class. Nonetheless, religious institutions and the clergy who depended on them for their social reproduction need to be considered as part of the social structural spectrum of Iranian society. Their objective existence as a homogeneous social class is perhaps less important here than the way the interests of the religious establishment were also threatened by the Pahlavi state. In any case, at least a sector of the clergy who presided over and depended on religious institutions may be regarded – depending on their exact social position – as part of the traditional middle class or even traditional bourgeoisie.

As recipients of religious taxes from traditional sectors of the population largely coterminous with landowners and *bazaaris*, the religious establishment was also affected by the economic decline suffered by these sectors. More directly, religious institutions became the direct target of the state's programmes to bring them under control by appointing government bodies to administer mosques, religious areas and pilgrimages to Mecca.[43] Under such conditions the clergy would be forced increasingly to 'become dependent on government handouts like any civil-servant'.[44] Moreover, although land reform had exempted the religious endowment properties (*awqaf*) administered by the clergy, an Endowments Organisation (*sazman-e awqaf*) came into existence in 1964 which began to make grants of *awqaf* to supporters of the regime and individuals who may have been thought likely to begin industrial enterprises on the land.[45] In other words, as part of its modernisation programme, the regime increasingly orchestrated efforts against the clergy that impinged on their institutional power and ability for social reproduction. Through the creation of a Department of Religious Propaganda and Religious Corps, the regime attempted to raise a stratum of 'mullahs of modernisation' loyal to the state.[46] But the cumulative impact of state policy was to stir significant antagonism from within religious institutions.

Finally, the growth in state activities during the pre-revolutionary decades resulted in the expansion of a modern middle class employed by the bureaucracy or related institutions in the education system and banking, as well as a burgeoning private sector of the self-employed such as doctors, architects, solicitors and engineers. Rapid economic growth in the 1960s and early 1970s resulted in increases in living standards for this fast-expanding class. It was arguably the support of this modern middle class that gave the shah's state a somewhat broader basis than that of a small dominant class during this period.[47] However, the post-1973 oil boom years resulted in inflationary pressures which adversely affected large sectors of this class. Those on fixed salaries were particularly hard hit. The sharp rise in housing costs as a result of speculation and inflation in this sector affected large numbers. While a small sector of this class enjoyed increased prosperity, many began to suffer materially. Moreover, a large proportion of them were increasingly educated at university level, able to travel abroad, and had developed greater political and economic expectations of the state. Despite its relative prosperity, the modern middle class formed a hotbed of political opposition to the state.

Thus, by the mid to late 1970s a large sector of the population, albeit heterogeneous in class terms, had considerable grievances against the state. Having shouldered a palpably visible role in the changing social conditions of various social classes in Iran, the state came to be targeted by them.

Evolution of a revolutionary discourse: international influences

The structural factors which underlie the outbreak of revolutions and their subsequent development are as important to the Iranian case as to any other, but one must also take on board the series of particular circumstances that enabled the forging of a popular coalition composed of diverging and often contradictory interests which led eventually to the toppling of the old regime. This popular ideology derived not only from the historical experience of the actors who participated in the Revolution, but also from the impact and influence of the prevailing system of ideas at the international level. An adequate analysis of the Revolution needs to take into account both these elements and their intricate interaction.

For the larger part of the twentieth century, the international system was defined by the cold war. This overriding cleavage may be conceptualised as a conflict between two distinct social systems – one of which was created as a result of a major social revolution – engaged in competition in the form of a universalising dynamic on both sides.[48] A major consequence of this situation was the existence of alternative socio-economic models within the international system. More specifically, social revolution was perceived as a means to radical social change and the route to an alternative set of social relations. Revolution was 'in vogue' as a model to be followed successfully to establish a new social order.[49] With the emergence of a multitude of newly independent states, and more generally those which were subsumed under the umbrella term of the Third World, revolution came to be seen as the solution to deep-rooted socio-economic problems arising out of the socio-economic backwardness and contradictory nature of those societies. The political imagination of the revolutionary elite in these regions reflected remarkable similarities deriving from the revolutionary tradition at the international level that Colburn terms a 'shared intellectual culture'.[50] These leaders were furthermore spirited by the fact that as revolution in the advanced capitalist countries came to be seen as less and less likely, the Third World could preserve the ideals of the entire left the world over, leading to enthusiastic support for its revolutionaries and revolutions.[51]

For the revolutionaries across the globe, the pressing issue was to find a solution to the widespread destitution and poverty of the masses: 'the social question'.[52] Here too a certain consensus prevailed as to the models to be followed. First and foremost, the role of the state was emphasised. 'Planning and state initiative was the name of the game everywhere in the world in the 1950s and 1960s and in the NICs until the 1990s.'[53] Second, the state was to initiate not only a programme of industrialisation but also a series of social reforms such as the provision of welfare, housing, utilities and, perhaps most importantly, dealing with the 'agrarian problem'.[54] Finally, the social question was intimately bound with the issue of 'development', which itself became a centre-piece of the ideas of revolutionaries with the evolution of the idea that 'dependency' led to 'underdevelopment' and that the goal of revolution in the Third World had to be national liberation and the freedom from imperialism. The emergence of these theories of development had a distinct impact on the imagination of revolutionaries.

Radical thought on the question of development came to be dominated in the 1970s by what is known as the 'dependency school'.[55] The centrepiece of the latter was that development in the Third World is blocked by participation in the capitalist world system because of the structural dependence of the 'periphery' on the 'core'. As long as peripheral states remained part of this system led by the principal imperialist power, the United States, backwardness would be endemic. The main issue around which dependency theory centred is the occurrence of exploitation on an international scale due to 'unequal exchange' between the centre and periphery which tends to worsen the terms of trade for countries in the Third World. This analysis provided the justification for 'de-linking' from the world market and the pursuit of strategies of import substitution, often following a state-led model.

The Iranian revolutionary movement occurred at a historical juncture at which the idea of social revolution was in vogue; revolutionaries were concerned with providing solutions to the 'social question' mainly through state-led policies and by attempts to 'de-link' from the international system or capitalist world economy. Many Iranians through contact and exposure to these ideas, became heavily influenced by them, contributing to the making of revolutionary ideology in Iran. The development of the Iranian left through the 1970s paralleled that occurring in other parts of the Third World, centring on 'underdevelopment' and seeking the roots of the latter in participation in the capitalist world economy. The rise of the 'new revolutionary movement' echoed an earlier development in Latin America that shared a similar revolutionary discourse of 'anti-imperialism, dependent capitalism, neo-colonialism and armed struggle'.[56]

A considerable number of Iranians were studying abroad during the 1970s.[57] Many of these students were opposed to the shah's regime and heavily influenced by the radical currents of thought prevailing in the milieu in which they were studying or active. Among these the Confederation of Iranian Students was not only the most significant, but also became increasingly radicalised and supportive of the guerrilla groups such as the *Fedaiyan-e-Khalq* (Fedai) and *Mojahedin-e-Khalq* (Mojahedin) operating in Iran. Militant students translated and read the works of Mao Tse Tung, Che Guevara, Regis Debray, Franz Fanon and others in secret discussion groups. Some guerrilla groups also had close ties to the Palestinian resistance, where they also found a forthcoming source of weapons. When revolutionary activities began, these groups had not only organisations and weapons, but also ideologies influenced by the international revolutionary intellectual culture of the time.

However, what distinguished the Iranian Revolution and is in need of explanation was the role of Islam and the religious establishment which eventually assumed its leadership. As Keddie has noted, the 1960s signalled a turning point in the emergence of activist Islam. The reasons underlying this moment are to be sought in domestic and international changes of the period. On the one hand, the shah's reforms impinged on the specific interests of religious institutions and prompted them to protest. Meanwhile, the failure of the nationalist and secular opposition in the 1951–53 period created disillusionment with this model of political protest, while the leaders of this movement were repressed; this development is perhaps best expressed in the intellectual trajectory of many secular young activists of the 1940s and 1950s, be they communist or radical nationalist. Arguably, the most potent source of the new Islamic activism may be sought at the international level in the 'shared intellectual culture of contemporary revolutionaries' and the very same ideologies that made such an impact on the secular opposition. For as religious figures came into contact with secular ideologies, especially Marxism and neo-Marxist theories prevailing at the time, they appropriated many modern concepts into their discourse, bringing their political vocabulary into concordance with that of many secular groups.

The resonance of this anti-imperialist discourse of Third Worldism with popular sentiment in Iran was the aggregate result of a semi-colonial past of intervention and foreign influence and the adverse effects of social changes on the lives of the population. Such changes were perceived as the encroachment of an alien way of life induced by a state dependent on and subservient to the West. The Pahlavi state was perceived not as an autonomous entity, but as the agent or puppet of external forces – more concretely the United States – whose influence in the country, exercised through the mediation of the state, had also to be curtailed. The historical reality of US involvement in Iran beginning with the 1953 *coup d'etat*, the stream of US military aid, political support and plethora of contacts led the United States to be irrevocably associated with the Pahlavi Regime and consistently denounced and condemned for social and economic shortcomings and the repressive political system in Iran. Calls for the elimination of US advisors, consulates and other 'American espionage nests' originated in the left-wing discourse at the time of the coup and later became more widespread as the intervention was criticised by left and right alike.[58] In December 1953 Tehran University students who protested at the visit of Vice President Richard Nixon and who met with severe state repression included both leftist and nationalist forces. In 1954 the ensuing agreement with the oil consortium which provided a large share for US corporations was severely criticised for establishing US influence in Iran and selling short Iran's independence. Militarily, Iran's membership of the Baghdad Pact and later CENTO was seen as a further instance of imperial control. Later, the programme of 'Western' reforms initiated by the shah in the 1960s also came under heavy attack.

For many of this generation, the shah's modernisation was an aping of the 'West' and modernisation came to be identified with

'Westernisation'. Thus, defence against 'Westernisation' became a major political issue. It comes as little surprise that the uniquely influential text of this period, Jalal Al-e Ahmad's *Gharbzadegi*, revolved around the notion of 'West-struckness' or 'Westoxication'. *Gharbzadegi* is a widely discussed text whose author has been labelled 'the dawn of Islamic ideology', on the grounds that the motive of his discourse was a culturally induced return to tradition.[59] However, the historical context of the failure of the secular movement and the social impact of the shah's rapid modernisation and reform programme provide a better explanation of the influence of this text, which was largely a critique of the simultaneous land reform and industrialisation programme. Al-e Ahmad argued against dependence on the West through importation and consumption of Western products, but concomitantly expressed a general scepticism regarding industrial society. In a telling paragraph he claimed:

> While we remain mere consumers – until we have produced machines ourselves – we are West-stricken (*gharbzadeh*). But the irony is that even when we do produce the machine, we shall be machine-stricken (*mashinzadeh*). Just like the West whose cry is raised against the autonomy of 'technology' and machine.[60]

Influenced – albeit without first-hand knowledge of many primary texts – by the discourse of contemporary Western intellectuals, Al-e Ahmad in effect articulated a Third Worldist discourse and a pessimism regarding the achievements of industrial society. That this text came to be seen as a nucleus of a sonorous and expanding discourse ultimately adopted and adapted by the religious leadership has arguably more to do with the global intellectual culture in which all of these ideas were articulated. At a time when the prevalent worldview of opposition forces was framed in terms of national liberation, anti-imperialism and socialism, by incorporating secular concepts, a new language of Islam began to emerge which closely corresponded to the secular Third Worldist rhetoric in its condemnation and denunciation of the role of the 'West' and in the gradual evolution of its revolutionary discourse.[61]

The borrowing of ideas of the left to propose solutions then presented as authentically Islamic was not peculiar to the Iranian case.[62] Faced with the challenge of rival secular ideologies, Islamic modernists began to seek new ways of opposition to the advances of the regime that did not involve identification with conservative Islamic tradition. The neo-Marxist theories prevailing at the time were perceived as rivals to religion and began to be studied by religious figures. In Iran, even students at the religious seminary in Qum in the 1960s and 1970s studied Marxist-inspired texts.[63] Islamic activists came into contact with their secular counterparts in a variety of ways, including imprisonment in common cells where they conducted debates regarding the social and economic system and forms of political actions, and through contact with Palestinian revolutionaries during periods abroad or in exile.[64]

Religious leaders targeted the West as the principal enemy. Following the legislative approval in October 1964 of the Status of Forces Agreement that granted diplomatic immunity to US military personnel and members of their households, including servants, the future leader of the Iranian Revolution, Ruhollah Khomeini, then at the Qum Seminary, delivered a speech against the granting of the so-called 'capitulatory rights to the United States':

> They have sold us, they have sold our independence. ... They have reduced the Iranian people to a level lower than that of an American dog. ... The government has sold our independence, reduced us to the level of a colony, and made the Muslim nation of Iran appear more backward than savages in the eyes of the world. ... Are we to be trampled underfoot by the boots of America simply because we are a weak nation and have no dollars? America is worse than Britain; Britain is worse than America. The Soviet Union is worse than both of them. They are all worse and more unclean than each other! But today it is America that we are concerned with.[65]

Other religious leaders who engaged more directly with secular ideologies began, by incorporating modern concepts, to present Islam as a progressive and activist religion able to enjoin social change and deal with the question of social justice. They wrote on socio-economic questions concerning the role of private property in Islam and its egalitarian disposition. Mahmud Taleqani's exegesis, *Islam and Ownership*, published in 1965, clearly depicts the close concern and engagement with Marxist concepts of ownership, labour power and class.[66] A transformation occurred in Iran, creating an activist version of religion enriched by the plethora of modern concepts and serving as an antidote to the ideas of the left. The need for freedom, independence, national liberation, anti-imperialism and the establishment of a more egalitarian society gradually entered the language of the religious hierarchy. As the participation of the religious leaders in the political process increased, the distinction between cleric and intellectual was dissolved.[67] The former were now perceived as 'intellectuals' educated at faculties of philosophy and not the traditional and passive clerics of the past.

The new 'Islamic ideology' of Ali Shariati, perhaps one of the principal ideologues of the revolution, reveals a basic reworking of the Marxist-influenced Third Worldist discourse of the period and the revolutionary ideologies of direct action. He propagated the myth of a revolutionary essence of early Islam, drawing the conclusion that political activity was urgent and a necessity for Muslims and the Third World in general. He attacked clerical compromises with the state and gave credence to the concept of Islam as a mass-mobilising ideology. He encouraged the exploited to world revolution, for which he justified the seizure of power by intellectuals through organisation and propaganda.[68]

This activist interpretation of Islam found its parallel in the views of some clerics, not least Ayatollah Khomeini. While his earlier writing indicated a more traditional attitude requiring only that the monarch respect religion and the state law conform to religious law, a clear transformation took place in his views on these matters while he was in exile in Iraq.[69] Khomeini's early writings, dating to the 1940s, constitute a defence of the hierarchical structure of the *ulema* and stress the Shi'i doctrine of the emulation (*taqlid*) of the clergy (*mujtahids*) by Muslims. This work was largely a reaction against modernist writers of the time who began to criticise religious institutions. For Khomeini, society's problems were to be resolved not by modernisation but by a return to Islam as practised at the time of the Prophet. There was little criticism of the monarchical regime or notion of revolution in these early declarations. Even later in the 1960s, when he in fact spoke out against the monarchy, he remained moderate in his demands by criticising practices rather than the principle of a monarchical state. In general, in this period Khomeini retained a traditional attitude to the state.[70]

The break in Khomeini's attitude to the state and society came during his exile in Iraq in the late 1960s. He put forward his novel ideas on Islamic government in a series of lectures later published as *Velayat-e Faqih: Hokumat-e Islami*. Here he introduced the necessity of the rule (*velayat*) by the leading religious jurisprudent (*faqih*). The novelty of this work was the insistence on control of the political affairs of the Muslim community by the religious elite.[71] As Sami Zubaida notes, although he was writing almost as if modern Western political thought never existed, the compatibility of Khomeini's ideas with modern concepts became increasingly evident.[72] Khomeini's doctrine was a radical departure in modern Islam. On the other hand, he drew, albeit implicitly, on modern sociological concepts of 'state', 'people' and 'nation'.

Concomitantly, he began to use more radical language in his depiction of society. While he had previously alluded to 'mutually dependent strata (*qeshr*)', he now adopted the terminology of the left to speak of warring classes (*tabaq'e*).[73] Increasingly, he stressed the need for action by Muslims. He attacked the quietism of 'collaborating mullahs'. He further came to insist on the inseparability of politics and religion, while the 'West' and Western corruption continued to be identified as the target for the unity of Muslims which was to be forged under the leadership of the *ulema*. He claimed that with the proper implementation of Shi'i Islam through the rule of the most learned *faqih*, the problems of Iranian society would be resolved. While his attitude to the status quo and monarchical regime – and his political language – changed significantly over a period of three decades, the kernel of Khomeini's thought remained the need to establish a 'true' Islamic society. Thus, it is important to bear in mind both elements of change and continuity in Khomeini's thought throughout the pre-revolutionary period. His emerging ideology and version of 'political Islam' was a synthesis of traditional (albeit evolving) Shi'i thought on the role of the state and *ulema* and more modernist language and concepts prevailing at the global conjuncture of the 1970s.

The exact source and origins of this new activist language are not clear. Abrahamian suggests the influence of the Shi'i *ulema* in Iraq during his exile and by younger lay and religious Iranian students and intellectuals including Al-e Ahmad and Shariati.[74] Akhavi concludes that there is little to suggest that Khomeini read Shariati's work.[75] Nevertheless, we may surmise that he was brought into contact with the ideas of younger scholars and activists during his exile and through his followers who visited him in Iraq. The Iraqi Shi'i leaders, with whom Khomeini was closely in contact, were highly susceptible to the ideas of the Iraqi Communist Party and appropriated many of the concepts used by the secular left in Iraq. On the other hand, Khomeini's religious followers, such as the future post-revolutionary President Akbar Hashemi Rafsanjani, visited him in exile in Najaf and brought him into contact with currents of thought amongst Iranian intellectuals and debates of the Palestinian movement, all in turn influenced by the prevailing global worldview.[76]

The themes incorporated into this discourse included national independence and anti-imperialism, and a commitment to the deprived and downtrodden and the banner of universalism and unity with the oppressed of the world. These are leitmotifs manifest in Khomeini's writings and speeches during the period of exile in Iraq in the 1970s. In his message to the Muslim students in North America in 1972 he wrote:

> The agents and servants of imperialism know that if the people of the world, particularly the young and educated generation, become acquainted with the sacred principles of Islam, the downfall and annihilation of the imperialists will be inevitable and also the liberation of the resources of exploited nations and

peoples from their control. ... Imperialism of the left and imperialism of the right have joined hands in their efforts to
annihilate the Muslim peoples and their countries; they have
come together in order to enslave the Muslim peoples and
plunder their abundant capital and natural resources. ... It is
your duty, respected youths of Islam ... to awaken people, to
expose the sinister and destructive designs of imperialism.[77]

Such slogans resonated with the social condition and grievances of the
various classes which were antagonised by the policies of the state and
the imperatives of state-led accumulation perceived to be directed by
external powers.

By 1978 state policies of accumulation and capitalist development
had antagonised large sectors of the population who were not experi-
encing the material rewards promised by the shah's grandiose claims
for the rapid socio-economic development of Iran. A popular cross-
class coalition of opposition forces emerged. The coalition which came
together and led to the successful outbreak of the Iranian Revolution
reflected a heterogeneity of social forces and diverging interests, bound
together by the perception that the Pahlavi state and its chief supporter
the United States were the root cause of Iran's problems. The significance of state intervention in capital allocation and accumulation in
pre-revolutionary Iran made the state the central target for the collective action of various classes and groups who were antagonised by
economic policies that included the licensing system, credit allocation
and the establishment of large agri-businesses.

The policies of the pre-revolutionary state had imposed a heavy cost
on large sections of the peasantry, urban poor and the urban working
class, the traditional middle class of the *bazaar* and sectors of the
modern middle class. These pressures were magnified as a result of the
rising inflation of the post-1973 oil boom years. The potential for cross-
class opposition to the state thus existed. Secular leftist political
organisations and the religious figures led by Khomeini shared a political language that could mobilise this popular force. The organisational
advantage, however, lay on the side of the religious elements. While
many secular activists were undeniably repressed by the shah's
regime, the clergy, equipped with the extensive network of mosques
and an independent financial base, were able organisationally as well
as intellectually to assume the leadership of the opposition movement.
Despite the attempted onslaught of the state, the clerical hierarchy
maintained its financial stability, independence and robust organisational structure. Religious educational institutions had been
strengthened and the collection of religious taxes took place on a more
secure basis.[78] Financial distribution to religious leaders was

centralised; accounting procedures were developed; religious schools, seminaries and mosques were founded; and Muslim missionaries were sent abroad.[79]

The increased institutional presence of the religious establishment was predicated upon their procurement of funds. Although the exact source and amount of financing is unclear due to the informal nature of the collection of religious taxes, estimates suggest that up to 80 per cent of the reserves of the religious institutions was provided by the *bazaar*. Opposition to large capitalists and their Western backers as well as a commitment to traditional values earned them the support of a large proportion of the merchant class. In any case, the *bazaar* financed many mosque activities and some *bazaaris* actively promoted ceremonies and gatherings held in mosques preceding the Revolution.[80] Moreover, a network of politically engaged clerics and 'Khomeini loyalists' had formed during the decades preceding the Revolution. Thus, when the first revolutionary protests broke out in 1978, there was a 'nucleus of a Khomeini organisation in place'.[81]

However, the Revolution was made possible by the participation of a broad coalition of social classes, each with its own interests and motives for the overthrow of the old order. Ultimately, the Revolution was made possible by the strike activities of the working class, among them most effectively the oil workers, supported by the *bazaar*, combined with popular demonstrations and the eventual breakdown of the shah's military and security apparatus. Thus, the old regime thus gave way to the new in February 1979.

3 Populism and the Revolution: domestic and international impact

The revolutionary coalition which overthrew the *ancien regime* of the shah was composed of various social groups and classes with diverging and sometimes contradictory interests. Less than a year later, however, power had consolidated in the hands of a small group of clerics intent on creating an Islamic state and exporting the Revolution to the region and beyond. This chapter explains the transformation from a modern social revolution to an Islamic state.

The immediate period following the Revolution was one of social and political indeterminacy as the old structures of the state had yet to be replaced by new ones. Struggles over property relations and democratic rights formed the backdrop to the disintegration of the revolutionary coalition, pulling the post-revolutionary state in opposing and contradictory directions. The key to the consolidation of power by the Islamic clerics and their ability to unify the broad class basis of the Revolution into a single revolutionary movement was Khomeini's hegemonic populism. This discourse incorporated many secular concepts and, crucially, adopted an 'anti-imperialist' mantle – most starkly symbolised by images of US hostages and the burning of the US flag. It also subscribed to a universalist ideology which called for the Revolution to push beyond the national borders of the Iranian state.

Populism and 'Khomeinism'

First, however, what do we mean by populism and how does it apply to the rhetoric of the Iranian revolution? Populism is one of the less precise terms in the vocabulary of social science.[1] It has been adopted to describe many diverse political phenomena ranging from US populism of the late nineteenth century and Russian populism in the pre-revolutionary period to varieties of Third World populist movements, in particular in Latin America.[2] Nevertheless, we begin with the assumption that there is some commonality between so-called populist movements. This is embodied in the rhetorical appeal to 'the people' in order to mobilise popular masses.[3] There can be no a priori demarcation of the social base of populism. In other words, a populist political discourse is not inherently the discourse of a particular class, but can constitute the ideological discourse of a class. Within a populist discourse, specific objectives of particular social groups may be presented as the general objective of the whole 'people'. Popular attitudes are called upon and appropriated by a particular group or class. Popular cultural symbols and traditions, the crystallisation of resistance to oppression in general, may be articulated into a discourse of a specific social group thereby neutralising their content. While populism may inform and constitute the discourse of dominated classes, dominant elites are also able to establish hegemony over a broad popular spectrum by appropriating the vocabulary of popular culture.

The emergence of a populist phenomenon cannot be detached from the socio-economic context, but is historically linked to a crisis of the prevailing dominant ideological discourse and is part of a more general social crisis.[4] Modern populist movements have in some way or other been responses to socio-economic change and upheaval, usually resulting from the global encroachment of capitalism. This uprooting experience has often affected the prevailing modes of existence of diverse social classes and formed the backdrop to the creation of broad cross-class coalitions ready to engage in social protest and unified by a populist discourse.[5] The particular responses in every case, and the popular-national elements articulated by the populist discourse, have varied according to specificity of the conjuncture. Nevertheless, a pattern in the form which modern populist movements have taken may be discerned. Modern populism of dominant elites has involved the mobilisation of support from underprivileged groups, often achieved through the personal appeal of a charismatic leader. Populist politics therefore entails an emphasis on the poor, disinherited or oppressed.

> Populist ideology is moralistic, emotional and anti-intellectual, and non-specific in its programme. It portrays society as divided between powerless masses and coteries of the powerful who stand against them. But the notion of class conflict is not a part of that populist rhetoric. Rather it glorifies the role of the leader as the protector of the masses.[6]

In Ervand Abrahamian's helpful account of the Iranian case, populism is defined as 'a movement of the propertied middle class that mobilises the lower classes, especially the urban poor, with radical rhetoric directed against imperialism, foreign capitalism and the political establishment'.[7] But by an a priori definition of 'Khomeinism' as a populist movement of the propertied middle classes and, therefore, a bourgeois revolution, such an account falls short in explaining the post-revolutionary struggles which determined the structure of the post-revolutionary regime or the ambivalence and equivocation in Khomeini's stance on the issue of land reform and property, which changed over time and reflected the contradictory nature of the revolutionary coalition and its different factional interests.

Khomeini's populism was crucially defined by its nationalist and anti-imperialist discourse, which rallied large sections of the revolutionary coalition behind him, as well as his claim to be the protector of the deprived masses. He was thus able to hold together and take command of the coalition which, in the immediate revolutionary aftermath, seemed on the verge of fragmentation.

The revolutionary centrifuge: a fragmenting coalition

The immediate post-revolutionary period was one of great political and socio-economic indeterminacy as the old structures had yet to be replaced by new ones. In the aftermath of the Revolution, Ayatollah Khomeini mandated a provisional government, headed by Mehdi Bazargan of the Liberation Movement of Iran, to run the administration of the country until regular political institutions could be established. Meanwhile an executive Revolutionary Council composed largely of religious figures remained in place. The provisional government, bereft of well-established state institutions, was beset by difficulties due to the interruption of economic activity on the one hand and a variety of social demands on the other.

Industry was disrupted during the revolutionary period and production could no longer be ensured as managers fled the country, and capital flight occurred on a large scale. Oil production – the principal lifeline of the country – also fell dramatically. Moreover, revolutionary consciousness in factories translated into demands for self-management by workers.[8] Workers' councils emerged gradually out of the former strike committees. The upsurge of the workers' movement continued through the latter half of 1979 with demands for higher wages and profit-sharing, establishment of a minimum wage, a 40-hour week and regional unions.

The provisional government found itself in a contradictory situation needing on the one hand to start up production in factories – and therefore to restore order – and on the other to maintain the semblance of being the protector of the interests of the underprivileged.[9] In fact, immediately after the Revolution, Ayatollah Khomeini issued a back-to-work decree denouncing anyone calling for continued strikes as 'treacherous'.[10] The councils represented a danger in their potential for becoming independent power bases, and although a faction of the ruling bloc paid lip-service to their importance, they conceived of these as state-run consultative institutions, rather than worker-run councils.[11] Various sectional interests opposed the demands of the workers. The *bazaaris* had believed that an Islamic government would protect private property, free them from government restrictions and controls, provide them with greater business opportunities, and tax them more lightly. The pro-*bazaar* factions of the government were openly against the workers' councils and the religious and conservative Hojjatiyeh Organisation, supported by traditional merchants and industrialists, actively opposed them as 'un-Islamic'. In this way, the struggle for workers rights and conditions continued within the immediate post-revolutionary context.

In the context of the relative post-revolutionary political freedom and the unprecedented increase in unemployment, large numbers of the jobless also organised to publicise their plight and make demands for unemployment benefits or loans.[12] The urban poor composed of slum dwellers and squatters also began more forcefully to express their demands for adequate housing. Led by young activists, they occupied vacant and deserted buildings in Tehran and other cities. This occupation of residential properties and hotels constituted another challenge for the new regime. The provisional government and sectors of the clergy committed to the sanctity of private property opposed the action vehemently. Leftist groups and radical clerical leaders encouraged the occupation. But while the radical clergy had the general political aim of undermining the provisional government, more conservative sectors within the regime identified the squatters with the secular left and opposed them on the grounds that they were acting at the behest of 'communist counter-revolutionaries'. For the most part, the religious authorities condemned the squatters and justified their eviction on religious grounds. Upper echelon clergy issued *fetwas* (religious edicts) ruling that occupying homes was *haram* (un-Islamic). However, the continued efforts of the squatters to organise themselves more systematically indicated that this issue over property rights remained unresolved.

The situation in the countryside was no less contradictory. The Iranian Revolution of 1979, like many other contemporary revolutions, harboured promises of socio-economic justice and equality and land reform. Among the landless and the poor peasants, the sense of deprivation and the expectation that the Islamic regime should do something was widespread. A nationwide assault on private landed property began shortly after the Revolution in February 1979.[13] Seizure of lands and demands for distribution became widespread. As a consequence, numerous open clashes occurred between peasants and landlords, prompting the government to take action. These conflicts were reflected in various tendencies of the post-revolutionary leadership. The provisional government emphasised the need to maintain order, stressed its respect for private property and viewed commercial farmers as successful entrepreneurs not oppressors of the masses. The Bazargan government attempted to play down the inequalities in land ownership and engaged in an extensive propaganda campaign against land seizure. Sections of the leadership, including some religious figures, on the other hand aligned with the leftist groups who maintained the slogan of the Revolution as belonging to the dispossessed masses. Ayatollah Bahonar, for instance, a member of the Revolutionary Council, announced that 'regarding large land ownership, the aim of the Revolutionary Council is to be able gradually to give these lands to those who work on them,' and Ayatollah Dastghaib, the Friday prayer leader of Shiraz, encouraged the youth and the farmers not to wait for the state to give them land. They themselves should act, seize lands from the feudal holders and landowners, and cultivate these lands under the banner of Islam.

Apart from the fundamental issue of social property relations and the conflict over the status of private property in this period, the question of the social and political rights of various social groups and the impending political structure of state institutions emanated in post-revolutionary debates. The most fundamental question for the political make-up of the state was the constitution of the country. The debate surrounding the form that the republic should take began in the aftermath of the Revolution with the provisional government's proposal for a 'Democratic Islamic Republic'.[14] In the event, however, with Khomeini's insistence and backing, the question was formulated to allow only the choice of an 'Islamic Republic', the content and constitution of which remained indeterminate. These debates revolved around the question of social and political rights, with significant implications for the democratic freedoms of numerous social groups.

Women constituted one such group. The participation of women in the Iranian Revolution was unprecedented, and although they did not necessarily begin with a feminist self-consciousness, their very role gave many women a new sense of confidence in their ability to organise and take action in the public sphere. This in turn prompted further organisation and activity after the outbreak of the Revolution.[15] However, once the Islamic Republic was established, the government began to rewrite the laws and rules relating to women's rights, attempting to force women out of the job market through a variety of methods such as closing childcare centres, enforcing the *hejab* (Islamic garb), compulsory redundancies and early retirement, and restricting access to certain subjects at university and later in schools.[16] On 7 March 1979, the day before planned demonstrations in observance of International Women's Day, Khomeini declared that women employees of government agencies should abide by the Islamic dress code and denounced International Women's Day as a Western phenomenon, irrelevant to Iranian women.[17]

In the aftermath of this declaration, during a five-day demonstration, alongside demands for equal wages and the preservation of the Family Protection Laws, women chanted slogans for the choice in what to wear and equal rights and freedoms. In response, *hezbollahi* groups threatened the demonstrators physically and verbally.

It was in this climate that Khomeini emerged as the charismatic leader of the Revolution, and secured hegemony over the majority of the population and the means for the gradual assumption of control of the instruments of the state. Khomeini and the religious leaders aligned with him, largely under the aegis of the Islamic Republic Party (IRP) which formed days after the successful outbreak of the Revolution, raised the banner of national independence, 'anti-imperialism' and protection of the deprived masses around which the majority of social groups rallied. Articulating this discourse, with their own brand of 'Islamic populism', religious leaders presented themselves as the champions of the Revolution. Thus they were able to establish hegemony over their secular counterparts.

Khomeinism: nationalism, anti-imperialism, universalism

Khomeini's Islamic populism was comprised of a number of elements. It firstly embodied a popular nationalist sentiment that was central to the Iranian revolutionary movement.[18] This widespread collective disposition related partly to a worldview shaped in conjunctural circumstances and influenced by a dominant international ideology coloured by 'Third Worldism' and 'anti-imperialism'. Its discourse reflected the populist rhetoric of the Revolution as on the one hand being the 'protector of the deprived masses', offering the solution to their social problems, and on the other being a movement for national independence and of struggle against global imperialism.

The Islamic discourse was imbued with that of 'Third Worldism' and dependency theory. One of the main tenets of Islamic social populism was that the social ills of society, inequality and oppression could only be eradicated by the termination of dependent relations with foreign powers and the severance of their influence in the country. The creation of 'Islamic government' that comprised an alternative more just social system entailed national independence through 'self-sufficiency'. The latter concept did not imply comprehensive 'de-linking' from the world economy, but revolved around the idea of independence from the world-dominating *states*. It was repeatedly stressed that purchases would not be made from the dominant *states*, but rather resort would be made to the world *market*. Khomeini also appeared to suggest that it would be preferable to forego economic development and material progress than to be 'dependent':

If we could erect a wall like the Great Wall of China between East and West, between the Islamic countries and whatever ... so that our country can be saved from their grasp and even if we do without their progress it will be to our benefit ... do not be under the illusion that our relations with America or our relations with the Soviet Union ... [is] advantageous for us. This relationship is like the relationship between a wolf and a lamb which is not very advantageous for the lamb. The East must stand on its own two feet ... free itself completely from the West, and if this is not completely possible, at least to save its culture.[19]

Overall, although 'Islamic government' was claimed to serve as an alternative social model to both the capitalist 'West' and the communist 'East', the thrust of the 'anti-imperialist' rhetoric was directed mainly at the United States.

The explanation for the nationalist sentiments of people lies not only in this worldview, however, but also in historical precedent and, in particular, the role of external powers in changing the course of modern Iranian history. Most significantly, as laid out in Chapter 2, the legacy of the nationalist hero, Mohammad Mosaddeq, whose popularity and importance to the Iranian mind must not be underestimated, and the role of external powers in the *coup d'etat* that toppled him, irrevocably contributed to the anti-Westernism of the Islamic Republic and the conspiratorial myth of a 'foreign hidden hand' behind major events in social and political life.[20] These then are the factors serving to reinforce the strength of a nationalist temperament which was then adopted and appropriated by the religious discourse of the Revolution.

Khomeini, of course, was at pains to stress the role of Islam and the 'Islamic Revolution' and denigrate that of nationalism by claiming that it was 'the culture of Islam, not nationalism or imperial culture' which had brought people to support the revolutionary forces.[21] However, revolutionary fervour and nationalist sentiment were so intertwined as to make such a distinction meaningless, and to accept it would miss the originality of the Khomeinist rhetoric in having been able to incorporate nationalism into its religious discourse. Richard Cottam rightly notes the advantage to Khomeini of having been able to manipulate national and Islamic symbols appealing to an inseparable 'national religious community'. Similarly Fred Halliday adopts a notion of a 'hybrid Islamic-nationalist ideology' to describe this articulation.[22] Religious leaders made frequent reference to 'the nation' (*mellat*) and the 'homeland' (*vatan*) alongside Islam and 'Muslim community' (*ummat*), to the extent that these terms often became interchangeable. Of course, the Islamic national-populist discourse was distinguished from the secular nationalism propounded by the shah, which drew upon pre-Islamic symbols. In its stead imagery was borrowed from the early days of Islam, though often articulated with the concepts of modern revolution, state and nationhood. Khomeini ultimately conflated nation and religion by insisting that the masses all belonged 'to the same nation, to the same Islam'.[23]

The Islamic components of the Iranian revolution, like many other movements in the region, were:

> looking to the common people for support against Western-oriented dominant social groups, institutions and parties: theirs is a populist nationalism with 'Islam' as the identifying emblem of the common people against the 'alien' social spheres in their own country which had excluded and subordinated them.[24]

However, Khomeinism cannot be regarded simply as 'national-populism', but entailed other elements. Khomeini's rhetoric was also driven by a commitment to the 'deprived' and 'downtrodden' masses in whose name the Revolution was made. The success of the Revolution was accompanied by promises of a more just and egalitarian society.[25] This appeared to signal a redistribution of wealth that questioned the status of private property, the role of the state and economic policy. Khomeini depicted society as divided into two conflicting classes. The deprived and disinherited masses, the *mostaz'afin* or *mahroomin*, had been exploited by the dominant class and oppressors, the *taghoutis* and *zalemin*, as a result of the socio-economic programmes of the shah backed by imperialist policies. His rhetoric promised to address this conflict and the widening gap between rich and poor, to redistribute land, to house the homeless and shanty-town dwellers and to provide welfare for the poverty-stricken masses.[26] This was the 'social-populist' element of Khomeinism.

Khomeini's writings nonetheless indicate little knowledge of economic theory. His directives on socio-economic questions merely postulate the defence of the interests of the deprived, with little acknowledgement of fundamental contradictions of class society.[27] There is no concrete programme for the restructuring of social relations or transformation of the economic system. The issue of social justice was simply couched in the language of religion. An Islamic social model was to provide the solution to the problems of the underprivileged masses, as religion was instrumentalised in the populist discourse as the *vehicle* for the expression of social demands. The lack of regard for the fundamental contradictions of class society and the problems of promoting a redistributive version of Islam under conditions of diverging interests of social groups was evident also in the tracts of other leading figures of the Revolution on 'Islamic economics', which claimed that Islam could serve as an alternative and unique model for the socio-economic organisation of society.[28] While criticising the inegalitarian nature of capitalist society and adopting an anti-capitalist position, their arguments rejected and claimed to go beyond secular Marxist analyses based on the class contradictions of capitalist society and presented Islam as an alternative means for social transformation.

The corollary of these arguments in favour of an 'Islamic society' and 'Islamic economy' was that the model was valid not only within the borders of Iran but universally. The Iranian 'Islamic solution' was the means by which the deprived masses across the globe would liberate themselves. In an uncanny reflection of Marxist ideas of the proletariat as the 'universal class' and the party as revolutionary 'vanguard', the Muslim masses of Iran were presented as the universal agents of revolution with their religious leaders – the network of clerics organised around Khomeini – as their vanguard. Khomeini thereby appealed to other Muslim masses to follow the Iranian example and leadership in revolutionary uprisings against their regimes.

The universalist drive of the Revolution was bolstered by presentation of the Islamic Republic as a 'third way' and alternative socio-economic system to the two prevailing models of capitalism and communism. The Islamic populist universalist discourse blamed the social ills of Muslim societies and the fundamental causes of oppression of the masses globally on foreign influence and domination. The image of the international system portrayed by Khomeini divided the world into the 'dominant' and 'dominated' nations. Thus, the solution to the social problems of the dominated and oppressed masses of the world would be to liberate themselves from the chains that tied them to the powerful states. The Islamic Republic was held to have set the precedent and achieved this status:

> Great things have been achieved, miraculous things, the defeat of *taghut*, defeat of the superpowers, today our country is independent, no one can interfere in its affairs and we will not allow left or right to interfere in this country, we will not let them exploit our resources.[29]

Regimes that did not follow the Iranian example in severing dependence on external powers and continued to be the servants and puppets of 'West and East' were denounced and their populations encouraged to rise against them. This formed the rationale for an ideology of 'export of revolution' beyond the borders of the Iranian state and served as an axiom of the Revolution which appeared to find a receptive audience in a number of states in the region. The disruption of prevailing modes of life through socio-economic changes of the previous decades had led to the disaffection of large sectors of populations in the region. This provided a fertile ground for the promotion of the Iranian 'Islamic alternative' across the world.

Khomeini's populism claimed to hold the solution to the problems of the deprived masses. He promised an egalitarian and more just society based on an Islamic model, the co-ordinates and framework of which nevertheless remained vague. One aspect of the creation of a new society free from social ills would be independence from the domination of foreign powers. The discourse of anti-imperialism and national independence formed the 'national-populist' element of Khomeini's rhetoric. We shall see in what follows that as the contradictions of the 'social-populist' rhetoric of protection of the deprived were revealed in light of the conflict of interests between different social classes and the status of private property, the 'anti-imperialist' and 'national-populist' element was drawn upon to a greater extent to maintain the unity of the revolutionary coalition.

Khomeinism's decisive moment: 1979–80

The national-populist rhetoric championed by Khomeini led on the one hand to the consolidation of power by a small faction of religious leaders who were able not only to discredit and delegitimise the so-called 'liberals' of the provisional government, but also to increase their control of the internal security apparatus, which would then be used against any protest movement now deemed the manifestation of imperialist conspiracy. On the other hand, the rhetoric signified a turning point in the international relations of post-revolutionary Iran by creating a situation of extreme tension with the United States and increasing the need for international allies and support. External issues thus became matters of greater significance in revolutionary rhetoric and policies.

Given the potency of the nationalist and anti-imperialist discourse in the revolutionary coalition, the establishment of hegemonic leadership could only be secured by articulating a national-populist rhetoric that incorporated these elements. Khomeini's resolute language, directed largely against the United States, enabled him to assume the leadership of the revolutionary movement and to ride the historical wave of nationalism and the general tide of anti-imperialism.

The nationalist predilections of the various sectors which participated in the Revolution rallied them behind Khomeini's leadership.

His resolute platform against foreign intervention and in favour of national-independence in the decades preceding the revolution had such an impact on the nationalist members of the Liberation Movement of Iran (Iranian Freedom Movement), including Bazargan who led the provisional government, that his opposition to the granting of diplomatic immunity to US military advisers had mattered more than his reactionary stance on female suffrage and democracy. Thus, in its November 1978 declaration, the Liberation Movement emphasised two points: firstly that the people of Iran wanted Islamic government, and secondly that Khomeini was to be recognised as foremost leader.[30] The weight and potency of the nationalist pitch in popular opinion was given concrete expression by a number of incidents in the revolutionary period. On the day of Khomeini's return to Iran from Paris the national anthem, which had been banned by the shah in favour of a monarchist version, was broadcast by the state radio, confirming the nationalist credentials of the revolution.[31] In the immediate post-revolutionary period, extensive ceremonies were held in honour of Mosaddeq, and the hundredth anniversary of his birth was celebrated with much fanfare.[32] Khomeini's slogan of 'Neither East nor West' reflected Mosaddeq's earlier policy of 'negative balance', adding to the legitimacy derived from acting as successor to the former nationalist leader.[33]

A wide spectrum of social groups also issued statements indicating their nationalist predilection. The *bazaaris* concomitantly blamed the shah and his 'foreign backers' for the country's social ills. In early 1978 they labelled the shah's government 'the servant of America and chained dog of international imperialism' and referred to how 'mineral resources and material and spiritual wealth have been plundered by a minority of dirty foreigners with the co-operation of internal servants.'[34] The working class, on the other hand, had grievances directly related to the rise in living expenses, which was attributed to economic unevenness and the dependent nature of the state on the United States. The demands of oil workers in Ahwaz in 1978, for instance, included 'Iranianisation' of the oil industry, use of the Persian language in all communications and the expulsion of foreign employees. In late 1978, the Common Syndicate for the Employees of the Iranian Oil Industry announced its participation in the revolutionary movement by stating that 'in unity with the fighting people of Iran, the purpose of the strike is to destroy despotism and eliminate the influence of foreigners in our country, and create an independent, free and progressive Iran'.[35]

Most telling of all, however, was the anti-imperialist and nationalist political vocabulary of the Iranian left. The word *melli* (national) also featured extensively in the discourse of the left, who enjoyed considerable

influence within factories and in some rural areas. Their slogans and literature were littered with praise of the 'national democratic revolution', the
need for an independent 'national' Iran and establishment of a 'national
economy'.[36] The prevailing neo-Marxist Third Worldist analysis reduced
the Iranian social formation under the shah to 'imperial-capitalist domination'. This was the source of all social ills and the next theoretical step
in the argument was therefore to brand all 'anti-imperialist' forces with
the 'progressive' label.[37]

Of the groups and parties of the left, the Mojahedin-e Khalq (*Mojahedin*), Hezb-e Tudeh-e Iran (*Tudeh*) and the Fedaiyan-e Khalq (*Fedai*)
may be counted as the most influential. On the eve of the Revolution,
bound by the Third Worldist and 'dependency theory' analyses of
imperialism, the leadership of each of the latter regarded 'anti-imperialism' as the principal feature of the revolution. Massoud Rajavi, one
of the leaders of the Mojahedin, claimed 'we are engaged in an anti-
imperialist revolution which is taking place with the participation of
all classes, layers and forces dependent on them. So naturally the
national issue takes priority over the class issue at the moment'. In
their new programme in 1979 the Mojahedin emphasised 'the need to
combat Western imperialism'.[38] While they saw the long-term objectives of the movement as being a 'classless society', their programme at
this stage was 'nothing but the complete destruction of imperialist
rule'.[39] Similarly, Noureddin Kianouri, Secretary General of the Tudeh
regarded Iran as being 'in the midst of a democratic anti-imperialist
revolution' the main demand of which was for the United States to
leave the country.[40] The minimum programme for the provisional
government published by the Fedai also declared 'the main aim of the
Revolution [as] the destruction of the dependent capitalist regime
through the overthrow of imperialist rule and its lackeys and the
comprehensive establishment of the rule of the people [*khalq*]'.[41]

The Mojahedin warned that imperialism was exploiting divisive
issues and stressed that if the nation did not remain behind Khomeini, imperialists would repeat the 1953 coup. They backed Khomeini's denouncement of the US Senate for criticising the type of
'revolutionary justice' being meted out in Iran, and repeatedly called
for national mobilisation to prepare for possible US invasion. Later in
1979 they criticised the social unrest in Tabriz on grounds that at a
time of national emergency all Iranians, irrespective of class and religion, had to stand against US imperialism.[42] At its Sixteenth Plenum
in February 1979, the Tudeh Party had declared its support for
Khomeini.[43] The party called for a people's democratic front against
imperialist threats to the Revolution. It thus became the leading
proponent of the idea of the 'progressive clergy' based upon the
latter's anti-imperialism and radical economic policies, including

extensive nationalisation, land reform programmes and commitment to the oppressed.[44] The Tudeh categorised every group that expressed opposition to the Islamic Republic as part of the 'united anti-revolutionary front', and called upon the regime to arm guards more heavily to defend the Revolution.[45] Of the large left organisations, the Fedai stood apart in expressing reservations and criticisms of developments in the new regime, leading to tensions and factionalism within the organisation. Nonetheless, while the Fedai initially called Bazargan's provisional government 'legitimate' and 'national', contrasting its respect for democratic freedoms to the 'reactionary fundamentalists', not long after they became critical of the government for falling in behind popular anti-imperialist objectives.[46] A commentary in *Kar*, the newspaper of the Fedai, emphasised:

a reactionary is one who is dependent on imperialism, the big bourgeoisie, the liberals and the feudals and defends their interests. A progressive is one who struggles against imperialism, the big bourgeoisie, the liberals and the feudals.[47]

Seeing the *maktabi* faction of the clergy as radical, anti-capitalist and progressive, the Fedai 'majority' tendency gave the latter full support. The Fedai decided to uphold the 'genuine anti-imperialism' of the radical wing of the regime, ignoring its profoundly anti-democratic aspects. Thus, unity of the 'anti-imperialist forces' was placed foremost on the agenda and overrode the commitment to democratic rights.

Most of the secular leftist forces thus developed analyses which led them either unequivocally to support the 'progressive clergy' or to criticise the provisional government for its lack of commitment to anti-imperialism, rather than protest against the reactionary stance taken on social and democratic issues. This position helped to shift the revolutionary discourse away from the struggle for social and democratic rights and allowed the religious leadership to establish its hegemony by riding on its anti-imperialist credentials.

Throughout this period Ayatollah Khomeini consistently referred to the need to maintain national independence and sever dependent relations with the West:

If we want the country really to be saved, the first priority is to save ourselves from Westoxification.[48]

Until this country extricates itself from Westoxification, it will not achieve independence.[49]

The main target of this rhetoric was the United States. The immediate post-revolutionary period was haunted by the very real fears of an externally engineered *coup d'etat* and a return of the shah or a military dictatorship subservient to the United States in a parody of 1953. These fears were reflected in large sectors of the media, which claimed time and again to reveal the numerous 'plots' and 'conspiracies' of the United States against the Iranian revolution.[50] The outburst of specifically anti-US sentiments was given one of its first major opportunities with President Carter's Middle East visit in the context of the Arab–Israeli peace negotiations. There were close links between Iranian revolutionaries and the Palestine Liberation Organisation (PLO), and PLO leader Yasser Arafat had declared his support for the Iranian Revolution as having 'threatened the interests of imperialism in the region' and made allegations about 'Carter's military conspiracy against the Iranian revolution'. These links stimulated rallies in protest against 'American plots against Iran and Palestine'.[51] The Tehran University 'anti-imperialist rally' in March 1979, attended by large numbers and with speeches by representatives of the PLO and the *Mojahedin-e Khalq* invited people to be vigilant against the plots of 'world-devouring global imperialism'.[52] In May 1979, when the US Senate issued a resolution protesting against the abuse of human rights in Iran following the execution without trial of officials of the previous regime by the Revolutionary Courts, the Iranian government responded with an official complaint. Ebrahim Yazdi, Foreign Minister of the provisional government, claimed the Senate resolution to be 'clear interference in the internal affairs of Iran'. Large-scale anti-US demonstrations, fervently supported by organisations and parties of the left, ensued.[53]

This rising tide of popular sentiment was reflected in Khomeini's revolutionary sermons and speeches. The greatest thrust of Khomeini's rhetoric continued to be directed against the United States. He repeatedly made references to a constant conspiracy directed from the United States, evoking fears of a repetition of past involvement which threatened the existence of the Islamic Republic. In the context of the various domestic social struggles taking place around the issue of social rights and the nationalities, the solution he insisted upon was the maintenance of unity. Soon any semblance of dissent from the 'principles of Islam' was delegitimised as playing into the hands of the counter-revolutionary US conspiracy:

> Today while the issue of confrontation with America lies at the top of our Islamic agenda, if our forces disunite, this will benefit America and now our enemy is America and all our resources must be directed against this enemy. ... Today whatever disturbance which is directed in any other direction will be to their advantage.[54]

This stance also had a decisive influence on the fate of the provisional post-revolutionary government. The Revolution resulted in the implementation of a number of policies to the detriment of the interests of the United States and the Western alliance. Iran had pulled out of the US-led regional military alliance (CENTO) during the course of the revolution. In July 1979, the Law for the Protection and Expansion of Iranian Industry was approved, allowing the nationalisation of heavy industries. Commercial relations with the United States were disrupted as payments for large orders of mainly military goods from the United States also ceased. However, in the immediate post-revolutionary period certain factors, including strong economic ties, served as impediments to the complete severance of relations.[55] Firstly, the cessation of payments to the United States prompted the US Department of Defence to take action in order to restructure or terminate contracts by sending an envoy to Tehran to negotiate with Iranian officials. The members of the provisional government, as the legitimate leaders and representatives of Iran, were locked into dealing with US officials on such matters. Additionally, the interpretation of the 'Neither East nor West' slogan by the provisional government was that the Islamic Republic should remain independent, but also avoid the 'communist threat' and therefore remain more open to the West. In the letter of the Foreign Ministry to the US government in May 1979, the wish of the Iranian government to 'establish friendly relations with the United States based on securing the independence of the country and national interests and mutual respect' was expressed.[56]

This led to increasing criticism of the provisional government. The greater the extent of contacts between the members of the provisional government and US officials, the more the likelihood of their being discredited as 'American agents' when these connections were revealed. In contrast, a prominent faction of the religious leadership associated with the Islamic Republic Party (IRP) maintained a strong anti-US attitude which resonated with the anti-imperialism of the leftist groups and rising mass sentiments. These trends contributed to the gradual replacement of the secular leadership by the religious elite as the rightful heirs to Mosaddeq's nationalist legacy.

The most significant moment for these developments came in early November 1979. The shah's admission to the United States for medical treatment on 22 October of that year, and the meeting between Mehdi Bazargan and Zbigniew Brzezinski in Algiers on 2 November, fanned extremism. This played a major role in the demise of the provisional government and had a crucial impact on subsequent social and political developments.[57] The shah's presence in the United States further raised the spectre of a conspiracy by the United States to engineer another *coup d'etat* and return the monarch to the country. In the popular rally of 3 November, Khomeini's speech was broadcast to the demonstrators castigating the United States for conspiring against Iran. In its resolution the rally demanded the return of the shah to Iran, but also warned of conspiracies, condemned alleged US interference in Iran, particularly in Kurdistan and other instances of social unrest, and demanded the annulment of all agreements with foreign countries contrary to the interests of the people.[58] Concomitantly, the Islamic Republic Party issued a statement to the provisional government revealing and severely reprimanding the meeting between members of the provisional government and US officials.[59] On the following day the US embassy in Tehran was stormed and occupied by a group identified as 'Muslim Student Followers of the Line of the Imam', who took as hostages the US diplomats in the embassy complex.

The occupation of the embassy and taking of hostages was celebrated not only by the clergy-dominated organisations such as the IRP, Qom Seminary, Mojahedin of the Revolution and the Movement of Combatant Muslims, [60] but also by the 'anti-imperialist left', such as the Tudeh Party, which had played a significant role in discrediting Bazargan's provisional government.[61] Following the takeover of the US embassy by the Muslim Student Followers of the Imam's Line, Tudeh's General Secretary Kianouri stressed the 'new phase of the Iranian Revolution', ending the domination by the United States and deepening of the Revolution's class content; he called for the continued detention of US personnel to prevent normalisation of relations with the United States.[62] The Mojahedin-e Khalq also gave their full support to the Muslim Student Followers of the Imam's Line. During this period the Fedai newspaper *Kar* denounced the government as 'comprador' and 'liberal bourgeois', as opposed to the 'anti-imperialist Khomeini', and blamed the Nationalist Front for conspiracy noting the 'role of imperialism and reaction'.

The domestic consequences

The events of November 1979 became a political tool with which to discredit opposition to the growing power of the clerics. Files and documents produced from the US embassy proliferated. The discovery of classified information by the groups storming the building led to revelations regarding every Iranian who had had any contact with the embassy, who was then potentially subject to prosecution.[63] The main victims of this turn were in the first instance the members of the provisional government, seen in derisory terms as 'liberals' who would return Iran to dependence on the United States; they were forced to resign following the embassy takeover.[64]

The political consequences of this moment in the Revolution were undoubtedly to concentrate power in the hand of a small group that was largely dominated by a number of clerical figures, and to detract from pressing social and economic problems. Moreover it assisted the passing of the Constitution of the Islamic Republic with its various reactionary clauses, which was presented as a matter of urgency in the context of the need to unite against the US conspiracy. While Bazargan had been in office, only one clause on the mandate of the *velayat-e faqih* (guardianship of the jurisconsult) had been passed. After his ousting, various clauses granting extensive powers to the highest-ranking religious leadership were added to the Draft Constitution then put forward for referendum. Khomeini urged the masses to unite in support of this proposed Constitution of the Islamic Republic against the common enemy:

> I will be voting in favour [of the constitution] on election day and I ask of all my dear brothers and sisters of all layers of society and from wherever they are to vote in favour of this fateful law. My beloved! Today while we face a satanic enemy ... do not allow the weakening of the foundations of the Islamic Republic.[65]
>
> If you believe in Islam, so you also have to believe in the Islamic state. Islam is in danger. And if you are nationalist, so your country is in danger. ... If there is disunity amongst us, this will be to the advantage of America and the great powers.[66]

The Islamic Republic's leaders used the anti-imperialist rhetoric to suppress the demands of various social groups for social and political rights and freedoms by denouncing them as agents of imperialism and counter-revolution, and also by professing an Islamic populism – a rhetorical claim to represent the masses – and therefore forging popular unity. Khomeini denounced human rights as the 'rights of the superpowers'.[67] Human rights organisations and the United Nations were all condemned:

> all these organisations and groups have been created to support the powerful and [these] associations have been created by the powerful to dominate the weak and suck the blood of the oppressed in the world. ... The notorious organisations they have there, which are there to serve the powerful and international capitalists, ignore the rights of the oppressed and [do] nothing except dominate the oppressed.[68]

Khomeini constantly referred to the 'conspiracies of the West-stricken' in thwarting the passing of the constitution and designated the concept of 'democracy' a Western construction irrelevant to Islamic society.[69] This process was perhaps most conspicuous in the rapid restrictions placed on women and their rights in this period.

Populism and the 'women's question'

In several of his messages and interviews from Paris, Khomeini had reassured women that they would have nothing to fear from his leadership and would have everything to gain in the society he envisioned. In fact, however, the idea of gender equality was for him a blasphemy and a Western plot, and the corrupting influence of the West was a repetitive theme in his popular statements. At the end of June 1980, announcing that every sign of the shah's rule must be destroyed, Khomeini decreed the requirement of Islamic clothing, *hejab*, for women. In a collective effort many women came to the streets in protest; in response, *hezbollahi* gangs chanted 'death to the foreign dolls'. Newspapers in support of the regime such as *Jomhuri-ye Islami* and *Ettela'at* denounced the protesters as supporters of the shah and Bakhtiar who were using the issue of women's rights to destabilise the Islamic Republic and the Revolution. Headlines and captions referred to them as 'American, CIA and imperialist agents'.

The Islamic leadership flaunted its own brand of 'female populism', and used this to undermine the secular women's movement and establish cultural hegemony in this area. Many held that discussion of women's rights was irrelevant to Muslim society since these rights were enshrined in Islam. Khomeini advised women to be happy with the status Islam had given them and not to allow the 'present day Satans' to deceive them and divert them from Islam in the name of freedom and human rights. In order to mobilise women, the regime declared 7 May 1980, birthday of the Prophet's daughter Fatima, as Women's Day and organised marches and demonstrations to commemorate, as well as extensive propaganda in the national media. A newly formed Islamic women's grouping, *Jame'eh-e zanan-e enqelab-e Islami* (Women's society of the Islamic Revolution), expressed its support for the spread of the 'Islamic cover' in a declaration issued in 1980 encouraging women to use the instrument of *hejab* in the fight against Western imperialism. In general, officials of the Islamic Republic politicised the concept by equating resistance to *hejab* with a conspiracy directed by the United States to destroy the republic. A major five-day seminar was organised by the society of Muslim Women Office Employees in Tehran in July 1980. President Bani Sadr's speech, read by a representative, noted that Iranian women should free themselves from the exploitation by the West in the form of blind imitation of their fashions and ways and establish 'real Islamic values' and not be diverted by side issues.[70]

Zahra Rahnavard, sister in law of Khomeini's future successor Ayatollah Khamenei, wrote a series of articles in *Ettela'at* and by July 1980 was given editorship of *Ettela'at-e Banuvan* (Women's *Ettela'at*), which was a medium for the regime's propaganda, encouraging a reduction in women's working hours and a return to their 'primary tasks' in the home. In July 1980 she wrote a series of articles in *Ettela'at* entitled 'Colonial Roots of the Abolition of *Hejab*'. Referring back to the enforced unveiling of women carried out in the 1920s by Reza Shah, she concluded that to gain back her lost identity the Muslim woman should wear the veil:

> Yes, we can use the *hejab* as an anti-colonial weapon against these looters. That is exactly why the planners behind the shah prevented veiled women's entry into universities and offices. And that is why the raising of this issue, the wearing of the veil as an anti-colonial dress, although I don't agree with the particular way in which it is done at the moment, has so angered these female servants of America. They protest against it to please their masters. This is precisely the protest of America that is voiced through its internal allies

In the meanwhile, as the regime encroached upon women's rights and activities, the left remained quiet.[71] The sole criterion for judging whether the leadership of the Revolution should be supported was whether the 'national liberation movement' took an 'anti-imperialist' stance, and this extended itself to the regime's reactionary policies towards women. As a result, most leftist groups showed little or no support for women's demonstrations, and the Mojahedin and Tudeh even criticised them for playing into the hands of imperialists and endangering the Revolution.

On 8 March 1980 an article in *Kar*, newspaper of the Fedai (majority section), described the women's protests of the previous year thus:

> last year on March 8 following Ayatollah Khomeini's statements that female employees of the ministries should wear the Islamic veil, a group of women, affiliated with the capitalist class, tried to divert the political demonstrations and protests of the progressive and revolutionary women and alter the revolutionary content of International Women's Day. Fortunately the conscious and combatant women of Iran recognised the infiltration of their ranks by the liberal and even suspicious women and neutralised the danger posed by the counter-revolutionary forces at that time.[72]

The influence of the groups and parties on the left pervaded women's organisations, and in particular the National Union of Women (NUW) which drew on classical Marxist-Leninist texts for the political education of its members.[73] The majority of leftist organisations did not acknowledge women's oppression as separate from class oppression or its solution as apart from the destruction of the class system, faithfully following the Third International's rejection of a 'special' women's issue which was to be resolved after the socialist revolution. In fact, an anti-feminist bias pervaded the left even among those who had studied abroad and come into contact with feminist thought and practice. The most common charge was that it is a specifically Western and bourgeois ideology.

On 1 May 1979 the National Union of Women issued their charter entailing six principles stating, 'we consider struggle against imperialism our primary objective, for it is capitalist society and dependent capitalism that exploit the toiling masses, cause the inequality of rights between women and men and turn women into consumers of luxury goods.'

When in November 1979 various women's groups organised the Women's Unified Conference, in the context of the recent occupation of the US embassy, half the points of the declared resolution dealt with the problem of fighting imperialism in Iran, declaring that 'Iranian women, as in the past, do not consider their struggle as separate from that of the toiling masses for liberation from the slavish dependency on imperialism.'[74] As a prominent figure in the women's movement, Homa Nateq, later noted, most left-leaning women's organisations 'saw imperialism and nothing else as our national problem'.[75]

Thus, the issue of democratic rights for women was also subsumed under the populist rhetoric of the religious elite, who effectively used their anti-Western and anti-imperialist credentials to discredit those who attempted to fight for these rights and resist the regressive policies advocated by the *ulema*. Once more, the dominant discourse of secular elements, in particular the left, meant that women were consigned to the heap of secondary issues, thus allowing the ruling elite to push through their programme.

Urban and rural social conflict

The populist rhetoric also served to discredit collective action on part of workers and encourage discipline. The anti-imperialist rhetoric of the regime was used to discourage 'agitators' as agents of 'internationally directed counter-revolutionary forces'. The regime's ability to discredit dissent was thus facilitated by its emphasis of the 'anti-imperialist' cause. This stance was again given legitimacy by Khomeini's statements:

These spies who call themselves devotees of the people ... set fire to the (crops) and stop the factories from working. ... Their spying has been proven, as has their connection with Zionism.[76]

Workers are the most valuable class in society ... workers' day is also the people's day. ... [A group of people] in the name of taking the side of the workers are preventing them from working. ... The criminal hand of America is behind these armed struggles.[77]

Existing workers' councils were discredited and dismantled, being replaced by 'Islamic associations' with the help of the Islamic Republican Party, which was moving towards ideological indoctrination of workers and employees. The party's populist, anti-imperialist and pro-dispossessed rhetoric appealed to many council members and most of the left-wing organisations, and disguised their general anti-democratic and anti-working class nature. The portrayal of the 'Islamic councils' as the true representatives of the workers, the new-found independence of the country and its industry and the need for unity against 'counter-revolutionaries' was bolstered by Khomeini in his speeches in this period:

> Strike after strike ... demonstration after demonstration [can be seen and heard]. ... I ask of all the layers of the beloved nation to rally to support the government which is to support the deprived and not to allow those who encourage disunity to gain influence among them.[78]

The Islamic Republic was presented as belonging to the deprived and under-privileged masses, and free of the class differences that were hallmarks of the previous regime:

> If there is ... a conspiracy ... in the Oil Company ... this has to be seen to ... be assured that your labour now belongs to you, the country belongs to you; it is not like the past when others would reap all the benefits.[79]
>
> I ask of the oil workers and employees for their support, to work for the country ... not to shut down. The country now belongs to them, the oil is their own. ... The compensation that they get is in return for work; if they don't work enough the compensation is *haram*.[80]

The working class was at this time structurally weakened by the continuing economic crisis that resulted in constantly rising unemployment which compelled workers to reduce their demands in order to keep their jobs. Furthermore, political differences between the secular leftist organisations that had influence among the workers and the ill-informed analyses of the regime added to the incapacity of workers. Thus, through its populist rhetoric, the regime was able more readily to bring the working class under its control and effect compromises with this social group. Controls were gradually increased as 'one-man management' was imposed in large factories. Eventually, the working class was disarmed of its most effective weapon, the right to strike, as the ruling clerics organised a gathering in February 1981 consisting of the 'representatives' of 170 Islamic associations of factories to condemn any form of labour strike.[81]

In many provinces, similar emphasis on the importance of unity in face of an external or foreign threat was utilised to suppress the movements for autonomy and national self-determination. These movements, which often evolved as armed struggles during the first post-revolutionary year, were largely concentrated in Turkmanistan, Kurdistan and Khuzistan. Khomeini put expressions of unrest down to the interference of external actors blaming US and British forces for the 'creation of divisions' in Iran.[82] The anti-US tide in the latter half of the year thus allowed these movements to be suppressed as counter-revolutionary and foreign-influenced:

> People who are dependent on America and the like are now in the universities ... in the desert ... in Kurdistan ... in Baluchistan. ...Where else have they got the money to pay two or three thousand employees not to work? ... Where are their funds coming from? ... Oh Fedai-ye-Khalq! Where have you obtained your weapons? [83]

In the rural areas and in respect of the issue of land reform and appropriations, the regime again emphasised the need for unity in face of the common US threat. On the other hand, the regime vied with secular forces by stressing its role in protecting the interests of the deprived peasant masses, emphasising their centrality to the Islamic Republic and establishing the organisation of a 'construction crusade' (*jihad-e-sazandegi*), which also served to undermine secular forces engaged in the peasant movements.

In fact an ambitious and radical land reform programme initially followed the resignation of the Bazargan government.[84] The radical stance taken by some religious leaders, and in particular members of the Revolutionary Council, had two major consequences. Firstly, it increased the revolutionary credentials of the religious leadership among the peasants and deprived masses, as well as giving cause for some secular leftist forces to rally behind the 'progressive clergy'. As in the case of industrial workers, the clergy were perceived to be taking the initiative in terms of offering radical reform programmes alongside a consistent policy of delegitimisation and repression. The belief that some ex-SAVAK agents and supporters of the shah were using every opportunity to destabilise the Revolution and attack the left became widespread, as the left became reluctant to blame supporters of the Islamic Republic for such activities.[85]

The second major consequence was that the issue of land reform became dependent on the interpretation of Islam with respect to the legitimacy of private property. Radical revolutionary factions undercut the legitimacy of private property. However, they were at odds with the interests of the landed merchants, who also provided the regime with financial support and who did not refrain from taking active measures to oppose the bill, ranging from propaganda and legislative lobbying to engaging in violent peasant/landlord conflicts.[86] Various conservative clergy with the backing and insistence of reactionary landowners mobilised against the land reform programme and issued *fetwas* (religious decrees) against it. The ambivalence which arose from this situation is well reflected in the non-committal position which Khomeini took on this issue:

> Ownership, if it is *mashroo* ... it is respected ... whether they call us reactionary or not ... and if it is not *mashroo* it is not respected. ... Let us suppose someone has property and his property is *mashroo*, but the property is such that the *vali amr* judges that this should not be as much as it is and is not to the benefit of the Muslim (community) then he can appropriate and occupy. ... The *vali amr* can limit this property.[87]

This very ambiguity about whether various land reform programmes are Islamic or not had one consistent consequence of giving leeway and flexibility to landowners and those who presided over various economic and coercive resources. It provided 'the best chance for arbitrariness to the warlords of the Islamic Republican regime [who could] do as they please in regard to both the land and the peasants'.[88]

The fate of the movement of the urban poor and unemployed was sealed in a similar manner. As Asef Bayat puts it, 'in the dramatic atmosphere associated with the seizure of the US embassy ... the concerns of the unemployed were lost in the noisy campaign of "Islam against the Great Satan".'[89] In fact, on the same day as the storming of the United States embassy, a large group of unemployed were demonstrating in Tehran, but their demands were stifled by the nationalist outcry of the embassy takeover. Subsequently, political pressure on the demonstrating unemployed and the groups organising their activities intensified. Sit-ins by the unemployed were disrupted by the armed

Revolutionary Guard. Friday prayer leaders would denounce the unemployed activists as agents of a counter-revolution.[90]

The urban homeless, who had taken to occupation of empty dwellings and hotels, were also faced with eviction. 'Knowingly or unknowingly, they had violated a fundamental property right that all the governments in the post-Revolution period were committed to protect.'[91] While a number of radical clerics encouraged occupations and takeovers, conservatives again upheld the sanctity of private property. Various tactics were used to force eviction of the squatters including public denunciation of the actions as 'un-Islamic'. The seizure of the US embassy helped to divide ranks amongst the organisers of the squatting activities and led to the evacuation of many hotels. Eventually, the squatters faced various limitations imposed by the state, and the advent of political repression curtailed activist support for the movement.

In sum, by concentrating on 'anti-imperialism' and the need to combat foreign – largely US – conspiracies, Khomeini's populist rhetoric served to establish the hegemonic leadership of a small clerical elite over a large spectrum of the population, to consolidate state power and to delegitimise the demands of various social groups in the post-revolutionary period.

International consequences

While Khomeini's 'anti-imperialist' populist rhetoric had a profound impact on the domestic balance of social forces, it was also a major influence on the international relations, foreign outlook and policies of the Islamic Republic. This largely concerned the stance of the Islamic Republic with respect to the superpowers – in particular the United States – the universalist tendency of the Revolution and the drive to export the Revolution internationally.

The Islamic Republic adopted a policy of hostility towards the international status quo dominated by the superpowers. The critical turning point in the external relations of the post-revolutionary regime was indubitably the occupation of the US embassy and the taking of US hostages in November 1979. From this moment, in the context of a tide of popular anti-US sentiment, a situation of extreme tension prevailed between the Islamic Republic and the United States and its allies. Souring of relations with the West did not, however, spell an era of flowering amicable relations with the Soviet Union as Iranian leaders continued to be reproachful of 'imperialism of the East' and, more specifically, the Soviet invasion of Afghanistan.

With the resignation of the provisional government following the storming of the embassy in November 1979, the foreign policy of the

Islamic Republic took a more extreme anti-US turn. While the Bazargan government had emphasised the need to maintain friendly relations with all countries on the basis of the independence of the country and the principle of non-alignment, there were now calls, supported by many of the leftist organisations, for the complete cessation of relations with the United States.

Khomeini, meanwhile, pandered to these anti-imperialist and anti-US sentiments. He refused all overt attempts by the Carter administration to negotiate the issue of the hostages in this period and referred to the United States as the 'Great Satan' and the source of all conspiracies against the Islamic Republic. 'Today there are underground treacheries in these embassies ... and the most important and main one is the one belonging to the Great Satan which is America.'[92]

As volumes of classified information held in the US embassy in Tehran were gradually released by those occupying the building, the accusations of treachery gained greater credence and momentum. As US warships began to patrol the Persian Gulf area, the Islamic Republic issued threats to execute the US hostages in retaliation. Popular demonstrations were held in Iran to celebrate the severance of diplomatic relations with the United States while the failed US attempt to rescue the hostages in April 1980 raised the stakes yet further and heightened tension between the two states.[93] More explicit and vehement threats were issued by the 'Muslim students' holding the US hostages:

> We assure you that if America tries to resort to these clumsy and cowardly tricks again, it will not only face the filthy, lifeless corpses of the hostages but all those responsible for these plots will be buried in the soil of Iran.[94]

These events helped to put the Iranian Revolution on a more staunchly anti-US trajectory. As the following radio commentary indicates, criticism by the more extremist elements of the new government and the relative moderation in its foreign relations gained momentum:

> Are the Iranian embassies abroad ... worthy of the Islamic Revolution? Did the Iranian ministers of foreign affairs not realise that in this critical post they should have first reformed the ministry itself and then the embassies so that they could prepare the way for exporting the Revolution to other countries? Is it in the interest of the Iranian Revolution that the Minister of Foreign Affairs should arrive in dependent countries like Bahrain and hold talks with its leaders at the time when those leaders send the Muslim strugglers in

their countries to the execution squads? Is it right that he should collaborate with America on the issue of the Muslim crusaders of Afghanistan whose torrent of blood washes away the army of blasphemy? Is it in keeping with the Islamic Revolution of Iran that the Foreign Minister sits at the same table with Ziaul Haq, the American dictator ... and Agha Shahi the direct agent of the CIA in the Middle East discussing Afghanistan and other Islamic issues – or is that a way of assisting the West?[95]

The hostility and tension with the United States was enflamed and exacerbated also by Soviet policy and statements at this time. Soviet leaders had an interest in the direction of the Revolution and the role of the Soviet-aligned forces of the left on the one hand, and in preventing the re-establishment of close ties with the United States on the other. Throughout this period the Soviet media consistently raised fears about the possibility of US intervention and counter-revolution in Iran through the Persian language 'National Voice of Radio', broadcast from the Soviet Union and the Soviet-aligned parties of the left.[96] In January 1979 the Soviet press and radio warned of an imminent US coup. Various forms of dissent within the new regime were attributed to the CIA or pro-shah forces as counter-revolutionary elements attempting to destabilise the fledgling revolutionary regime. Soviet radio broadcasts in March and April 1979 regarding the regional move-ments for autonomy in Kurdistan, Baluchistan and Turkmanistan were a prime example. The Soviet newspaper *Pravda* ran an editorial on 9 November 1979 on the meeting in Algiers between Bazargan and Brzezinski, stressing the economic exploitation by the West, the issue of the shah's wealth, frozen assets and the evils of capitalism. In the aftermath of Washington's failed attempt to engineer a rescue mission for the US hostages in Tehran, *Pravda*, in its 1 May 1980 issue, spoke of the invasion of Iran and on the following day referred to the mission as a cover for a *coup d'etat* against the Iranian government in which Khomeini was to be kidnapped. The overriding effect of this propa-ganda directed from Moscow was to raise fears about a repeat of the 1953 incident and allow the radicalisation of the revolutionaries in their witch-hunt for 'agents of imperialism'.

However, while the leadership of the Islamic Republic adopted much of this anti-US propaganda into their own rhetoric to raise fears of the prospect of intervention and counter-revolution, the hostility and confrontation with the 'superpower of the West' did not have as its corollary close relations with the 'superpower of the East'. A resolution issued by demonstrators in January 1980 following the Soviet invasion of Afghanistan stated:

The struggling Iranian nation led by the Imam Khomeini, while preparing itself to struggle against the United States, is also opposed to the blasphemous colonialism ruling the East and is under no circumstances prepared to lose its independence and freedom. ... The Iranian nation denounces the Soviet military intervention in Afghanistan and wishes success to the combatant Afghan brothers who are waging battle against the iniquitous Soviet intervention for the independence of their realm.[97]

The need to maintain a modicum of relations with its northerly neighbour, the lesser threat of Soviet intervention due to historical reasons, the Soviet attitude to the Iranian Revolution and the alignment of the left with the regime all meant, however, that anti-Soviet rhetoric did not match the slogans directed at the United States. As the Iranian Ambassador to the Soviet Union put it:

Of course all that [dispute with the USSR] is not substantial enough to disturb the friendly relations between our country and the USSR. We do have trade and economic relations with the USSR and there are many issues which we approve.[98]

Although diplomatic relations were maintained with the Soviet Union, however, the Islamic Republic maintained a strict notion of 'non-alignment' in its slogan of 'Neither East nor West'.

The hostile stance of the Islamic Republic towards the dominant states within the international system can be traced to a specific history of influence and involvement which we discussed in Chapter 2. The maintenance of this posture in foreign policy had two particular consequences for the external relations of the Islamic Republic. Firstly, it led to the more vociferous international promotion of the Islamic Republic as the vanguard of the oppressed peoples and the global alternative to 'imperialism of East and West'. This extended beyond 'non-alignment' and fed into the universalising discourse of the Revolution in the encouragement of revolutionary movements in other countries based on the Iranian model. 'Brotherly commitments towards all Muslims and protection of the deprived of the world' became a principle of foreign policy enshrined in the constitution of the Islamic Republic.

Secondly, the Islamic Republic found itself in a situation of international isolation. Furthermore, the potential threat of intervention or interference continued to loom both in the popular mind and in the calculations of state leaders. Under such conditions, apart from the ideological element of the 'export of revolution', there existed a very practical consideration of the need for international support and allies in order to counter-balance the hostility of the international system. As Abol-Hasan Bani Sadr, first president of the Islamic Republic put it, one aspect of the regime's foreign policy would be:

> aid to all the freedom movements of the world [for] if we do not help these movements we shall not be able to achieve release from the domination of the superpowers, for helping them is in reality helping ourselves for if we do not help them the world powers will be able to defeat them and will eventually defeat us too.[99]

Both of these dynamics powered the universalist engine of the Islamic Republic. In other words, both the ideological premise of the Islamic Republic and the need for allies in a context of international isolation gave impetus to the policy of promotion of 'Islamic Revolution' abroad.

Export of revolution: Iraq, Palestine, Lebanon and the Gulf

The language of 'export of the Revolution' littered the vocabulary of the religious leadership. This rhetoric began to gain momentum as religious leaders, now setting the pace of political events, more explicitly called on peoples to rise up in revolutionary movements and overthrow other regimes. Regional states that maintained their ties to the superpowers or remained within military or economic alliances were denounced as collaborators of global imperialism and the puppets of external powers. Local populations were encouraged to engage actively in opposing these regimes by following the Iranian example. Moreover, and conversely, the Iranian Revolution served as a source of inspiration for movements of opposition across the region. The revolutionary movement, which had overthrown the palpably strong state ruled by the shah, came to be seen as a model for social action against the prevailing socio-economic and political status quo in a number of states of the region. While specific social grievances, historical experiences and forms of organisation differed from place to place, revolutionary struggle began to be conceived as a viable alternative to other, often more conciliatory forms of resistance. The leaders of the Islamic Republic, on their part, did not hesitate to draw on this revolutionary potential of populations in order to promote 'Islamic Revolution'.

In their sermons and speeches, Iran's revolutionary leaders pointed to the need to export the Revolution 'by means of words and bringing the message of the Revolution' and 'awakening all the people who are like us'.[100] Support was expressed for various movements across the globe, including the Muslims of Afghanistan, Eritrea, Philippines, Southern Lebanon, Palestine and the Polisario, as the Islamic Republic was presented as the vanguard of the oppressed of the world.[101] The ardently internationalist slogan of the Islamic Republic Party proclaimed 'Glory to the international Islamic Revolution. Final victory to the oppressed'.[102] Extensive international networks of active supporters and propaganda issued from Tehran aimed at the over-throw of regional states and the establishment of parallel regimes aligned with Iran. In order to promote revolution globally and fulfil the internationalist aspirations of the regime, a foreign radio broadcasting service was established primarily aimed at the Arabic-speaking popu-lations of the region, but also including broadcasts in various other languages.[103] Additionally, an Office of Liberation Movements (*vahed-e nehzat-ha*) was formed, initially under the auspices of the newly formed Islamic Revolutionary Guard Corps (*sepah-e pasdaran-e enqelab-e eslami* hereafter *Pasdaran*).[104] The constitution of this office spelt out its main premises and political aims:

> The world in which we live is full of inequality and injustice. The arrogant powers and the exploiters have divided the world into two blocs of East and West and each is plundering the meek nations. ... It is incumbent upon this Muslim nation to unite and liberate the oppressed nations. ... Our Aims: 1– ... the formation of a strong global Islamic force ... 4– to raise the consciousness of the meek people and nations across the world, 5– assistance and co-operation with all the justice-seeking forces which have revolted against the oppressors without being dependent ... 7– armed struggle against any regime which does not follow the true path of Islam even if it goes under the name of Islam, 8– the preparation of all the oppressed for revolt against the oppressors on a particular day ...[105]

The regime also organised a number of international conferences in Tehran and other Iranian cities for Muslim leaders and Friday Imams thereby helping to create a network of organised Islamic opposition that found its fulcrum in the Iranian regime.[106] The final resolution of the World Friday Imams' Congress in Tehran in May 1984 thus declared the aims of a 'united movement of the world of Islam' and 'support for liber-ation and independence movements'. Regional propaganda focused on 'the struggle of the Muslim, Lebanese and Palestinian revolutionaries and other Muslims of the world', urging them to foil 'all the plots of international arrogance and reactionaries'.[107] Further afield, the Islamic Republic declared support for 'all liberation movements against West and East' including the 'justice-seeking and freedom-loving people of Ireland' and the 'oppressed Afro-Americans'.[108] The greatest thrust of the Islamic Republic's urge to export revolution was, nevertheless, aimed largely at regional Muslim populations and most directly at the Iraqi masses who were encouraged to rise in an Iranian-inspired movement to topple the Ba'th regime.

The quest for revolution in Iraq

The religious leadership in Iran had close contacts with Shi'i leaders in Iraq and believed there to be a revolutionary potential in the neighbouring country that would simultaneously remove a regional threat, in the shape of the secular Ba'th regime and provide the Islamic Republic with a close ally at its doorstep. Thus, the Iranian leadership hastened the radicalisation of the Islamic opposition in Iraq by encouraging *al-da'wah al-islamiyah* (the Islamic Call Society) and prompting the formation of *al-mojahedin*.[109] They also increasingly called on the Iraqi people at large to rise against their oppressive regime. Numerous Iranian media reports condemned the Iraqi regime for conducting a 'police state' and claimed the Iranian Revolution to be the aspiration of the Shi'i majority in Iraq. In early 1980 Ayatollah Montazeri denounced the Iraqi regime for mistreatment of the Islamic opposition within the country and conspiring against Iran through regional policies:

> we have received news that some of our Muslim brothers have been executed in Iraq. Now the role that Mohammad Reza [Shah] used to play here is being assumed by that gentleman [Saddam Hussein]. He is becoming the gendarme of the region. He is conspiring against Iran. His ambassador has spread pamphlets against Iran in Beirut. Their footsteps have been found in dear Kurdistan and Khuzistan.[110]

In January 1980 a popular demonstration in Ahwaz against the Iraqi Ba'th Party directly condemned the Iraqi government and issued several anti-Iraqi slogans including:

Death to Saddam Hussein
The Ba'th Party is defeated – Islam is victorious
The Iraqi brother must be freed
Under Islamic government there is no Arab and non-Arab
Death to the three corrupt : Saddam, Sadat, Begin.[111]

Bani Sadr as president, referring to the neighbouring government as a puppet of the superpowers, claimed that the Iraqi people would soon bring the regime to its knees.[112] In its Arabic broadcasts, the Islamic Republic's principal message to the Iraqi people was to rise against their oppressors.[113]

In Iraq meanwhile, following the success of the Iranian Revolution, the confidence of the Islamic leadership was boosted. Strong links were established with Iranian counterparts. In this period, leaders of the Islamic movement in Iraq appear to have concluded that peaceful demonstrations would have to be abandoned as a means of anti-regime protest. The Revolution 'turned the gaze of the Shi'is increasingly toward Mohammad Baqer al-Sadr, the leading Shi'i leader, who send his closest disciple, Mahmud Hashimi, to represent him in Tehran.[114] In June 1979 Sadr was put under house arrest by the Ba'th Regime. Inspired by the Iranian revolution, Iraqi Shi'i supporters who came to demonstrate in his support proclaimed allegiance not only to Sadr but also to Khomeini chanting:

In the name of Khomeini and Sadr, Islam is always victorious.
Long live, long live, long live Sadr, Islam is always victorious.[115]

The Iraqi regime responded with brutal force, and in June and July 1979 executed a large number of clerics. While under house arrest Sadr dispatched tape-recorded messages to the Iraqi masses, stressing the need for a 'fighting position' and for *revolutionary* organisation. In July 1979, the newly formed Islamic Revolution Movement issued a statement supporting active struggle against the Ba'th Regime with reference to the Iranian Revolution as a source of inspiration:

The Islamic Revolution in Iran has induced the people to speak out. Popular zeal was soon translated into numerous delegations pouring on [sic] Ayatollah Mohammad Baqer al-Sadr from all over Iraq – expressing allegiance to him and accepting his leadership of the Islamic Revolution. ... The Islamic Liberation Movement shall resort to all means to deprive the Ba'thist regime and the Saddam Hussein faction particularly from [sic] their power to dominate and tyrannise the people of Iraq. ... The Islamic Liberation Movement in its present form represents a coalition of the main Islamic Parties that have been operating in Iraq for decades. The aims of the Liberation Movement are to: 1– Expose the fallacy of the Ba'thists to the people of Iraq in particular and to world opinion at large; 2– Mobilise the people of Iraq to speak out against the Ba'thist regime; 3– Win the support of other movements in the world and particularly in Iraq; 4– Isolate the Ba'thist regime from their power to control and brainwash the people.[116]

When the Iraqi regime finally executed Sadr in 1980, Ayatollah Khomeini was already publicly inviting and encouraging the Iraqi people and army to overthrow the Ba'thist regime.[117] Following the execution, the Iranian Foreign Ministry declared that the Iranian regime would not rest 'until the final overthrow of the criminal, imperialist and Zionist agent regime of the treacherous Saddam Hussein'.[118] The formation of the 'Iraqi Islamic Council' and the 'liberation army' was concomitantly announced, calling for mutiny in the regular Iraqi army with the ultimate aim of overthrowing the regime in Baghdad and replacing it with one aligned to the Islamic Republic.

The Iranian Revolution and the Arab–Israeli conflict

Another *leitmotif* of the Islamic Republic's universalist discourse was the Palestinian and Lebanese resistance against Israel. The aims of liberating Palestine and supporting the Lebanese Muslims served in fact as a fulcrum of the Islamic Republic's revolutionary foreign policy. It symbolised the regime's role as vanguard of the oppressed and foremost leader in the struggle against US imperialism and international Zionism. Declarations of support for the Palestinian Liberation Organisation were rife in public statements and the media. Many participants in the Revolution had strong ties to the Palestinian Liberation Organisation, largely through pre-revolutionary military training in Palestinian camps. These relations were further cultivated in the aftermath of the Revolution. The Israeli embassy in Tehran was replaced by a Palestinian counterpart, PLO officials frequently paid homage to the Iranian Revolution and regime and became frequent visitors to Iran.[119] As Ayatollah Montazeri, with whom the Office of Liberation Movements was closely affiliated, later urged, the promotion of revolution amongst Palestinian Muslims continued:

> liberation of beloved Jerusalem is an important issue to us. Consequently, in order to realise the solution 'today Iran, tomorrow Palestine' ... it would be appropriate for the guards to implement certain programmes both inside and outside the country to strengthen the foundations as well as the promote and expand the religious knowledge of Palestinian Muslims.[120]

In Lebanon too the revolutionary Iranian leadership endeavoured to encourage a revolutionary movement which would pull the rug from under the feet of the more moderate Amal organisation. The establishment of the Islamic Republic had significant consequences for political mobilisation of the Lebanese opposition, largely through radicalisation of the Shi'i community. The Revolution provided them with a more effective model for political action at a time when many were becoming disillusioned with the tactics and policies of the Amal.[121] A small contingent of *Pasdaran* troops (Iranian Revolutionary Guard) was dispatched to Lebanon in 1980 and their presence was officially endorsed through *majles* (parliament) legislation in June 1981. This provided an embryonic foundation for the foundation in 1982 of *hezbollah*, a radical Islamic Shi'i-dominated organisation aligned with and supported by Iran.

The universalist flames of the Revolution, were subsequently fanned by the 1982 Israeli invasion and occupation of Lebanon.[122] The event led to a substantial influx of Iranian aid and resources to Lebanon. The *Pasdaran* announced the dispatch of larger forces 'in order to engage in face to face battle against Israel'. The *Pasdaran* contingent set the scene for the expansion of Iranian operations in Lebanon. A number of individual clerics and revolutionary organisations, such as the Office of Liberation Movements and the Ali Akbar Mohtashami network, become involved in these activities. The *bonyad-e shahid* (Martyrs' Foundation) established a public and international relations department through which co-operation with 'Islamic liberation movements' was arranged. Branches of the organisation were set up in Lebanon and Syria to co-ordinate 'financial, medical, educational and social affairs'.[123] This provided a broad network of activities through which Iranian influence could be exercised and the ground prepared for the formation of a broad revolutionary movement.

The Arab Gulf States and beyond

Beyond Palestine and Lebanon, the Iranian Revolution was promoted as the model for the masses of the region to follow to topple prevailing oppressive regimes and to establish a 'just Islamic society'. The Gulf monarchies were severely reprimanded for acting in the interests of imperialism and being 'puppet regimes'. In the immediate aftermath of the Revolution the Iranian leadership instigated Islamic opposition groups in the Gulf states, proclaiming support for 'all the freedom movements of the world, especially those of Palestine, Lebanon, Iraq, [Saudi Arabia] and any other movement which has risen to break the idols under the banner of "God is Great".'[124]

The impact of the Iranian Revolution on the opposition within the Gulf States, particularly the largely disadvantaged Shi'i groups, was considerable. Before the Iranian Revolution these groups were not generally disposed towards militant political opposition, and only after 1978 did they began to engage in more radical action.[125] Khomeini appointed an Iranian-Iraqi cleric, Hadi al-Mudarrisi, as his personal representative in Bahrain. Mudarrisi's preaching gave rise to a number of demonstrations in the Gulf States in 1979, leading to clashes with the authorities and detention of the Islamic leaders. The Iranian leadership responded by encouraging the spread of 'revolutionary culture' and forming the 'Islamic Front for the Liberation of Bahrain' in Tehran. Similarly, in 1979, Khomeini appointed Abbas Muhri as his personal representative in Kuwait. In November 1979 the US embassy in Kuwait was attacked by demonstrators and in February 1980 demonstrators bearing Khomeini's portrait engaged in riot activities.[126]

Iran's efforts to influence the Islamist opposition in a bid to encourage parallel revolutionary successes were not confined to its Arab neighbours. Islamic Revolution was deemed the only solution for the crisis of the state in Turkey, while an Islamic Revolution in Pakistan was forecast as the outcome of unrest in Islamabad.[127] In Afghanistan also, the seizure of power by the secular leftist People's Democratic Party of Afghanistan (PDPA) in 1978, and the Soviet invasion in the following year, further prompted the Iranian leadership to play an active role in assisting sections of the Islamic opposition and armed groups. In their final resolution on 25 March 1980, Iranian demonstrators condemned the 'plots and violations by the Eastern colonialists', in particular against the 'Islamic brother country of Afghanistan'.[128] Iranian influence in Afghanistan was most effective amongst the Shi'i minority who, as Olivier Roy has noted, were inspired by the Revolution and adopted Iranian religious practices and the political slogans of the Revolution into their own discourse.[129] The Afghan *Sazman-i Nasr-i Islami* (Nasr), a pro-Iranian group formed as a result of the merger of pre-existing activist groups including the *geruh-e mostazafin* and *ruhaniyyat-e mubariz*, received financial aid and logistical support from Iran.[130] Later the Iranian *Pasdaran* encouraged the formation of the *Sepah-e Pasdaran* in Afghanistan which received a limited supply of weapons from Iran and recruited from young Afghans living in that country.

In sum, in the immediate aftermath of the revolution, Iranian leaders endeavoured to incite revolution beyond Iranian borders and claimed leadership of various and diverging movements of opposition. As the populist discourse of the revolutionary leadership in Iran expressed international solidarity with other – mainly Muslim – oppressed masses, the potential of similar revolutionary movements reverberated through the region. As we shall see in the next chapter, concerns about political stability and order at home and more widely in the region led to the formulation of policies by regional states designed to encounter the impact of the Iranian Revolution and contain its global repercussions.

4 International containment of the Islamic Republic

This chapter deals with the dynamic of challenge and response between the post-revolutionary Islamic Republic and international actors. The first section of the chapter assesses the policy of the United States, whose hostility towards the new regime not only entailed the pressure of diplomatic and economic sanctions, but also contributed to the invasion of the post-revolutionary state by the neighbouring Iraqi regime in direct and indirect ways. The second section then considers Iraqi and other regional responses to the Iranian Revolution and regional policies of containment of the Islamic Republic. The attitude of other states in the region to the Revolution is necessarily considered in the context of the war and from the perspective of their respective policies towards the two belligerents. The following section addresses the impact of the Revolution on the interests of the major capitalist states. In the final section we show that the Islamic Republic's policy of direct export of revolution showed little sign of success in the 1980s, in part due to the policies of containment but largely due to the specific contexts of neighbouring states.

After the hostage crisis

The storming of the US embassy in Tehran in November 1979 and the ensuing hostage crisis not only led to the severance of diplomatic relations between Tehran and Washington, but marked the onset of an intense and long-drawn period of hostility between the two. The initial concern of the Carter administration following the *fait accompli* of the Revolution and formation of the Islamic Republic had been to explore possibilities of negotiations with 'moderate elements' within the new provisional regime with the objective of safeguarding strategic interests in the Gulf. Its second aim was to protect US private property threatened by nationalisation, expropriation and repudiation of debt. The course of events in the early post-revolutionary period resulted in varying degrees of success in attaining these goals.[1]

The Carter administration responded to the taking of US hostages in Tehran by immediately halting the shipment of military spare parts to Iran, imposing visa restrictions on Iranians, imposing an embargo on oil imports from Iran, and ultimately freezing all deposits in US banks and foreign subsidiaries.[2] A military response was actively considered from the first moment of the seizure of the hostages. However, there were several constraints on such a policy.[3] On the one hand, there was concern about the economic repercussions of a military operation. Moreover, bearing in mind the continued impact of the Vietnam War on the political process in the United States, the administration was determined to avoid a situation where the United States would be trapped into an escalatory cycle leading to land combat in Iran.[4] Most importantly, the implications both for superpower relations and Soviet–Iranian relations bore heavily on US strategy, whose dilemmas had been made particularly acute by the Iranian Revolution and the disruption of the strategic and military regional alliance structure of the United States.

Decision making in Washington was greatly influenced by the Soviet invasion of Afghanistan. Sick notes the belief that 'a U.S. declaration of war against Iran at that juncture would have disrupted the Islamic consensus building against the Soviet Union and would have provided the USSR with a golden opportunity to pose as the protector of regional states against the "aggressive" designs of the United States.'[5] Although the option of declaring war continued to be discussed seriously in Washington, the constraints on such direct action were ostensibly too overbearing. The 'Carter Doctrine', spelt out in President Carter's State of the Union address in January 1980, stated that 'any attempt by any outside force to gain control of the Persian Gulf region will be regarded as an assault on the vital interests of the United States of America and such an assault will be repelled by any means necessary, including military force.' The serious implications of escalation in the region appeared thus to tie Washington's options in the hostage crisis to a strategy of applying diplomatic and economic sanctions and attempting to negotiate a deal for the release of the hostages.

With a proposal for UN economic sanctions facing veto by the Soviet Union in January, US state officials engaged in extensive lobbying of other major capitalist allies to secure active support for the sanctions.[6] The Washington administration appeared to have realised that the appetite of its allies to take parallel measures against the Islamic Republic was limited, and was also concerned not to jeopardise the international consensus on condemnation of the Soviet action in Afghanistan by taking unilateral moves.[7] The application of sanctions against Iran also raised the dilemma of whether this would lead to a suspension of Iranian oil supplies to the capitalist industrialised countries.[8] Requests did nevertheless stream from US officials to other heads of state for co-operation and signals to the Iranian government of such support.[9]

European states were extremely reluctant to break economic relations with Iran. Thus, as a means of bolstering their resolve, 'Washington let it be known through a veritable torrent of leaks, public hints, and private statements that the alternative would be a unilateral interruption of Iranian commerce through some military action, specifically the mining of Iranian ports.'[10] The European Economic Community (EEC) and Japan, while eschewing retroactive measures, came in May 1980 to suspend all contracts concluded with Iran since the taking of hostages.[11] Although some West European companies offered to sell Tehran arms and other banned goods, and Austria, Switzerland and Sweden did not join the EEC in supporting the US-led sanctions, Iran had to pay premiums on certain imports and use Dubai as a transit port for many of its imported items.[12] By June 1980 there were already signs that the sanctions were taking a toll on the Iranian economy, and in August President Bani Sadr conceded that they were having considerable effect.[13]

The measures taken by the administration in Washington in general, and the freezing of Iranian assets held by US banks in particular, had two consequences in serving US public and private objectives. Firstly, although the full range of strategies adopted in order to ensure the release of the hostages may not yet have fully come to light,[14] the impact of the sanctions and freeze on assets undoubtedly created pressure for a settlement of the crisis as oil exports fell, foreign exchange reserves not covered by the freeze were running low, factories were working at one-third capacity and there was a shortage not only of technicians but also of spare parts.[15]

The second consequence of the US measures was the protection of private property, as the assets were ultimately used for the repayment of US claims against Iran. The resolution of the crisis through the Algiers Accords provided the funds for the full repayment of all claims of US corporations and private interests against Iran 'to a degree unprecedented in any compensation programme after a revolution or a war'.[16] This effectively protected the property of US individuals and companies, particularly banks, against any move by the new government to repeal the contracts or arrangements of the *ancien regime*. The Revolution threatened the interests of a number of US banks by leaving them exposed to loans authorised by the shah without constitutional status, which were subject to annulment by the revolutionary government. The freezing of the Iranian assets, by ensuring that these would ultimately be set against loan payments, thus safeguarded the banks against financial difficulties.[17] The freeze on assets was removed by the US administration (19 January 1981) only after the *majles* approved a law allowing international arbitration in the disputes with the United States. As a result of eventual negotiations, the government agreed to repay over $5bn in syndicated and non-syndicated bank loans from US and foreign banks, and to set up an escrow account with a further $1bn against claims filed against Iran by US firms and citizens.[18] The issue of unpaid Iranian debts to US entities was referred to the Hague tribunals, which continued for a number of years and came to find largely in favour of the claimants.[19]

The actions of the US administration had a significant impact on the Iranian economy for a number of reasons. Firstly, the United States could not immediately and easily be replaced as a trading partner. As other capitalist countries bowed to the US-led sanctions, oil exports and foreign exchange reserves sank. Clearly, in conjunction with the sanctions imposed on the regime in Iran, the blocking of assets cut off access to much needed reserves and also dealt a severe blow to the state of the Iranian economy in the precarious post-revolutionary period. These difficulties were then exacerbated by the Iraqi invasion of post-revolutionary Iran on 22 September 1980. The release of the US hostages may not have been a direct result of the Iraqi attack. Nevertheless, the latter made a significant contribution to the urgency for the Iranian regime of the revocation of sanctions and other economic measures.

Though there is no evidence of direct encouragement from Washington for the move by Baghdad, within a context of heightened hostility with revolutionary Iran in the midst of the hostage crisis there was a clear confluence of interests between Iraq and the United States. US–Iraqi relations began to improve, signalling a *rapprochement* between the two countries. The initial US strategy of fostering Arab nationalism as an 'indigenous force' against communism in Iraq had backfired, with the breaking of diplomatic relations and the Iraqi Treaty of Friendship with the Soviet Union. Diplomatic relations between the United States and Iraq had not improved, and in December 1979 the Carter administration listed Iraq as a 'country that supports terrorism'.

Nonetheless, the strategic position and policies of the Ba'th Regime fitted in with the broader and long-term goals of successive US administrations. The Carter administration began to make moves for closer relations in the 1970s and high-ranking officials were sent to Baghdad in 1976 and 1977.[20] This was partly motivated by strategic interests of limiting Soviet influence, and also partly by economic interests in exporting US goods and services during the proliferation of rapid economic development programmes in the 1970s. But from November 1979 onwards, the US attitude to Iraq was also inevitably shaped by the hostage crisis and Washington's ensuing hostile relations with revolutionary Iran. In an official memorandum in March 1980, National Security Advisor Zbigniew Brzezinski, despite voicing concerns about Iraq's increasing naval power in the region, stressed:

the situation in Iran has changed the nature of our relations with Iraq somewhat. The hostage situation and the Afghanistan problem make it highly desirable to maintain correct relations with the Iraqi regime for the moment.[21]

In April 1980 Secretary of State Cyrus Vance and Brzezinski announced that there was 'no fundamental incompatibility of interests between the United States and Iraq'.[22] They then recommended the sale of eight General Electric engines to Italy for use in the manufacture of frigates destined for Iraq.[23] Despite early awareness in Washington of tensions between Iraq and its revolutionary neighbour, and recognition of 'the outbreak of war as a distinct possibility',[24] the State Department approved this sale in August 1980 while also announcing the consideration of the sale of five Boeing Commercial jets to Iraq. Though the latter deal was later cancelled as a result of Congressional pressure, these moves undoubtedly contributed to confidence in Baghdad that a military attack on its revolutionary neighbour would not incur a heavy-handed international response. It appears that though officials in Washington considered that public support of Iraq would have been imprudent, the war was thought initially to contribute to the pressures on Iran to resolve the hostage crisis. As a Congressional brief suggested:

> Iraq is currently seeking diverse, independent relations with both East and West. ... Iraq's edging away from the Soviet Union and Iraq–Iran tensions may provide new opportunities for increased contact between Iraq and the United States, although public support for Iraq's struggle against Iran could be imprudent and could jeopardise the hostages' safety.[25]

All in all, the policies of the United States towards the Islamic Republic during this period were conditioned by the hostage crisis, though clearly other objectives were also pursued, to varying degrees of success. Apart from the loss of future Iranian trade and investment, the interests of US private corporations were largely unscathed. The Carter Doctrine laid the foundations for a greater US presence in the region and the guarantee of the flow of oil essential to the reproduction of the capitalist system. On the other hand, the beginnings of a *rapprochement* with the Iraqi regime served, at the very least, to embolden Baghdad to invade its revolutionary neighbour.

The Iraqi response: onset of the Iran–Iraq war

While US policy seems at least to have signalled a green light to the Iraqi regime, domestic developments in Iraq independently contributed to the decision to launch a full-scale military attack on the Islamic Republic in September 1980. These related largely to the reverberations of the Iranian Revolution within Iraq and the impact of the revolutionary movement on internal social and political relations. The potential repercussions of the Iranian Revolution were acutely feared by the governing Ba'th Party in Iraq. The Iraqi regime was particularly aware of its own internal opposition and the danger posed by Iran's revolutionary propaganda and influence for a number of reasons.[26] The Shi'i majority in Iraq constituted a potentially powerful social force. A large part of the population had experienced significant social dislocation as a result of the state-led development programmes of the previous decades. On the other hand, the organisational and political cohesion of the Iraqi *ulema*, whose social and economic position was also threatened by state-led secular modernisation, provided a focus for revolutionary activity. Signs of this potential had already been manifested in the 1970s in the course of a number of popular struggles.

Protests in the aftermath of the Iranian Revolution led to heightened trepidation amongst the ruling clique in Baghdad. The perceived threat of an Iranian-inspired uprising was initially expressed in the execution of the Shi'i leader Baqer al-Sadr, deportation of Iraqis of Iranian origin (called 'Iranians living in Iraq'), and the support for the Iranian opposition. The Iraqi regime also became concerned about the co-operation of Islamic *Da'wah* with Iranians in Qum to draw up plans for the overthrow of the Iraqi government and Khomeini's calls for the transfer of Najaf's seminaries to Qum.[27] The increased activity of opposition groups was apparent also in assassination attempts on the lives of Iraqi officials, including Deputy Prime Minister Tariq Aziz in April 1980 and Saddam Hussein in June 1980, leading to severe responses by the Ba'th regime. Under these conditions, the Iraqi regime, clearly threatened by the impact of the Iranian Revolution in Iraq and the revolutionary potential of the Iraqi masses under the leadership of the clergy, resorted to violence and repression of opposition at home. It also engaged directly in activities against the neighbouring regime, including both support of the exiled Iranian opposition and eventual invasion of Iran in September 1980.

The Iraqi regime had begun to assist exiled Iranians even before the events described above.[28] In summer 1979 the National Movement of Iranian Resistance (NAMIR) was formed by the exiled former Prime Minister of Iran, Shahpour Bakhtiar, with the goal of replacing the Iranian regime with a 'government of national unity'. Between 1979 and 1980, while the belief that the regime could easily be overthrown was maintained, NAMIR was funded largely by the business community, including the shah's entourage. As the Islamic Republic gradually became stronger, the tactics of the organisation altered accordingly. A secret NAMIR-affiliated political-military organisation, *Neghab*, infiltrated the Iranian military establishment with the aim of engineering a military coup in 1980. The role of Iraqi assistance in this operation was crucial. In May 1980 NAMIR began broadcasting the clandestine 'Radio Iran' under the aegis of the regime in Baghdad, which also provided financial assistance estimated at around $30–70 million and a monthly additional budget of $200,000 to $250,000.[29] Strategically the Iraqi regime assisted the plotters by keeping the Iran–Iraq border in a constant state of mobilisation and allowing the plotters access to fully armed fighter planes ready for take off. The foiling of a coup planned by NAMIR (the Nojeh Coup) by the Iranian regime and failures of the organisation in this period no doubt contributed to the eventual Iraqi decision to launch a full-scale attack on its revolutionary neighbour.

Although the precise reasons and the circumstances of the Iraqi invasion of Iran remain unclear, various economic and political factors influenced the decision.[30] It was also made in the context of perceived domestic conflict and instability of Iran in an indeterminate post-revolutionary situation where new state institutions were yet to be fully established and while the regular army, being in the process of widespread purges, was in disarray.[31] Perhaps most critically, the post-revolutionary regime was caught in a situation of international isolation. Relations with both superpowers were tense. In particular, in the context of the extremely hostile relations with the United States, the Iraqi government could be certain that there would be little direct military or strategic support for the Islamic Republic in response to an Iraqi attack.

These circumstances provided the grounds for a calculated offensive strategy and in September 1980, (mis-)perceptions of a weak and unstable post-revolutionary regime in Iran encouraged the Iraqi regime to meet the challenge of revolutionary Iran with 'a military policy of both containment and aggrandisement'.[32] The resulting war between the two states had profound repercussions on both societies. The impact of the war on the Iranian state and society will be considered in the next chapter. For the Iraqi regime one propitious consequence was indubitably that it complicated the problems of the opposition and made it easier to curtail opposition activities.

Regional policies of containment: the Gulf states and beyond

The repercussions of the Iranian Revolution were felt not only in Iraq but elsewhere, and contributed to the policies of containment of the Islamic Republic devised by other states of the region.

The Iranian leadership denounced the neighbouring regimes in the Gulf for impiety and subservience to foreign powers. This posed a threat to these regimes as it called their political legitimacy and religious credentials into question. Iranian encouragement of dissent amongst Muslim populations was perceived potentially to delegitimise the prevailing status quo in the Gulf region and lead to social dissent.[33] Moreover, for the Arab states in particular, Iran's radical position on the issue of Palestine and Lebanon was an additional implicit challenge. While claiming to represent the Arab cause against Israel, the Arab Gulf States had economic and political interests, including their relations with external powers, that made them unwilling or unable to match the radical rhetoric of the revolutionary regime; this put their own regional legitimacy at risk.

The ensuing signs of popular discontent and unrest in the aftermath of the Iranian Revolution gave concrete cause for consternation for regional rulers. The potential impact of the Revolution on significant Shi'i populations, which formed a majority or sizeable minorities and occupied strategic locations within the socio-economic order, was a perceived threat.[34] The social and material circumstances of these populations, coupled with a sense of deprivation, fortified the potential for religious identity to serve as a locus for the formation of a popular consciousness and collective will determined to overthrow the prevailing status quo. The stimulation of such latent social tension by the events in Iran threatened rulers throughout the region. Extensive propaganda emanating from the Arabic language service of the Islamic Republic and repeated condemnation of regimes in the region exacerbated their apprehension.

In Saudi Arabia the Iranian Revolution appeared to have given the Shi'i minority courage to challenge the Saudi monarchy and make demands for a fairer distribution of wealth, an end to discrimination and reduced ties with the United States.[35] In November 1979 the regime faced domestic opposition in the form of demonstrations against the ruling family as the Grand Mosque in Mecca was seized and occupied. Shortly after the Revolution, the *munazamat al-thawra al-islamiyya li-l-tahrir al-jazira al-arabiya* (Islamic Revolution Organisation for the Liberation of the Arabian Peninsula) was formed in the Shi'i-dominated Eastern Province and became engaged in anti-regime activities, often in association with secular dissidents.[36] Public protests and demonstrations against the House of Saud took place in this region during the November occupation of the Grand Mosque. Throughout the ensuing decade, Iranian-inspired disturbances at the time of the annual pilgrimage to Mecca (*Hajj*) fuelled the fears of the Saudi regime.[37]

The gravity of these events for the Saudi monarchy stemmed from a number of factors. Firstly, the Shi'i minority's strategic location in the eastern region where they constitute a significant percentage of the workforce in the oil industry created the spectre of a disruption to the operations of ARAMCO and the lifeblood of the kingdom.[38] Secondly, a concern shared by most rulers in the region was that their regimes could be threatened by direct foreign (especially Iranian) influence amongst the opposition. Finally, a 'domino theory' prevailed, in that the cycle of Iranian propaganda and unrest was perceived as contagious and had the potential to spread throughout the Gulf and destabilise the region as a whole.

The 'domino theory' of the impact of the Revolution was given particular weight by the events of 1981 in Bahrain, where a number of demonstrations supportive of the new Iranian regime had already taken place in 1979. A coup attempt in December 1981 reverberated well beyond the borders of the state, not least due to an account of the events published in a London-based weekly, *al-majallah*. The article alleged that the 'Iranian conspiracy' behind the coup was not aimed at Bahrain alone but targeted other countries, including Saudi Arabia.[39] Bahrain's interior minister charged the group arrested with belonging to the Islamic Front for the Liberation of Bahrain, headquartered in Tehran. The Saudis, on the other hand, 'behaved as if they were even more threatened than the Bahrainis themselves' and called on Iran to stop 'sabotage activities' in the Gulf.[40]

Similar apprehensions arose when a number of bombings and signs of social unrest also sporadically threatened order in Kuwait. These included the *ashura* demonstrations in 1982 by sympathisers of Khomeini, suicide bomb attacks against the US embassy and French consulate in December 1983, and an attempt on the life of the Kuwaiti ruler Sheikh Jaber al-Ahmed al-Sabah in 1985.[41] Kuwait's geographical situation and proximity to Iran, and Iranian violation of Kuwaiti airspace in 1980 and 1981, also raised fears of military vulnerability. All these events led not only to internal measures to fortify the security apparatus and deportation of suspected Shi'i activists, but also to further co-operation amongst the Gulf states to contain the Islamic Republic and to formulate regional policies during the course of the Iran–Iraq war.

The threat posed by the Revolution and the Islamic Republic as perceived by the majority of the Gulf rulers served to shape the evolution of policies forged in regard to their relations with both the Islamic Republic and the Iraqi regime.[42] There is also evidence to suggest that the Iraqi plan to attack Iran was forged with the prior knowledge and complicity of at least the Saudi Arabian and Kuwaiti regimes.[43] The subsequent prosecution of the war following Iranian air raids on Kuwaiti territory and installations further strengthened the perception of Iran as a direct military foe. In view of the Iranian Revolution and the Iran–Iraq war, the impetus to create a diplomatic forum and framework for the formulation of co-ordinated policies by the conservative Gulf monarchies accelerated sharply, leading to the formation of the Gulf Co-operation Council (GCC) in May 1981.[44] The image of Iran as a regional threat created more of a necessity for the Gulf states within the Council to 'maintain official neutrality [in the war] while in fact stepping up effective support for Iraq'.[45] This 'tilted neutrality', led largely by Saudi Arabia and Kuwait, continued throughout the war, taking the form of diplomatic initiatives, strategic co-operation and considerable sums in financial assistance.

In the first year of its formation, GCC policy had been to lend indirect support to Baghdad without forthrightly condemning the Iranian regime or declaring alignment with Iraq. During its third meeting in Bahrain in November 1982, however, following Iranian offensives in the war, the GCC declared 'support of Iraq in its attempts to put an end to this war by peaceful means'. A Saudi radio commentary in the same month announced that there would be 'no way to thwart those (Iranian) plans and foil them except by supporting Iraq financially and militarily in order to destroy the Iranian war machine'.[46] By 1984, after attacks on shipping in the Gulf, the GCC forthrightly condemned 'Iranian aggression on the freedom of navigation to and from the ports of [the GCC states]'.[47] The 1986 Iranian offensives led to condemnation by all the GCC states and effectively moved even regimes in Bahrain and Qatar, which had maintained a somewhat more ambiguous position, further towards support of Iraq.[48]

The Saudi–Iranian relationship in this period has been characterised as one of a 'cold war'.[49] The kingdom moved to form a 'real alliance' with Iraq, evidenced by the extent of strategic assistance and finances extended to the Iraqi regime. Saudi-owned AWACs (Airborne Warning and Control Systems aircraft), supplied mainly by the United States, provided crucial intelligence information on Iranian military tactics and targets to Baghdad. Financially, Saudi Arabia led other Gulf states in providing loans to Iraq that made possible the pursuit of Iraq's 'guns and butter' strategy. By the end of 1982 the approximate distribution of funds per Arab donor was $14 billion from Saudi Arabia, $6 billion from Kuwait, $2–4 billion from the United Arab Emirates and $1bn from Qatar. These loans added up to a total of around $25–30 billion by 1983 and exceeded $40 billion by the end of the war.[50]

Furthermore, Saudi Arabia and Kuwait engaged in counterpart oil sales whereby crude was provided for sale to Iraqi customers or in payment of contracts and deliveries to Iraq. As early as 1980 Saudi Arabia had provided 'war relief' crude in order to prevent Iraq from losing its customers. In July 1982 a deal between Iraq's State Organisation for Marketing Oil Products, Mobil (an ARAMCO partner) and Mitsubishi of Japan allowed oil deliveries to the latter in part payment of Iraqi contracts, while other arrangements effectively meant that Saudi Arabia was paying for Iraqi purchases of French weapons.[51] In 1983 official government-to-government arrangements for counterpart oil sales were made between Iraq and both Saudi Arabia and Kuwait. From 1983 to 1988 about 300,000 barrels per day of crude oil from the neutral zone between Kuwait and Saudi Arabia were sold by the latter states on behalf of Iraq.[52] In order to facilitate the transportation of Iraqi oil, a pipeline was allowed to run through Saudi territory to the Red Sea with no transit fees charged to Iraq.[53] Furthermore, Saudi Arabian financial aid was used to pressurise the Syrian government to alter its position of supporting Iran in its war with Iraq.[54]

While Syria and Libya remained the Islamic Republic's regional supporters, policies adopted by other Arab states, principally Jordan and Egypt, amounted to support of Iraq. The Jordanian regime remained resolute in this role throughout the war, permitting the passage of military and other supplies through the port of Aqaba, financing Iraq's suppliers, and allowing Iraqi oil to pass through pipelines running across the country.[55] The Egyptian regime also remained concerned about both the policies and regional impact of the Islamic Republic and the praise for the Iranian Revolution by Egyptian Islamic scholars.[56] Consequently, Iraq was supplied with much-needed Soviet-made military hardware and spare parts, while Egyptian pilots participated in the Iraqi air force and migrant workers relieved the strain on the Iraqi economy as the net of conscription was widened. Under the banner of pan-Arabism, relations between the two states improved through the decade. Face-to-face contacts between high-level officials in France in 1982 culminated in President Mubarak's visit to Baghdad in 1985.[57]

We may thus conclude that the overall objective of regimes in the region was the containment of the Iranian revolution, which was perceived not only to be a source of inspiration for opposition groups threatening the status quo, but also to be actively engaged in inciting such movements. An Iranian victory was seen as a prelude to regional domination by the Islamic Republic. In order to thwart such an outcome, most of these rulers acted to assist Iraq financially as well as through diplomatic and other material support.

The United States and the West: policy in the 1980s

The Iranian Revolution had detrimental consequences for the economic and strategic interests of the United States and its allies. The fall of a principal regional ally, withdrawal of the post-revolutionary regime from the CENTO alliance, and abrogation of military co-operation and commercial contracts of the previous regime all constituted an assault on these interests. Throughout the 1980s, the US administration played a proactive role in responding to the Iranian Revolution to protect its interests, although this needed to be set against a broader backdrop of the Cold War. Moreover, against the background of common interests of the major capitalist states, each had more specific strategic and commercial interests that mediated their policies.

Both Iran and Iraq, as major oil exporters, were lucrative markets for the major capitalist states, which were reluctant irrevocably to impair relations and risk foregoing the economic benefits. Nevertheless, while economic calculations were of import, political concerns regarding the regional balance and the potentially destabilising impact on capitalist interests of the spread of the Iranian Revolution were crucial factors in the formulation of policies towards the two belligerents during the Iran–Iraq war. Firstly, the fear of a radical version of Islam spreading in the region and destabilising allied regimes figured prominently in the strategic considerations of the Western allied states. The adverse repercussions of such a trend for the interests of the latter would include disruptions to the supply of oil with severe consequences for their economies and the world capitalist system as a whole.

Secondly, the oil imperative and other commercial and strategic interests were tied to the maintenance of relations with Arab Gulf states which were crucial exporters of oil, served as lucrative markets for the exports of advanced capitalist states and were major investors in many of the latter's economies. Moreover, a pre-occupation with the Soviet threat in the cold war framework and the siren calls of impending 'communist infiltration' in post-revolutionary Iran also informed, to a greater or lesser extent, the policies of the Western allies. US interests defined capitalist interests as a whole, and it was imperative to defend and protect the international interests of capitalism. These common interests notwithstanding, it is important to distinguish between the attitude of the administrations in Washington and their counterparts in the other capitals, for differences amongst leading capitalist states – stemming largely from particular commercial interests – led at times to diverging and contradictory policies.

United States policy towards Iran during the Reagan administrations evolved in a contradictory manner. The most convincing explanations for this point to the intersection of the various interests of the US in the region and the diverging tendencies of the personnel and departments within the administration. A 'Soviet-centric', 'Israel-centric' and 'Arab-centric' tendency within the administration could be discerned, while within each of these tendencies, different strategies were adopted to achieve certain policy goals.[58] Furthermore, the administration also yielded to the anti-Iranian sentiment of the US public, which followed the hostage crisis.[59] Though various factions within the administration adopted different strategies and recommended varying policies towards Iran, the centrality of the Persian Gulf region to 'vital' US interests was never questioned. Nowhere are the contradictions of these interests more clearly spelt out than in the statement given by George Schultz before the House Foreign Affairs Committee on 8 December 1986 in the aftermath of the revelations of the arms-for-hostages deals of the Reagan administration:

> The Persian Gulf is important to the United States – and for many or our key friends and allies as well. A quarter of the free world's oil flows through the Persian Gulf and an even higher percentage sustains the economies of our allies in Europe and Japan. It is vital that Western access to that oil continues. The region is a strategic focal point – one in which the Soviet Union has long sought to expand its presence and control. We have an important stake in denying them such expansion. We have major political interests with individual gulf states both in their own right and because of their influence on events in the Middle East, Afghanistan and elsewhere. Therefore we want the states of the gulf to enjoy a peace and political stability free from threats of Soviet intimidation, external aggression or internal subversion. We wish to sustain productive relations with these states of the region, in part so that the supply of oil to the West can continue unabated. ... Our dealings with Iran are shaped by a strategic dilemma. We have a 'northern' concern – to keep Iran free of Soviet influence – and a 'southern' concern – to keep Iran from dominating its gulf neighbours. Because Iran continues to resist Soviet influence but threatens the gulf our near-term priority must be to reassure gulf Arab states of our support and stand fast on our anti-terrorism and arms embargo policies. Meanwhile, we must use alternative channels to bolster Iranian resistance to Soviet influence and focus on shared interests such as Afghanistan. Similarly, stability in the gulf will affect our efforts to encourage meaningful movement in any peace process between Israel and its Arab neighbours.[60]

The policies forged by the Reagan administration towards the Islamic Republic were thus mediated by its 'northern' and 'southern' concerns. The 'northern' threat of Soviet influence in Iran loomed despite the 'Neither East nor West' policy proclaimed by the leadership of the Islamic Republic. Throughout this period there was an influential current of thought which feared the ability of Moscow to influence a post-Khomeini regime in light of the lack of US influence in the Islamic

Republic.[61] These apprehensions translated into both the overt strategic and military policies of the administration and the covert manoeuvrings entailed in the secret deals with the Islamic Republic. The Reagan administration continued to adhere to the Carter Doctrine – readiness to deploy military force to secure its 'vital interest' of the flow of oil through the region. Furthermore, the Rapid Deployment Force (RDF), the build-up of which had already been accelerated under the previous adminis-tration following the Iranian Revolution, was superseded by the new permanent military command (CENTCOM) in the Indian Ocean. On the other hand, in view of the perceived Soviet threat and influence in Iran, conclusions drawn by CIA and NSC officials were to allow sales to Iran of 'arms that would not decisively affect the war with Iraq but would show Tehran that it had alternatives to reconciliation with and depend-ence on Moscow'.[62] This perspective formed the kernel of the Reagan administration's secret dealings with the Islamic Republic.[63]

However, US interests were not confined to the 'maintenance of Iran's territorial integrity as a buffer between the Soviet Union and the Gulf', but also the prevention of 'an Iranian revolutionary crusade' that would destabilise the oil-producing Gulf Arab states.[64] The US administration's 'southern concern' to 'keep Iran from domi-nating its gulf neighbours' and to contain the Iranian Revolution within Iranian borders was largely concretised in the policy of preventing an Iranian victory in the war with Iraq. Secretary of State Alexander Haig noted that US neutrality in the war did not mean indifference, and in May 1982 Defence Secretary Casper Weinberger stated more explicitly that 'an Iranian victory is certainly not in our national interest'.[65] This was also expressed in a study by the National Security Council in 1983, publicly declared by Reagan in 1984, and spelt out in a 1986 Congressional Report which stated:

> the preservation of Iraq's territorial and political integrity is in the US interest. ... Should Iraq collapse, the installation of a revolutionary Shi'ite regime in Baghdad would raise the poten-tial for increased stability in the Gulf Arab states and the possibility of an Iranian-Syrian axis which could threaten not only the Gulf region, but also Jordan, Israel and US interests in the Eastern Mediterranean. Destabilisation would tend to open opportunities for increased Soviet influence in the region. ... US policy concerns currently centre on the possibility that Iraq, despite moves on the part of its supporters to sustain its economic and military capacities, ultimately might collapse as a result of the war of attrition to the detriment of American regional interests. ... The US has an interest in preventing Iranian revolutionary military expansion in the Gulf region.[66]

The regional policies adopted by the Reagan administration were thus not only an increased direct strategic presence, but also a visible shift towards the support of Iraq in its war effort.[67] The first overt signals of an US rapprochement with Iraq manifested in early 1981 when Secretary of State Haig sent a delegation including the Deputy Assistant Secretary of State (Morris Draper) to Baghdad in April, after which trade increased and the sale of the previously barred Boeing jets was cleared.[68] Despite declaring neutrality in the Iran–Iraq war, US arms were shipped to Iraq via third countries, through which Baghdad was also provided with intelligence information.[69] The main factor in this policy was the strategic position of Saudi Arabia in the Washington administration's regional policy. AWACs were initially stationed in Saudi Arabia, which passed reconnaissance information to Baghdad. Later, despite much Congressional resistance, the administration pushed through the sales of the aircraft to the Saudi government. In a statement before the Senate Foreign Relations committee on 5 October 1981, Haig reasoned that this arrangement would be necessary in order to protect the United States as 'our enemies and the enemies of peace have not been idle. Just last week the Iranian planes bombed oil facilities in Kuwait.'[70]

But the support of Iraq also extended to more direct bi-lateral economic and strategic ties. Iraq was removed from the list of countries allegedly supporting international terrorism in February 1982. From December 1982 the United States Department of Agriculture Commodity Credit Corporation agreed to guarantee credit for sales of agricultural commodities to Iraq, and the sale of 60 helicopters capable of being converted to military machines was authorised by the Reagan administration in 1983. Full diplomatic relations between the United States and Iraq were restored in 1984, and by 1985 a co-operation agreement between the two countries was concluded to cover industry, agriculture, energy and telecommunications.[71] Furthermore, not only did the Reagan administration raise no objections to the large military sales to Iraq by West European allies, but it also encouraged Gulf Arab states to increase or at least maintain their financial support for Iraq.

Meanwhile, official policy was directed towards limiting the flow of arms from third countries to Iran.[72] While first steps towards this objective began in 1983 as 'Operation Staunch', the legal basis for its realisation lay in the designation of the Islamic Republic as a state supporter of international terrorism by Secretary of State George Schultz in January 1984. Subsequently, a number of legal measures came into effect with respect to Iran and were effective in limiting the regime's capabilities in the acquisition of war materiel: the Foreign Assistance Act prohibited economic assistance; the Arms Export Control Act forbade the transfers of any munitions item or the provision of export licences for such transfers; and the Export Administration Act required the securing of a validated licence for the exports of goods or technology.[73] US officials engaged in extensive diplomatic efforts designed to prevent the strengthening of the Islamic Republic and its potential consequence, the fall of Iraq.

Clandestine organisations of the Iranian opposition were also supported by official sources in the United States. In 1981 an exiled organisation, Ali Amini's 'Front for the Liberation of Iran', had been launched with CIA support. By 1984 co-operative relations were established between the United States and the National Movement of Iranian Resistance (NAMIR) headed by Shahpour Bakhtiar. By 1985 NAMIR's 'Operation White Star' aimed at the overthrow of the regime was taken seriously by the United States, and from March 1986 the organisation began to receive financial assistance from US official sources.[74]

Thus, the containment of the Iranian Revolution and spread of radical Islam in the region appears to have been a fulcrum of US foreign policy in this period, mediated only by parallel concerns regarding Soviet influence in the region. This strategy was concretely advanced by the clearly discernible tilt towards Iraq on behalf of successive administrations in Washington.

The inclination towards Iraq was broadly reproduced in the policies of other major capitalist states during the Iran–Iraq war. Nonetheless, a degree of equivocation may be detected, largely stemming from particular commercial interests of public and private concerns. There was a degree of reluctance to break trade and investment links with Iran, which formed a lucrative market for the capitalist states. However, the respective attitudes of the Iraqi and Iranian regimes towards foreign economic relations in themselves created an imbalance of policies towards the two warring states. The Islamic Republic maintained an ideological policy of eliminating its foreign debts and reducing 'foreign dependence'. The Iraqi regime on the other hand continued to borrow on the international market and became reliant on international lines of credit. Commercial considerations had their place in the extension of credit arrangements to Iraq, which of course were intended for purchases of both civilian goods and military equipment.[75] This also meant that various interests were tied to the survival and financial viability of the Iraqi regime forming another – now commercial – incentive to prevent the downfall of the Iraqi regime.

Ultimately, for both political and commercial reasons, the major capitalist states had a general interest in preventing the fall of the Iraqi regime and Iranian victory in the war. While political interests and the commercial concerns of both private and public entities committed the capitalist states to the Iraqi regime for a number of reasons, a strong parallel case for Iran could not be made. Firstly, the

Iranian post-revolutionary regime maintained a commitment not to borrow money abroad. Thus, the Islamic Republic engaged in numerous counter-trade agreements and 'oil-for-goods' deals while also limiting loans to short-term letters of credit.[76]

Secondly, the blocking of assets covered a large part of Iranian debt, particularly to US companies, carried over from the pre-revolutionary regime and the ensuing claims process. For example, the French government was able to cover claims for compensation for financial damage suffered by several major companies following the Revolution by blocking funds totalling over $1bn from a loan advanced by the shah.[77] That Iran still had pre-revolutionary debts outstanding to Britain in 1988 may also go some way towards explaining that country's greater willingness to trade with Iran despite cooling of relations.[78]

Thirdly, the export guarantees extended for imports into Iran in the form of letters of credit did not constitute significant threats to financial and corporate economic interests. This was partly due to the magnitude and terms of the advances and partly due to confidence in Iran's ability to obtain oil revenue. Moreover, there was little question of the Iranian Republic being defeated in the war, while the regime appeared also to be stabilising internally with the elimination of serious challengers to the clerics' rule. In other words, as the Islamic Republic did not seem likely to *lose* the war, the objective became the prevention of an Iranian *victory* and Iraq's *collapse*. All in all, this meant that even where neutrality was publicly announced, concrete policies worked towards preventing the defeat of the Iraqi regime through war, the effects of which would have reverberated through the strategic and political configuration of the region. This however, did not prevent the capitalist states from maintaining commercial interests and ties, including through trade in arms,[79] insofar as this did not upset their strategic interests or tip the balance of the war towards Iran

The combined strategy of international actors resulted in extending the Iran–Iraq conflict over a period of eight years by keeping a balance and parity of resources between the two sides. In effect this spelt a general tilt towards Iraq, even where neutrality or an interest in ending the conflict was announced. Since an Iraqi victory was seen to be out of the question, efforts were concentrated on preventing Iranian preponderance and regional domination.

In sum, the Iranian Revolution provoked responses from actors regionally and internationally through its efforts to export the Revolution and encourage similar movements elsewhere in the region. It threatened the domestic political legitimacy and credentials of regional leaders by serving as a potential source of inspiration and direct instigation. Fear of regional domination by a powerful revolutionary state added to the overall concern of regimes in the region to contain the revolution. The most decisive form of international reaction to the Revolution was, of course, foreign invasion, and throughout this chapter we have set out how the Iran–Iraq war mediated wider policies towards the Islamic Republic. Overall, the strategy of the United States and its allies resulted in lengthening the conflict by keeping a balance and parity of resources between the two sides – a strategy to which the Soviet side of the cold war also contributed for its own reasons. In effect, this spelt a general tilt towards Iraq as efforts were concentrated on preventing an Iranian victory. The Iran–Iraq war certainly changed the political map of the region and its dynamics. It undoubtedly made it more difficult for the Islamic Republic to export its Revolution in the region. But the failure to export Revolution in the 1980s cannot be put down to containment alone.

Exporting revolution: a unique failure

The universalist populist discourse of the regime had rested on the belief that the 'Islamic Revolution' would in fact be exported and that parallel revolutions or 'Islamic states' would be established. These would then not only serve as a legitimising factor for the Islamic Republic, but also provide a source of support and allegiance in an otherwise hostile international context. However, while the Iranian Revolution undoubtedly sent shock waves around the region and beyond and contributed to popular religiosity and Islamic mood, there was little sign of successful 'export of revolution' beyond the Iranian state.[80] The Islamic Republic pursued an official policy of pan-Islamism aimed at bridging the gap between Shi'ism and Sunnism and propagating Islamic unity. However, this policy was, by and large, a failure.[81] Although the regime did draw on the resurgence of Islamic movements as a source of legitimacy, few of the latter declared explicit allegiance to the Islamic Republic. Most were home-grown movements with their own dynamic and momentum. A number of reasons for this lack of international allegiance may be singled out.

Firstly, contrary to the rhetoric of Islamic leaders, buttressed by essentialist notions of 'Islam' in academic scholarship, these were movements grounded in differing social structural conditions.[82] What it meant for each organisation and movement to be 'Islamic' differed from place to place, counteracting the centripetal forces that the Islamic Republic's calls for unity attempted to animate.[83] Even in Iraq, for instance, where there is arguably greatest correlation and correspondence between the Shi'i *ulema* of the two states, and where many of the followers of Iraq's Ayatollah al-Sadr accepted Khomeini's leadership, prominent members of the *da'wah* never accepted the concept of *velayat-e faqih* as envisaged by Khomeini.[84] In Saudi Arabia, although in the early 1980s the leaders of the Shi'a movement followed the Iranian line, a shift in their discourse occurred which took the movement away from the rhetoric of revolution and Khomeinism.[85] Furthermore, the organisation and leadership structure of various movements – often transposed onto traditional structures of local politics that incorporated patronage networks and the like – stood in the way of unifying them under one leadership.

Secondly, the identification of the Iranian Revolution and Islamic Republic with Shi'ism and Shi'i minorities led to the creation of what Olivier Roy has termed a Shi'i 'ghetto' in which the Islamic Republic was boxed.[86] Of course, the Revolution did compel Shi'i minorities in the region to identify with the Iranian phenomenon and to mobilise, on account of both the push factor of their constituting marginalised communities and the pull factor of Iran as the centre of global Shi'i activity. However, this very identification led to a distancing by Sunni Islamists as *political* divisions between different groups prevailed.[87] Perhaps the clearest manifestation of such a sectarian division, exacerbated also by ethnic cleavages, could be observed in Afghanistan. The Afghan Islamist resistance was a broad popular movement unified by the mediating discourse of religion, which informed the popular consciousness, but which was also fractured by localism, personalised politics, factionalism and ethnic divisions. 'Islam' was interpreted in diverging ways by the different participants in the movement.[88] Here, apart from the limited influence in some – but emphatically not all – Shi'i groups, the Islamic Republic could find few sources of allegiance.

Thirdly, Islamist movements and governments were often happy to receive Iranian aid, including financial donations, military training and other resources, but ideological and political alliances did not necessary follow. The leaders of these movements, in a bid to advance their own political goals, were ready to receive aid from any source that would provide it. The support of Islamist movements by other international actors served as a further factor working against a global Islamic movement under the leadership of the Islamic Republic of Iran. One instance of this may be seen again in Afghanistan where Pakistani officials, with the complicity of Washington, supported conservative Islamist groups that crystallised and reinforced ethnic and religious tensions with pro-Iranian counterparts. Furthermore, Saudi organisations subsidised and assisted Arab *Mojahedin* from conservative Wahhabi and Muslim Brotherhood groups to fight in the Afghan resistance and challenge Iranian influence there.[89]

The regime's failure to realise its goal of 'exporting revolution' during its first decade was best symbolised by the absence of 'Islamic Revolution' in neighbouring Iraq, where the likelihood of the event was estimated to be the greatest by Iranian leaders and external observers alike. The toppling of the Ba'th regime in Baghdad and its replacement by one allied to Tehran would have eliminated the pressures of military conflict. It would also have provided the Islamic Republic with much needed international recognition and support both diplomatically and strategically, in addition to reaffirming the legitimacy of the regime at home. Despite the regime's repeated calls for an 'Islamic Revolution' in the region, and in particular for an uprising of the Shi'i population of Iraq, and the formation of *al-majlis al-a'la l-il thawra al-islamiya fi al-iraq*, Supreme Assembly of the Islamic Revolution of Iraq (SAIRI) in Tehran in 1982, however, there was little sign of success of a popular Iranian-inspired movement.

While the Iranian Revolution initially served as a source of inspiration for the Iraqi Islamist opposition, several more specific factors limited its further evolution. Firstly, the war itself sharpened nationalist and patriotic feeling in Iraq. The close embrace of the opposition by Iran led to a growth of latent resentment as the Iraqi Shi'i wanted 'things to grow on their own soil'.[90] Secondly, in an attempt to neutralise the impact of the Islamic opposition, the Iraqi leadership embraced religion. Thus, the previously secular Ba'th regime began to incorporate religious symbols into its rhetoric. In 1983, an Islamic conference was convened in Baghdad legitimated by the presence of Ali Kashif al-Ghita, a Shi'i cleric aligned with the regime.[91] Various other demonstrations of allegiance to Islam subsequently mushroomed in Iraqi rhetoric and symbolism. Thirdly, the repressive measures of the Ba'th regime had a severe impact on the Islamic opposition.[92] In May 1983 over 100 members of the al-Haki family, influential in SAIRI, were arrested, and six of them were executed immediately. Ten more were executed in February and March 1985. Estimates indicate that over 5000 Islamists were killed by the regime by the mid-1980s.[93] All these factors had a decisive impact in curtailing the activities of the Iraqi opposition led by religious figures and reduced the potential of a successful Islamic Revolution in Iraq.

Faced with the absence of a popular uprising in the neighbouring country, Iranian leaders began increasingly to encourage the formation of guerrilla groups and the training of the Iraqi opposition in military tactics and operations against the Iraqi regime in the hope of inducing revolutionary change.[94] In June 1987 plans were announced by the Islamic Republic Guard Corps (IRGC) to fortify the military role of popular forces inside Iraq, while the Iraqis were encouraged to continue the war themselves. All-Iraqi units, were formed from the forces which had been participating in Iran's war effort and Iranian directives called for the establishment of 'Hezbollah brigades' inside Iraq.[95] In January 1988 the sixth meeting of SAIRI was organised in Tehran, giving reports on the progress made in heeding Ayatollah

Khomeini's directive to organise inside Iraq. However, the repressive moves of the Iraqi regime, including the use of chemical weapons against Iraqi civilians, added to the problems of the Islamist opposition in Iraq. The Iraqi state thus proved resilient and resistant to the universalist rhetoric of the revolutionary leaders, thereby denying Iran's post-revolutionary state its much needed allies, and sources of support and legitimacy.

5 Populism, war and the state

Foreign invasion, war and international pressure on the post-revolutionary Iranian state irrevocably shaped not only the development of its external relations but also the domestic balance of social forces. These conditions had significant implications for the relations of the state and social classes. As we saw in Chapter 3, social and political struggle ensued in the immediate post-revolutionary period, leaving indeterminacy in the institutional make-up of the post-revolutionary state. As we show in this chapter, war and the subsequent national mobilisation provided the conditions for state managers to expand their own role, leading to the consolidation of a new ruling state elite. The articulation of Islamic populism with a national revolutionary discourse formed the basis for an effective *levee en masse* for war. Many social groups were rallied behind the policies of a narrow religious elite who, in the process, consolidated their control over the instruments of the state. Having originally constituted the populist discourse, 'social populism' was abandoned in favour of 'war populism'. The material demands of large sectors of the population were also delegitimised through the excuse of wartime emergency conditions and the preponderance of national security. The war contributed to the establishment of a repressive and coercive state apparatus, while those in control of state apparatus prevailed over the means of surplus extraction.

'War populism' and revolutionary images of the international system

The Iraqi invasion of 1980 and the ensuing war augmented the national-populist rhetoric of the leadership. Khomeini presented the war as a counter-revolutionary plot of imperialist powers to destroy the revolution. This helped to rouse patriotic feeling and evoked the memory of counter-revolutionary interference in Iran. Not only the experience of the past but also the reality of the policies of external powers towards the Revolution – including more recent events such as the US attempted rescue of hostages in April 1980 and the external activities of the Iranian opposition in exile – played a part in radicalising nationalist sentiment. The inclination towards Iraq by major foreign powers added credence to the national-populist rhetoric and rallied the nation behind the religious leadership in an act of mobilisation for national self-defence. The immediate consequence of the outbreak of war was therefore to concentrate the attention of the population on the issue of defence of the nation and revolution, and to forge a national alliance which proved instrumental in consolidating the foundations of the Islamic Republic.[1] Khomeini repeatedly warned of the imminent danger which the Revolution faced:

> The blow that you have delivered to the superpowers is unique in history. Do not expect them to sit idly by as mere spectators. They are active. If they can they will attack us with military force.[2]

Other leaders continued to raise the spectre of foreign intervention in Iran through the media and in prayer sermons throughout the duration of the war. In his Friday sermon in January 1982, for instance, Ayatollah Emami-Kashani claimed:

> international imperialism and its agents throughout the world see a great threat in Iran's Islamic Revolution. ... O nation of Islam, what must we do? They are seeking to destroy Islam. Do we have any choice other than to resist arrogance and achieve unity among Muslims? ... You now face your historic response.[3]

One of the key images of this rhetoric was that of a global collusion of the superpowers against the Islamic Republic. This not only played a part in rallying the population, but also helped to reinforce the image of the strength of the Revolution in resisting counter-revolutionary forces.[4]

US policy was regarded as a clear sign that the 'Great Satan' and 'world-devouring imperialism' aimed to use all their might to destroy the Revolution. The Islamic Republic's leadership condemned any direct US presence in the region and the support of allied states. The approval both of the Saudi Arabian request for the despatch of US AWACs and of their later direct sales were proclaimed as moves 'intended really to provide a cover for a new US strategy in the Middle East' aimed at domination of the region.[5] The Reagan administration's plans for a new permanent military command (CENTCOM) came under virulent attack for regional interference.[6] Improved US–Iraqi relations were denounced alongside the presence of the US navy in the waters of the Persian Gulf as 'nothing less than an act of aggression and blackmail against the countries of the region and ... support for the aggressive and defeated regime of Iraq'.[7]

As this rhetoric corresponded to the reality of the protection of US economic and strategic interests and assertion of US hegemony in the region, the leadership was able readily to exaggerate its claims, leading to the erratic projection of omnipotent 'American hands' behind various regional events. The US position was depicted as hegemonic and unitary, rejecting any notion of internal and domestic disputes within the US administration over regional policies. Congressional debates on the sales of AWACs to Saudi Arabia were, for instance, presented as a mere show that was part and parcel of a plot to deceive the Saudi regime that it had gained a major achievement.

Though the revolutionary leadership frequently repeated the steadfast conviction that they were fighting US imperialism and that the United States was the major protagonist in the region,[8] condemnation extended to France and Britain for sales of arms to Iraq and to regional states which then provided the Iraqi regime with intelligence information, financial assistance and military supplies.[9] Closer to home, heads of the 'puppet regimes of the region' were condemned for carrying out 'the wishes of the Great Satan'.[10] The creation of the Gulf Co-operation Council (GCC) in the aftermath of the outbreak of the Iran–Iraq war was seen as the direct result of US plotting.[11]

The Soviet Union was likewise condemned for the provision of military equipment to Iraq.[12] Through the slogan of 'Neither East nor West', the Islamic Republic was proclaimed to be the only truly non-aligned state, and thus the United States and Soviet Union had colluded against it through their puppet and tool, Saddam Hussein. According to the Political Office of the *Pasdaran* (Revolutionary Guard Corps), Iraqi possession of Soviet manufactured military equipment illustrated that 'the Russians using their T-72 and even T-74 tanks' came to 'serve the US in this war'.[13]

The failure of the UN Security Council to condemn the Iraqi invasion of Iran and to identify Iraq as the aggressor meant that international law was easily represented as a 'tool in the hands of the superpowers' to reinforce and legitimise their stronghold on world politics. The absence of 'any form of condemnation by the world community of the Ba'thist aggression' left no doubt as to 'the international conspiracy against the Islamic Republic'.[14] Later neglect of the use of chemical weapons by the Baghdad regime led to a further flood of criticism of the Council.[15]

Attempts at bringing about a ceasefire through various peace missions were dismissed as having behind them conspiratorial foreign hands aimed at 'imposing' a peace contrary to Iran's interests. Rafsanjani claimed that 'an onslaught has been launched in the world to impose a certain sort of peace on Iran, when they failed to achieve any conclusive results by imposing this war on us.'[16] Both the unilateral attempts by third parties and proposals for negotiations by envoys and delegations from international organisations, such as the United Nations or Islamic Conference Organisation, were rejected as initiatives directed by and in the interests of Washington and Moscow:

Washington endeavours to keep Saddam in power by establishing peace. ... Moscow along with other Western countries concentrated its efforts in the UN in order to play a part in imposing the ceasefire upon Iran. These efforts intensified as Iran's resolution to continue the war grew firmer.[17]

The Political Office of the Revolutionary Guards (*Pasdaran*) inferred that there were only two outlooks on the war. On the one had there were 'compromisers [who] were thinking of holding negotiations and compromising with the enemy' and on the other 'followers of the line of Imam Khomeini ... renouncing any imposed peace and compromise and not to favour, even under the most difficult circumstances, peace missions which wanted to complement Iraqi aggression and to subdue the Revolution'.[18] The populist images of the international system reflected in the war rhetoric and expounded by the Khomeinist leadership served to strengthen and impose the latter position.

In an extension of his populist-universalism, Khomeini portrayed the war as the struggle against imperialism not only by and on behalf of the Iranian people, but also for the liberation of the oppressed the world over. He incorporated various international and regional events into this schema and utilised them to make more plausible the Khomeinist vision of the world: that world imperialism aimed to destroy Islam and the Islamic Revolution in Iran for having created the alternative model of society for the deprived masses of the world.[19]

Iranian war aims were thus defined as defence of the Revolution, which in turn was equated with defence of the deprived of the world against world imperialism. The Israeli invasion of Lebanon in 1982 contributed to the coalescence of the war and the cause of the masses of the region in a way that justified the continuation of war into Iraqi territory as a liberating and 'humanitarian' cause, since it was a precondition for liberating Israeli-occupied territories:

> we declare that we shall not rest until the complete liberation of the occupied territories and, particular, beloved Jerusalem, from the pawns of Zionism. God willing, with the overthrow of Saddam we shall march victoriously towards beloved Jerusalem.[20]

Khomeini repeatedly stated that the 'liberation of Jerusalem' could only be realised consequent upon an Iraqi defeat.[21] The continuation of war into Iraqi territory would provide access to the Palestinian and Lebanese battlefronts enabling Iranian forces to fight against the invasion of Israel:

The liberation of Iraq from the injustice of Saddam and his regime can only be achieved through advancing along all the fronts in order to eliminate the Iraqi clique which rules in Baghdad, liberate the holy shrines and begin the march to liberate Jerusalem, Lebanon, the Golan Heights and Jordan.[22]

The stance taken by the Islamic regime became less and less conciliatory, and the war effort and the defence of the oppressed masses against world imperialism and mobilisation towards these aims were declared as religious duties.

The war with Iraq thus contributed to the hegemonic discourse of the leadership as the war was conflated with imperialism in the populist rhetoric. The hegemonic policies of the US administration and the regional policies of other states, including Israel, were used to give greater validity to the idea that the 'Great Satan' and 'World Zionism' were aiming to destroy Islam and the Revolution, and to encourage a more massive 'defensive' mobilisation and to advance the universalist cause of the 'export of Revolution'. Khomeini's rhetoric projected the image of a conspiratorial international system standing in polar opposition to the Iranian Revolution. Evocation of the national-popular memory of external intervention served to heighten the urgency of mobilisation in an act of defence of the nation, revolution, religion and the fight against imperialism. Victory in war was defined by the regime as the most urgent total aim of the Revolution. This, as we shall see in what follows, had profound consequences for the domestic policies of the regime and the balance of social forces within post-revolutionary Iran.

Popular mobilisation and war contributions

Khomeini's hegemonic populist rhetoric and effective use of the means of mass communication and media were key to mobilising the population by galvanising a *levee en masse* for total war. He decreed that 'the whole nation from the military and armed forces to the bazaar, university and everywhere, farmers, workers, employees, all the layers of the nation all of these must be the guards of Islam.'[23] Khomeini called upon all of the Iranian nation, 'people from all walks of life', to remain decisive and equipped in the defence of Islam and to prepare for the war as it was a war for the defence of 'Islam, Muslims' dignity and honour, the holy Koran, the Iranian nation and other nations'.[24] Though he emphasised the need to fight for *Islam*, he appealed to popular national sentiment by emphasising that defeat would be a *national* disgrace.[25]

Khomeini eulogised the war for awakening the masses and inculcating activity and awareness within them. He presented war as having the positive effect of revealing the 'inner capacity' of man and shaking off feelings of 'slackness and inactivity'.[26] He applauded men for their heroic feats at war, appealing also to chauvinistic and *macho* sentiments, comparing the zeal to attend the war fronts with the male lust for the 'nuptial chambers'.[27]

Women were urged as the mothers of warriors to encourage their children to volunteer for the fronts. On the Islamic Republic's Women's Day in 1983 Montazeri, referring to the early days of Islam, congratulated mothers for their generosity in giving their children up as martyrs for God.[28]

However, the mechanisms of mobilisation also included institutional devices using material incentives as well as more coercive methods. In their various capacities, the heads of the revolutionary institutions, maintaining their loyalty and adherence to the 'Imam's line', set about immediately to put the clerics' calls for war mobilisation into practice. The *Pasdaran* expanded the recruitment of volunteers.[29] The activities of the affiliated *basij*, through the organisation of the local mosques, were stepped up. Khamenei, as president and Chair of the Supreme Defence Council, established as a wartime executive committee, stated that 'any trained person in any part of the country must be ready to present himself to the mobilisation centres of Islamic Revolution's Guard Corps for dispatch to the battlefronts against global arrogance.'[30] Numerous appeals resulted in large numbers – mainly stemming from the regime's traditional and religious social base in the poorest sections of the population, often with rural backgrounds and illiterate or semi-literate – volunteering for the fronts.

The regime took to the employment of child-soldiers as schoolboys between the ages of 12 and 18 were encouraged to join the *basij*. Large numbers of schoolboy volunteers were given plastic keys to hang around their necks, symbolically providing entry to paradise and the realm of 'Martyrdom'. In order to provide greater incentives for young volunteers, plans for the creation of 'pupil guards' were announced for the recruitment of boys between the ages of 15 and 19 with educational incentives and easier access to universities subsequent upon service.[31] By 1987, a large percentage of pupils in secondary schools had reportedly undergone some kind of military training.[32] Likewise, schemes for the rotation of university students for the war were set in place as the Revolutionary Guard called for university staff and students to register for service.[33]

Other revolutionary organisations such as the Construction Crusade (*jihad-e sazandegi*) also contributed to this mobilisation. The *jihad-e sazandegi* which had been formed following Khomeini's edict in June 1979 was intended, as prescribed in its charter, to mobilise the existing 'potential and resources of the people and the state to co-operate in effectively and rapidly elaborating and implementing the construction projects and in reviving society in all its material and spiritual dimensions while taking into consideration and emphasising the needs of the villages and the remote regions of the country'.[34] Having developed a nationwide organisational structure through a network of village councils, which were largely supervised and run by clerics, its resources were, directly and indirectly, channelled into the war effort.[35] The *jihad* contributed both in its 'engineering in war' capacity and by mobilising volunteers; collecting money, clothes and food; providing medical facilities; and producing and distributing Korans and propaganda material for the war.[36]

When the need for greater mobilisation arose, women, who had initially been assigned a behind-the-scenes role in the war, were also called upon for military combat. Khomeini, in his 1986 address on the Islamic Republic's Women's Day, reversed the supposed Islamic ruling that women were not to take part in combat by decreeing that the defence of Islam and an Islamic country was also a requirement for women, and as Iran's conflict with Iraq was a defence against an 'imposed war', women should also learn military skills and join the army.[37] Thus, training programmes for women volunteers were also organised by the Revolutionary Guard. A 'day of the *basij* of the sisters' was announced during Basij Week in December 1987, stressing their contribution to the war effort and employment in arms industries.[38]

The *basij* also presided over various headquarters for the attraction and organisation of popular assistance. Provincial war centres were set up comprising the regional governor general, Friday Imam, *Pasdaran* command and officials of the *jihad-e sazandegi*, all engaged in increasing the mobilisation effort.[39] A Supreme Council of War Support was formed in 1986 and 'village war councils' were established for the despatch of further forces from rural areas.[40] The government approved and encouraged the participation of state employees at the fronts.[41] A ministerial order in 1986 decreed the formation of a war committee (*setad-e omur-e jang*) in every ministry under the direct supervision of the respective minister, in order to 'deal with the needs of the war'.[42] Shortly afterwards, the government ordered all ministries and organisations that drew upon public funds to despatch 20 per cent of their employees to the fronts should the *Pasdaran* or *jihad-e sazandegi* demand this.[43] In order to encourage employees to volunteer for the war, extra benefits were awarded, including additional wages, employment security in compensation for time at the war fronts and greater opportunities for promotion.[44] The following International Labour Day in 1987 was used as an opportunity to dispatch greater numbers of government employees to the fronts.[45]

The people were also called upon to make war donations in a

[103]

variety of ways. 'The noble and honourable people of Iran' were urged to show their revolutionary fervour by 'donating from what little they have to the Muslim people who are fighting on the battlefronts'.[46] Rafsanjani called for the payment of 300 billion riyals in religious dues (*khoms*) on a national scale.[47] Khomeini explicitly made it a duty to help in the war effort under conditions where the government alone was unable to 'cope with the difficulties' of 'defending the country's population and property as well as safeguarding Islam'.[48] Under the explicit direction of Khomeini, the Supreme Council of War Support, proclaimed both direct mobilisation and 'financial jihad' – material assistance for the government's conduct of war – as duties. Thus, the leadership appealed to the population to assist the government in financing those fighting at the fronts. A number of special bank accounts were set up to facilitate popular donation for the war. Ayatollah Montazeri, for instance, had various accounts set up for donations to the fronts.[49] In order to mobilise further assistance, contributions made directly by the public to the war effort – ranging from basic commodities such as wheat flour and detergents to gas stoves, trucks and, of course, cash sums including the donations of a proportion of wages – were extensively publicised in the media.[50] Particular appeals were also made to the traditional and wealthy merchants of the *bazaar* and their large donations, such as the contribution of 10,000 million riyals by the *bazaaris* of Qom, as well as those by the clerics, were made public as evidence of their religious and devout credentials and to provide role models for the population at large.[51]

War, populism and repression

Although the war initially led to popular mobilisation for defence, this by no means spelt the resolution of post-revolutionary social conflict stemming from a fragmenting revolutionary coalition and the diverging interests of different social groups. The tightening of control and shrinking compass of the ruling circle resulted in active engagement with the domestic opposition, which included both party activists and less formal groups. Various political groups and parties that had initially participated in the Revolution took to opposition activity. The most important of these was the *Mojahedin-e-Khalq* (Mojahedin). The pro-Soviet *Hezb-e Tudeh* (Tudeh) was the last of the secular left parties to be cast into the banned opposition.

The regime adopted a number of ways to deal with such protest. Firstly, using populist rhetoric foreign hands were blamed for any sign of disruption and opposition was repressed for being the 'agent of imperialism'. Opposition was demobilised by using the imposed war as an excuse for shortcomings and material scarcities. Meanwhile, the coercive instruments of state were also fortified and increasingly placed in the hands of a new elite who employed them to control the population.

Armed domestic opposition was manifested in a series of demonstrations, assassinations and bomb explosions during 1981. These activities, largely attributed to the by then banned Mojahedin, constituted perhaps the most serious active challenge to the Islamic Republic in its early years. They were dismissed by the regime as an alternative measure of 'the vampirist imperialism' which, finding direct military intervention costly, was trying through 'its agents within the country, spies and fifth columnists' to change the course of the Revolution by spreading rumours and inciting sedition and sabotage.[52] While the country was at war, these activities were doubly nefarious for being treacherous to nation and Revolution. The circle of allegedly exposed US agents extended beyond the underground activists to those who had, until then, remained close to the ruling clerics including the first president of the Islamic Republic, Bani-Sadr, who was finally ousted from his post. In the *majles*, the former prime minister of the provisional government, Mehdi Bazargan, was silenced after voicing opposition to the regime's policies as deputies denounced him claiming 'he's American', 'down with the American lackey' and 'down with America'.[53] Khomeini, rather ironically, discredited those who attempted to resist the concentration of power in the hands of the clerics for being dictatorial as well as under foreign influence.[54]

Attempts at mediation in the war were also linked to the plot of 'global imperialism'. When the headquarters of the Islamic Republic Party (IRP) were bombed in 1981, the coinciding arrival of peace missions in Tehran was taken as evidence that all these efforts formed an integrated plot of 'agents of the US CIA to distract the attention of people from the war'. The activities of the internal opposition were regarded as having the parallel aim of preventing the Islamic Republic from fighting the war.[55] From 1982, objection and resistance to the increasing control and coercion of the regime and its policy of continuing the war into Iraqi territory multiplied. These voices were again branded the counter-revolutionary voice of foreign imperialist agents and traitors. *Jomhuri-ye Islami*, the newspaper of the Islamic Republic Party, rejected such calls and recommended that the only answer of the Iranian nation should be 'vigorous struggle with the aggressor enemy who through the support of East and West has attacked our Revolution'.[56] Khomeini repeatedly discredited demands for an end to the conflict as 'wanting an American Peace'.[57] Peace would be 'against Islam, the Koran, wisdom and all human values'.[58] Koranic verses and images of legendary battles during the early days of Islam were adopted to legitimise his view:

The Koran says war until sedition is removed from the world, therefore it would be wrong for anybody to think that the Koran has not said war, war until victory.[59]

Domestic opposition focused, however, not only on the war but also on socio-economic issues. As people became increasingly discontented with the failure of the Islamic Republic to improve their material lives, a number of strikes and street protests emerged. Such forms of protest were harder to attribute to foreign agents, and often the war itself was used as an excuse to suppress these demands. Shortages were blamed on the war, which in turn was alleged to be the result of the policy of the superpowers.[60]

Other protests were expressed in the form of strikes at industrial plants and other organisations and anti-government and anti-war demonstrations. As various sectors of the population protested against working and social conditions, the war was called upon as a ready excuse to neutralise their demands. The case of the Tehran bus drivers' strike is a poignant one. Initially the strike was quite successful and the government was unable to break it. It came to an end, however, when the government brought in the bodies of dead soldiers and paraded them across the picket lines. They protested that while people were being killed at the front, bus drivers were demanding increased wages and creating problems for the government.[61] Women's complaints against the imposition of the *hejab* (Islamic garb) were countered by a similar technique as Interior Minister Mohtashami claimed that when the 'dear combatants' came to the cities from the fronts and saw the 'misuse of Islamic garb' by some women, their morale would be harmed.[62]

Any opposition to the increasing concentration of state power, the prolongation of war and the policies of the new ruling clerics was put down to the conspiracies and agencies of an omnipotent 'world imperialism'. This tactic was clearly deployed against particular individuals who spoke out against the regime and organised opposition groups and parties, but also effective in suppressing the demands of numerous social groups. However, ultimately, the power of persuasion through populist rhetoric had to be backed up by coercive force and the war itself provided the means to establish the instruments of state coercion.

Development of the instruments of state coercion

Wartime emergency conditions became the banner under which the new state apparatus was strengthened. Mechanisms for the control, subjugation and surveillance of the population were reinforced. War conditions led to control not only of the military and security apparatuses but also of other state institutions, including media and education.

In the immediate aftermath of the outbreak of hostilities in late September 1980, Khomeini, in his address to the nation, ordered unconditional obedience to the Command Council, restrictions on the broadcast and print media and the unity of 'all layers of nation and government bodies'.[63] The establishment of the Supreme Defence Council, invested with considerable executive power, reinforced centralised control.[64] Restrictions were imposed on the forces of opposition, including factions in dispute within the leading elite as well as social forces from below. In March 1981 Khomeini issued another decree in which he not only emphasised limits to be imposed on the media, but also restricted officials of the government, including the president, from voicing their views in public.[65] On the basis of the emergency wartime conditions, the activities of groups and parties were circumscribed. They were required to have permits from the newly formed Ministry of Islamic Guidance for publications, permission from the Ministry of the Interior for the holding of meetings and demonstrations, and were forbidden from encouraging or inciting strikes, go-slows, sit-ins or any other disruptions in government organisation.[66]

A Wartime Offences Court was set up to investigate violations and crimes and to 'establish security and avert calamities emanating from the enemy'.[67] Active in the elimination of internal opposition, the court called upon the population to identify and report the alleged 'agents of SAVAK and other dregs left over from the previous regime [who had] been taking part in the meetings of the fascist American groups who are fighting against the Islamic Republic'.[68] The war was repeatedly used as a justification for clamping down on the media. The Wartime Publicity Office, set up in May 1981, ordered the mass media, institutions, civil and military organisations to coordinate all reports relating to the war through its staff.[69]

The new institutions were used to impose severe restrictions on the organs of the opposition both within the ranks of the government and among groups outside its formal structures. Thus, several newspapers were banned in June 1981 for 'publishing troublesome articles ... particularly during the war'; these included *Mizan*, *Jebhe-ye-Melli* and *Enqelab-e-Eslami*.[70] Khomeini and other leaders persistently stressed the importance of propaganda and use of the media in general, and the broadcast media in particular. Much of television programming had a directly religious content and, during the war, military marches and revolutionary songs were increasingly prevalent.[71] The formation of an Information Ministry resulted in extensive legislation stipulating that all ministries, government organisations and military and security forces filter information through it. This ministry became increasingly active in the domain of intelligence gathering and internal security.[72] Its activities were not confined to the control and repression of opposition amongst the population at large, but also extended to the surveillance of those within the ruling elite who deviated from government policy, which was increasingly formulated by a narrow circle. Universities, a traditional locus of political activity, were also increasingly brought under the control of the state. As institutions they were discredited by Khomeini for promoting 'foreign and un-Islamic culture'.[73]

In response to the threat that opposition groups might come together through organisation within universities, these institutions were closed by the regime. The war continued to provide the excuse for their protracted closure until extensive purges had been carried out and a 'cultural revolution' had been carried through.

Finally, war naturally affected the evolution of military and para-military institutions of the post-revolutionary regime. The new leadership remained wary that the distrusted army might reassert itself and a potential *coup d'etat* be led by the military. Their apprehensions were increased by the cautions of the left, warnings of an imminent *coup* and calls for the establishment of a 'people's army' or 'people's militia'.[74] Under these conditions, the re-organisation of the military entailed purging the higher echelons of the regular army as well as developing the emergent revolutionary militias into a loyal command structure. Prior to the war many officers had been executed. A programme of 'ideologisation' of the rank and file was laid out with the aims of 'propagation of Islamic ideology' and putting the armed forces at the disposal of the government, while the necessity of further purges and 'purification' continued to be stressed.[75]

Though the war rallied and mobilised the army for national defence and necessitated its re-entry into the arena, concomitantly, the formal training and organisation of the Islamic Revolution Guard Corps (*Pasdaran*), who had developed as a revolutionary paramilitary, were encouraged. The *Pasdaran* was formally established in May 1979 following Khomeini's decree, and its role of 'defence of the Revolution and safeguarding its achievements' was enshrined in Article 150 of the Constitution. The 'mobilisation of the deprived' (*basij-e-mostazafin*) was initiated as a people's militia following Khomeini's call for an 'army of 20 million' (*artesh-e-bist milioni*) in the aftermath of the taking of the US embassy in Tehran. Nevertheless, these organisations were still in their infancy in 1980 and remained loose and decentralised.[76]

The war had important consequences for the organisation and re-organisation of these paramilitary forces. The activation of the *Pasdaran* was accelerated and more resources were channelled into developing its academic, ideological, political and military programmes.[77] Strengthening ties between the *Pasdaran* and a number of religious figures provided the new elite with a loyal military institution. These ties emerged more as a relation of control by the clergy through the role of Khomeini's representatives (*namayandeh-e imam*) and their supervisory duties. The religious and ideological training of the Guards were not only taken over by these clerics, but also this function was later centralised following the establishment of a *Pasdaran* research centre in Qum – home of the country's largest religious seminary – which assumed responsibility for educational and propaganda material.

The numbers of *Pasdaran* personnel grew dramatically in the first years of the Revolution from an estimated 5000 in 1979 to 50,000 in 1981, 150,000 in 1983 and 250,000 in 1985.[78] The war was central to the rapid augmentation of numbers within this organisation as its task of defending the Revolution naturally came to entail an active role in countering international counter-revolution. But participation in the war did not detract from the part played in enforcing internal security. This latter role could now be played more effectively not only due to a numerical increase of membership, but also as a result of greater institutionalisation through the establishment of the Ministry of Revolutionary Guards in November 1982 and an intelligence unit within it.[79] Furthermore, the *Pasdaran* also controlled the *sarallah* and *jundallah* urban patrols, which maintained a strong presence on the streets and played an important part in surveillance of the population. More generally, the internal functions of the *Pasdaran* included the surveillance of urban areas, countering organised opposition, suppressing popular demonstrations against the regime, confronting and arresting 'counter-revolutionaries', protecting sensitive government institutions and organisations, conducting intelligence-gathering operations and propaganda activities.[80]

Similarly, the war radically changed the organisation, functions and political role of the Mobilisation Corps (*basij*). With the outbreak of the war the *Pasdaran* took charge of mobilising the 'army of 20 million'. Recruitment took place through the co-operation of the *Pasdaran* network and the local mosques thus helping to organise and centralise the *basij* which officially took the title of the *Basij* Unit of the Guard Corps (*vahed-e basij-e sepah-e Pasdaran*). The background and pressing socio-economic requirements of the majority of the volunteers meant that the *basij* could serve as a 'prime revolutionary machinery of patronage for low-income youths'.[81] By 1985 government sources claimed to have trained over 3 million volunteers, 600,000–700,000 of whom had assisted at the war fronts. Though some returned to previous occupations after service, high levels of unemployment left a vast number of personnel to engage in activities such as propagation of Islamic ideology, security and political repression which would open up channels of mobility through the state bureaucracy.

Ultimately, the Armed Forces Bill comprehensively defined the goals of the *Pasdaran*, *artesh* (regular army), security forces and police as defence of the nation *and* the Islamic Republic of Iran as well as the support of the oppressed Muslims and nations.[82] Meanwhile, an independent organisation for the protection of intelligence in the armed forces, the head of which was to be directly appointed by the leader, would co-operate with the Ministry of Information to ensure that the coercive apparatus of the state remained directly subordinated to the rule of the clerics.[83] The Armed Forces Law also formally defined the duties and recruitment criteria for the employment of members of the *basij* under the aegis of the *Pasdaran* thereby creating a category of personnel loyal to the regime and entrusted with ensuring the internal and external security of the state.[84] The importance of the creation of these military organisations to the longevity of the Islamic state under the aegis of a small group of clerical leaders cannot be overstated. These organisations did not only provide the recruiting ground for the war and followers of the regime. They also provided a military force of not inconsiderable strength directly loyal to the spiritual leader and ready for mobilisation in defence of the Islamic Regime.

To summarise, the internal impact of the war was to allow greater control of security inside the country as 'counter-revolutionaries' and 'traitors' were discredited, universities remained closed and government agencies were purged. It also made for the strengthening of revolutionary organisations, especially the paramilitary, media and propaganda, and intelligence services. The prolonged war provided the means and justification for fortifying the coercive apparatus and institutions of the state. As the circle of those in power narrowed, defence of the Revolution, Islamic Republic and liberation movements across the globe was equated with the defence of the government in power. The state maintained the banner of representing 'the people', but the interests of the people were simply defined by the policies of the state.

The categorical expression of this development was Khomeini's decree on the powers of Islamic government in early 1988.[85] This empowered the government of the day, under the jurisdiction of the supreme religious leader, to define the interest of Islam, nation and revolution. Khomeini famously confirmed the primacy of the state over all other matters:

> the ruler can close down mosques if need be or can even demolish a mosque which is a source of harm. ... The government is empowered to unilaterally revoke any Shari'a agreements which it has concluded with the people when those agreements are contrary to the interests of the country or of Islam.[86]

The gradual assumption of control of the state apparatus that found its ultimate expression in this decree was crucial in allowing a small elite to define and dictate the policies of the state and to conduct the war for almost eight years.

Abasement of 'social populism'

As the national effort and resources of the country were concentrated on the war, other policies and programmes regarding the transformation of the socio-economic structure were largely disregarded throughout the first post-revolutionary decade. 'War until victory' was the primary slogan of the Revolution, at the expense of alternative objectives such as the redistribution of wealth, egalitarianism or development planning. The interests of the 'deprived' were, rather, interpreted in new ways devoid of a socio-economic content.

While a 'social-populist' tendency could be said to have co-existed with or intersected the 'war-populist' one, it was subordinated during the eight-year Iran–Iraq war. This, it must be emphasised, is not to say that the post-revolutionary regime, having initially held to a progressive socio-economic programme, was subsequently deflected by the 'external factor' of war as a number of scholars, wittingly or unwittingly serving as apologists for the failures of the Islamic Republic, have suggested.[87] Though the post-revolutionary state was the victim of foreign invasion, the continuation of the war by the regime was a consciously pursued policy that was far from inescapable. Nevertheless, the post-revolutionary regime cannot be regarded as an undivided and cohesive whole. Different factions and tendencies existed even within the leadership and we need to explain how one tendency came to prevail over others.

Khomeini's populist rhetoric entailed a strong element of social justice and protection of the interests of the deprived (*mostazafin* or *mahroomin*). While failing to offer an economic theory or comprehensive socio-economic model for society, he had initially called for greater redistribution of wealth, concentrating on the destruction of big capital in favour of the 'deprived layers' of society. During the immediate post-revolutionary years, the importance attached to the question of social justice was evident in the First National Economic Plan (1983/4–1987/8) submitted to the *majles* in August 1983.[88] The plan emphasised social justice and redistribution over and above goals of capitalist accumulation and industrial growth. The general objectives were the expansion of education and culture, securing the interests of the *mostazafin*, economic independence, the provision of social security, health care, food and clothing, housing and finally elimination of unemployment. However, throughout the decade, the war came to be awarded priority over not only economic planning and development, but virtually all areas of social life and the objectives of the Plan were largely abandoned in war's favour. Even prior to the presentation of the First Plan, Prime Minister Mousavi clearly stated, 'at a time when we have set the victory at war as our priority and most important goal, it is natural that all the government's programmes and resources are mobilised and directed for achieving that victory.'[89]

By 1985, in presenting the annual budget bill to the *majles*, Mousavi reiterated that the war was the main axis of all political and economic activities and proposed a 12.5 per cent increase in the defence budget, while noting that government expenditure aside from the war had decreased.[90] The objectives spelt out in the revised version of the national plan finally approved by the *majles* in 1986 were then limited to a series of generalities, while budgets approved or amended by the *majles* consistently announced spiralling additional expenditure for the war.[91] Industrial development was largely concentrated on military production. In an effort both to economise on foreign exchange earnings and to reduce dependence on imports of arms, the post-revolutionary regime, not unlike numerous other 'third tier producers', adopted a strategy of import substitution military industrialisation.[92] Extensive nationalisation and state ownership of the means of production meant that industry could be directed towards production for the war effort and military self-sufficiency. Towards these aims, a special Industrial and Engineering War Commission was established in 1985 and a war affairs headquarters set up in every ministry.[93] Thus, in the sixth year of the war Prime Minister Mousavi could claim that 'It is quite clear that one of our most important industrial bases ... for the future of our country will be these military industries' and by the end of 1987, 50 per cent of national heavy industrial product was utilised for the war effort.[94]

Meanwhile, in the context of the war, the redistributionist and egalitarian populist element of Khomeinist politics translated into a romanticist abstention from material wants and a return to an austere past. Khomeini repeatedly implored the people to refrain from making material demands and not to endanger 'our honour, our Islam, our lives and the lives of our youths because meat or fruit is expensive', and appealed to them to eradicate the mentality of wanting to become 'palace-dwellers'.[95] Such demands were to be deplored under the exceptional war conditions.[96] References were made to the early days of Islam and the sacrifices and hardships endured by the Prophet in his efforts to promote Islam. Khomeini repeated again and again that the 'deprived and afflicted classes of the Revolution' had not endured as many trials and tribulations as the Prophet of Islam throughout his life; that compared with the 'suffering tolerated by the Prophet and his dear wife' their problems were negligible; and that 'the nation or the *umma* of that great Prophet' would not complain if goods were scarce'.[97] The masses were urged to follow the example of Muslims at the dawn of Islam in leading frugal lives. Khomeini famously suggested that the Prophet and Imam Ali had maintained themselves on a single date a day. As economic conditions deteriorated in post-revolutionary Iran, Ayatollah Montazeri reminded the nation at war that during the battles of early Islam, Muslims had in fact 'lived on one date a day for every *two* men'![98]

The government maintained the populist banner of representing and protecting the interests of the deprived. However, throughout the war the deprived came to be conceptualised differently. They were no longer the property-less and poverty-stricken, but the 'barefoot masses' which encompassed a motley coalition of social classes. Khomeini presented Iranian society as being free from class divisions or interests and united through Islam: 'Nowhere else in the world ... are farmers sitting alongside the president and workers alongside the prime minister.'[99] As he put it:

They might say this government has done nothing for the people ... but the people should realise what the government has done for them. ... It was the people who established this government and this republic. Not all the people but the bare-foot masses. The burden has been on the shoulder of the *bazaaris*, the middle class and the oppressed. That is, the deprived stratum.[100]

The deprived were now to be identified not by deprivation in terms of any socio-economic category but by support of the regime and participation at the war fronts:

All those who sacrificed their young people came from the deprived masses [slum dwellers and the deprived strata]. Let us count how many of the well-to-do, how many of those who are criticising the Islamic Republic have gone to the war fronts. How many of them have been martyred? You will be hard pushed to find even one. ... All of our martyrs come from the deprived masses. Our deprived are not only the slum dwellers; some *bazaaris* are deprived, some workers are deprived, some farmers are deprived, they might come from different walks of life. Those who are serving on the fronts come from those masses. Those who are trying so hard to guard the country and Islam come from those masses.[101]

Thus, the dismissal of material demands and economic development in favour of the war had two strands. Firstly, the demands themselves were dismissed as extravagant and a reflection of the excesses of Western culture such that their expression under the particular conditions of war was considered abhorrent, un-Islamic and unpatriotic. Secondly, as the government retained its label of representing and protecting the deprived, those who opposed the government could no longer belong to the 'deprived class'. It was therefore the deprived who had to be redefined to entail supporters of the regime, war volunteers and families of 'martyrs'. But this also meant that increasingly coercive instruments were to be deployed to deal with protest from social groups which did not come under this umbrella and whose interests were not protected by the policies of the regime. Wartime conditions led to the creation of a state apparatus ready and willing to use coercive means against social opposition while the state elite pursued bellicose objectives. The regime would use this state apparatus to repress opposition in the years to come. It was increasingly able to do so through control over the material resources which underpinned the state.

Social basis of the war

We have seen how the national-populist rhetoric of the revolutionary elite and control over instruments of the state, including the means of mass communication, organisation and education, encouraged total popular mobilisation for war during the 1980s. Domestic resources for the war thus included direct donations of cash and goods as well as human lives. On the other hand, the complicity of powerful classes, which remained an independent source of financial support for the religious elite, could only be secured by ensuring that their material interests were met. As we shall see, the continuation of the war served these interests and strengthened the arm of the pro-war faction in the regime. Meanwhile, state and para-state ownership of the means of production and state command over oil rents provided surpluses for the war.

The ownership of the means of production by the state and para-state bodies allowed those in control of the state apparatus to make autonomous decisions regarding expenditure. In the 1980s, this enabled them to increase the proportion of revenues earmarked for the war. As a consequence of extensive nationalisation in the aftermath of the Revolution and the expropriation of assets of previous owners who left the country, direct state ownership and control of a large number of industries made revenues for the war more readily accessible to the regime.

The Law for the Protection and Expansion of Iranian Industry, approved by the Revolutionary Council in the immediate revolutionary aftermath, allowed the nationalisation of heavy industries,

industries owned by specifically named individuals who had allegedly acquired their wealth by corrupt means, and industries which had liabilities exceeding their assets and were facing economic crisis and bankruptcy.[102] By the mid-1980s only smaller industries remained in private hands. State and corporate ownership facilitated the creation of what may be called a 'state-class' – a class of personnel who depended on the state for their reproduction, had at their disposal the surpluses accrued to the state and who, in this instance, were able to channel these resources towards the war.

The expansion of the public sector led to a dramatic increase in the numbers employed by the state, thereby leaving the extracted surpluses at the disposal of those controlling the administrative apparatus of the country.[103] In a bid to maximise these surpluses, the regime adopted policies that resulted in a deterioration of the living conditions of the working class at large. A total wage freeze was effected between 1979 and 1989, while the official rate of inflation during the same period averaged 25 per cent per annum. Real wages therefore showed a downward trend for the whole duration of the war.[104] Concomitantly, an intensification of the labour process was encouraged as the population was urged to increase production and work harder and more intensively behind the scenes due to the exceptional war conditions. The resolution of a state-sponsored rally in Tehran in April 1981 stated that the country was engaged in a war between Islam and blasphemy and called upon workers, farmers and government employees to increase production.[105] Industrial schools, factories and all production units were also urged to raise output of military hardware by doubling their efforts.[106] Increasing production was ranked alongside fighting on the battlefields as a form of war. Rural labourers were assured by the clerics that their hard work in 'breeding cattle' and producing 'high yields of sugar beet, wheat or barley' were just as valuable as participation at the fronts.[107] In the absence of secular trade unions and the limited role of 'Islamic councils' in representing the material interests of workers, the compound result of such policies was, of course, intensified exploitation of the working class.[108] With much of national industry under the ownership of the state, the leadership was able effectively to cast its net over the surpluses produced and divert them into the private coffers of a new 'state-dependent' class or the war chest of those factions continuing to beat the drum of battle. The latter faction was provided further means to pursue these goals due to the strength of large religious corporate bodies.

Though the industrial assets of the old capitalist elite were nominally 'nationalised', they were only partly controlled by the government as the *bonyads* (religious foundations) took charge of a considerable proportion of these assets.[109] These para-state organisations took possession of the

properties confiscated by the Islamic Revolutionary Courts in the immediate aftermath of the Revolution. The most important and influential of
these, the *bonyad-e mostazafin* (Foundation of the Oppressed) was established in 1979 under the orders of Khomeini to take control of over 200
confiscated industrial, agricultural and trading corporations previously
owned by the Pahlavis. By 1983, it owned over 200 factories, 250 trading
companies and 45 agro-industrial complexes, and by 1985 the companies
owned by the *bonyad-e mostazafin* numbered over 600.[110]

Khomeini also decreed the foundation of the *bonyad-e shahid*
(Martyrs Foundation) in February 1980. This organisation was nominally charged with protection of the interests of families of martyrs of
the Revolution through the use of appropriated assets and funds
assigned to it from the national budget. By 1985 the Foundation was
responsible for the management of 68 industrial factories, 79 trading
companies, 19 construction businesses and 17 agricultural plants.[111] It
became engaged in heavy industrial production, imports of industrial
goods and raw materials, and highly profitable economic activities
such as the internal distribution of consumer goods such as tobacco
and household durables.[112]

Throughout the 1980s, the *bonyads* made a significant contribution
to the military effort. Exempted from the usual government controls,
they presided over considerable revenues, particularly through
trading and real estate affiliates, and increasingly acted as holding
companies making significant profits.[113] These profits could readily be
channelled into the war effort as they came largely under the jurisdiction of the religious leadership. These sprawling organisations were at
the disposal of the clerical leadership in general and Khomeini in
particular, as they were controlled by the religious leadership and not
the government, and ultimately accountable only to the leader.[114] As
the head of, the *bonyad-e mostazafin*, Khomeini presided over 50 per
cent of all its profits, which were paid directly into his personal charity,
and he thus controlled the means of distribution of these funds for
whatever purpose he chose. Likewise, although there were attempts to
establish a constitution (*asas-nameh*) for the governance of the *bonyad-e-
shahid*, Khomeini decreed that it should operate without formal
regulation, thus allowing greater flexibility both for its management
and pursuit of projects as well as the destination of its funds.

Nominally charged with protecting the interests of the poor and
deprived, these massive conglomerations, contributed to the conduct of
war in two ways. Firstly, as the war took priority over other goals, the
direction of activity of these foundations also shifted. They became a
direct source of finance through donations for the support of the war. In
1985, for instance, of the total payments of 7 billion riyals made by the
bonyad-e mostazafin, the publicly divulged allocations included 1.5 billion

riyals for the war.[115] Secondly, they contributed to popular mobilisation by providing material incentives for participation at the fronts. A *bonyad-e shahid* company was formally placed under the ownership of the children of those killed in the war, thus providing their families with a source of income. The families of 'martyrs' were assured of a monthly income and regular investment account for each child in addition to a lump sum payment to the family and preferential treatment in receiving scarce goods and services.[116] The *bonyad-e shahid* also ensured its clientele priority in admission to all educational institutions from primary school to university, priority in obtaining basic economic needs and employment, exemption from fares on all state-owned city transport and the payment of half-fares on intercity transport, medical insurance and a special card for the purchase of medicines, hospitalisation and treatment of the disabled and wounded including, if necessary, their dispatch abroad.[117] These incentives were taken up by large numbers from the regime's social basis in the 'marginal' urban and rural population that was comprised largely of the unemployed and lower middle classes, thus assuring their complicity with and loyalty to the Islamic Republic's leadership. The *bonyads* became important institutions in the make-up of the state; a source for rallying support through the provision of material incentives to the regime's followers well beyond the war years.

In summary, by the end of the first decade of the Islamic Republic, an elaborate and coercive state apparatus had been established under the control of a religious revolutionary elite which had seemed determined not only to propagate the Revolution at home but also to export it abroad. The successful mobilisation of the population for the war and its financing by public revenue that was extracted internally and externally made continuation of the war a viable option for a number of years. The regime's populism led to a popular mobilisation resting on nationalist and universalist themes. On the other hand, the capacity of the regime to continue with the war effort depended on the extraction of internal and external revenues. In the next chapter we show how a combination of internal and external pressures constrained the post-revolutionary regime and led to a period of change in the 1990s.

6 State crisis and change

During the 1980s, the Islamic Republic was marked by revolutionary policy at home and abroad. In contrast, the second decade of the Revolution saw a number of changes in policy as well as leadership. In July 1988, the leadership abandoned their revolutionary goal of 'war until victory' and agreed to end the war with Iraq. August 1989 saw the death of Khomeini and the replacement of the hegemonic populist leader with a more divided leadership, as well as a number of constitutional changes. New watchwords of post-war reconstruction and economic development entered the vocabulary of the regime. Finally, in 1997, a new president was elected on what seemed to be a popular wave which would pave the way for genuine reforms.

As the 1990s began, many spoke of the socialisation of the Islamic Republic and the end of a revolutionary era. This was the start of a notably different 'Second Republic'.[1] It signalled a process of normalisation, an Iranian *Thermidor* or *Perestroika*.[2] In 2007, however, the benefit of hindsight reveals this at best to have been a contradictory and crisis-ridden period: a *Thermidor* whose twilight was already in sight at the beginning of the decade and whose definitive end came in 2005 with the election of a hard-line president who reverted to the revolutionary language of the 1980s.

The changes in policy and practice during the second decade seem at first glance to vindicate the notion of socialisation or normalisation generally presented in orthodox accounts of international relations to indicate the de-radicalisation of the policies of revolutionary states over time. In this chapter we propose to examine this supposed process of 'socialisation'. As we shall show, the conjuncture of domestic and international pressures resulted in a crisis of the Islamic Republic at the end of the 1980s which could only be alleviated by a revision of its immediate policies. The concrete policies pursued as a result were intended to strengthen the Revolution at home before promoting its cause abroad. They included reconciliatory policies with respect to a number of regional and global states and a substantial revision of previous economic strategies. These changes may appear to lend credence to the idea that the Islamic Republic was in the process of 'socialisation' or 'normalisation' that had been launched at the end of its first decade with the end of the war with Iraq, the death of Khomeini and the inauguration of the 'Second Republic'. But the return to several policies of the early post-revolutionary period and radical posturing on foreign policy more recently, throws this view into grave doubt. More generally, the history of the Islamic Republic in its second and third decades, as we shall elaborate later in this chapter, shows that a number of continued tensions within the post-revolutionary regime posed obstacles to 'socialisation', making this putatively linear process equivocal and unpredictable.

State, revolution and class: a theoretical explanation

Many observers of Iran over the last decade have remarked on the contradictory nature of the regime and its policies.[3] The Islamic Republic's foreign policy since 1989, in particular, has been singled out as sending 'mixed messages'.[4] However, most explanations of the regime's policy changes tend to rely on factional divisions within the leadership.[5] While it is of course correct to point out the differences amongst the religious leadership, the attribution of the policies of the 'Second Republic' to the strengthening of one faction or the other is questionable. Many changes in policy were advocated by those very same erstwhile radical revolutionary leaders. Some more interesting explanations have focused on the changes in the preferences of the regime.[6] However, even these have not gone on to explain why the regime has undergone changes while continuing to veer between this or that policy.

The argument here is that the change in policy was impelled by changes in economic circumstances that were due to both international and domestic factors, including pressure from the popular classes on whom the regime depended. As a result, state managers perceived a threat to their own position and ability to reproduce themselves socially. Under wartime conditions the means of administration, production and distribution were increasingly controlled by state managers.[7] This increasing domination led to the further emergence of a 'state-class' – a bureaucratic ruling class whose social reproduction depends on the ability of the political administration of the state to extract surpluses. On the one hand this can be conceptualised as the 'autonomy' of state managers from the previously dominant private capitalist class under the exceptional circumstances of revolution and war.[8] On the other hand, however, this is not a situation of absolute autonomy of the state from class interests. Firstly, the social interests and influence of other dominant social classes need to be taken into account. As we have seen, these interests were often tied to merchant capital during the period of the war. Secondly, a fusion of state and class was realised in the emergence of a new bureaucratic dominant class with a composition different to that of the previously existing (pre-revolutionary) ruling class.

Faced with a reduction in state revenues and social discontent, the ability of the new post-revolutionary bureaucratic class to reproduce itself socially was endangered. As Block has noted:

those who manage the state apparatus – regardless of their own political ideology – are dependent on the maintenance of some reasonable level of economic activity. This is true for two reasons. First, the capacity of the state to finance itself through taxation or borrowing depends on the state of the economy. If economic activity is in decline, the state will have difficulty maintaining its revenues at an adequate level. Second, public support for a regime will decline sharply if the regime presides over a serious drop in the level of economic activity with a parallel rise in unemployment and shortages of key goods. Such a drop in support increases the likelihood that the state managers will be removed from power one way or another. And even if the drop is not that dramatic, it will increase the challenges to the regime and decrease the regime's political ability to take effective actions.[9]

The final years of the Iran–Iraq war of the 1980s saw such a drop in the revenues accrued to the post-revolutionary state due both to external and internal developments. According to Block, the structural position of state managers gives them an interest in aiding the accumulation process.[10] This is the reversal which we observe in the case of the leadership of the Islamic Republic. As the regime felt the pressure of popular unrest from below, it was prompted firstly to remove the burden of military conflict and also to attempt to increase the level of economic activity and increase revenues.[11]

The economic failures of the Islamic Republic and the experience of war had made clear that without a productive base and strong national economy, combined internal and external pressures on the state would remain as obstacles to the achievement of the ultimate goals of the Revolution. Economic issues and the re-evaluation of economic strategy were thus elevated in the political agenda of the government to the extent that even the president himself began to take weekly lessons in economics![12] During the initial post-revolutionary years the regime had laid claim to an alternative and viable 'Islamic model' for the organisation of society, including a distinctly 'Islamic economics'.[13] The social aspect of Khomeini's populism had centred around redistribution of existing wealth on the one hand and austerity on the other while rejecting economic growth or capital accumulation as an explicit aim. Meanwhile, the economic circumstances of the majority of the population had deteriorated substantially.

Under such conditions of economic downturn, decline in business confidence and falling popularity of the regime, two options are viable: either state managers capitulate to the international and domestic business community (capitalist class) and eliminate price, import and exchange controls designed to insulate the domestic economy in order to increase 'business confidence', or there is a move to 'socialise the economy', by which is meant the taking over of private firms and extensive nationalisation.[14] The regime veered between the two options.

The alternative of full nationalisation or socialisation was not an option for the Islamic Republic's leadership for a number of reasons. The dominant tendency in the early years of the Islamic Republic followed a populist-statist model of imposing limitations on private property while nevertheless recognising its sanctity. While large sectors of industry and services were nationalised following the Revolution, the economic system sat uncomfortably between state ownership characterised by the 'state-socialist' model on the one hand and a capitalist market on the other and may more usefully be described as having been a 'managed war economy' in the 1980s.[15] From the beginning, the state's takeover of major industries was not intended to eliminate private property, but was rather a response firstly to the immediate post-revolutionary circumstances and then to the war.[16] With powerful interests vested in the protection of private property, the outcome was a series of *ad hoc* regulations and a lack of a coherent economic model or plan. While during the war the role of the state had grown, the political basis or will for full-scale nationalisation simply could not be asserted.

This, however, is not to say that the automatic response was for the state immediately to act in the interests of private domestic and international capital. In fact, public ownership and control continued to be widespread through the 1990s. While the rising financial needs of the government and the lack of profitability of the public sector pushed in the direction of privatisation, this resulted in a 'series of disputes between political and economic leaders, and a great deal of propaganda to convince the general public that privatisation was not necessarily the return of the industrialists of the pre-Revolution days'.[17]

The actual strategy of privatisation that was undertaken is also crucially explained by conjunctural international developments. The revolutions in Eastern Europe and the subsequent disintegration of the Soviet Union posed dilemmas for the regime. As the model of state-led development was discredited, lessons were to be learnt.[18] In the absence of a serious ideological challenge, the extension of capitalism on a global scale accelerated in the post-cold war world. Under conditions where the Islamic Republic had to compete with many other regions for the attraction of internationally mobile capital and where the less developed countries were losing the struggle for access to investment flows, its chances of success in attracting the required investments and technology were reduced as long as it did not conform to the internationally circumscribed economic rules and norms. The only option that seemed to present itself to peripheral states was to conform to the exigencies of the world economy and the neo-liberal strategies of the global financial institutions regarding structural adjustment and the establishment of free markets.[19] In this context, the 'state socialist' model of socio-economic organisation was branded with the stamp of failure by the new government.[20]

Finally, changes in economic and political circumstances rekindled the interest of private capital in investment and accumulation in Iran. This created a 'push factor' towards further privatisation. Both the revolutionary circumstances and the war had adversely affected the opportunities for investment in productive capitalist enterprise. Revolutionary opposition to large domestic and foreign capitalist enterprises, and subsequent political instability, led to a reduction of capitalist investment. In general, under wartime conditions, the influence of the domestic and international capitalist class is reduced.[21] Moreover:

> as long as the war conditions prevailed, the private sector had no incentives to acquire the public enterprises. If it acquired the public enterprises it would have encountered the same obstacles facing the government in maintaining and modernising these facilities.[22]

With the end of the Iran–Iraq war, however, as Behdad aptly puts it, the capitalist class 'demands its "fair share"'.[23] Meanwhile, conditions of political repression ensure there is only limited action by the working class against capitalist enterprises. Thus, at this juncture, potential investment opportunities for domestic and foreign capital once again emerge.

To summarise, the changing policies of the state cannot simply be attributed to a change in the ruling faction within the leadership. Nor can we leave the altered disposition of the state managers unexplained. Policies were changed in response to socio-economic crises which threatened the existence of the state. The response was not one by state managers acting autonomously of class interests to protect their own position. It was that of a ruling bureaucratic class taking measures to ensure its own survival and social reproduction. Under the prevailing political and economic circumstances, the strategies available to state managers in pursuing this objective were circumscribed.

The critical conjuncture: external and internal pressure and the economy

Towards the end of the 1980s, the limits to the state's pursuit of external and internal goals became more and more evident. Domestic pressure and the limits to revenue hindered the regime in its pursuit of external goals of exporting revolution and establishing the Islamic Republic as a viable alternative model of social organisation.

Domestically not only was there a lack of improvement in the material circumstances of the vast majority of the population – including the 'deprived' in whose name the Revolution had been made – but indicators signalled a real decline in living standards. There are few reliable statistics on incomes or wages in post-revolutionary Iran. Official inflation figures are often significantly underestimated, rendering calculation of real wages even more problematic. Using private consumption on a *per capita* basis as a proxy, living standards were stagnant during the first years of the war and then actually declined by over 11 per cent per annum over the final years from 1985 to 1988. Under such circumstances, not only did signs of public discontent begin to emerge, but there was even protest from within the ruling elite.[24]

One consequence of the failures of the Islamic Republic both at home and abroad was a dampening zeal for mobilisation reflected in the falling numbers of war-volunteers, forgery of exemption papers from military service, increasing frequency of official calls for people to participate in the war, tightened conscription regulations, and the arrest and imprisonment of absentee conscripts.[25] Under the weight of an increasing economic burden, not only did popular participation and enthusiasm diminish, but also seeds of discontent began to grow into public expressions of dissatisfaction. More direct forms of popular protest included a number of mainly unreported demonstrations against the government.[26] A strike in 1986 by medical doctors, a relatively advantaged socio-economic group, and vocal protests against the war by 'legal opposition' figures including former provisional Prime Minister Mehdi Bazargan, as well as several well-attended demonstrations in the major cities of Tehran, Tabriz, Mashad and Hamedan in 1987, brought home the extent of popular dissatisfaction.[27] Under such circumstances, the regime could no longer rely on the compliance of the population at large and their direct and indirect, human and financial, donations for the war effort. As 'voluntary contributions' subsided, the conduct of war would come increasingly to rely on more 'official' sources of income through the internal and external extraction of surpluses. As we shall see in what follows, however, here also the state came under fiscal and financial duress.

Lack of industrial growth, fixed domestic capital formation and productivity in post-revolutionary Iran limited the surpluses available to the state. Gross domestic fixed capital formation, which stood at around 30 per cent of gross domestic product (GDP) in the immediate pre-revolutionary period, fell dramatically throughout the war years. Thus, between 1979 and 1988 real gross domestic capital formation declined by an average annual rate of 7.8 per cent.[28] There are several reasons for the lack of capital formation and industrial growth under the Islamic Republic. Of these, the most significant are capital flight, stagnant productive growth as a result of hugely uneven relative opportunities for merchant and industrial capital, as well as policies of 'import compression' and concentration of capital in the defence industry. The flight of capital from the country took place on a massive scale in the aftermath of the Revolution and continued throughout the following years.[29]

Meanwhile, opportunities for reaping exorbitant profits from trading activities expanded under the Islamic Republic, including through the black market, reduced incentives for investing in productive capital. The war years provided economic benefits to anyone privileged enough to receive foreign exchange quotas, import licenses, output allotments from publicly managed industries, or other entitlements, who could therefore take advantage of the prospering black market in commodities.[30] The black market in goods, exacerbated by the rationing of basic commodities during the war, also meant that access to the domestic product or the official channels for the distribution of goods – the government-controlled internal market – provided a source of easy profits to which those with administrative control, including members of revolutionary organisations such as the *Pasdaran* or *komitehs* had ready access. Furthermore, government control over the local distribution of basic goods translated into a massive form of hidden taxation of the population which relieved the strain on state revenues and released resources for war expenditure.[31]

In 1983, import permits were imposed and these permits, which were issued to merchants by the Ministry of Commerce and often available through political influence and patronage within the regime structure, provided access to foreign currency at the overvalued official rate of exchange. They contributed to the 40 per cent increase in imports from March 1983 to March 1984 as the merchant class benefited from rates of return of the order of 2000–3000 per cent.[32] Although most of these profits poured into the private pockets of the merchant bourgeoisie, corporate and semi-public interests, also reaped the profits of this ill-defined legal framework. Under such conditions, there was little incentive, particularly in an uncertain political and legal environment, to invest capital in productive industry. But concomitantly, merchant profits provided an unreliable source for state revenues through taxation due to extensive political power and influence, particularly with some clerical factions in the regime. Despite government attempts to impose taxes on private sector trade, parliamentary supporters of the *bazaar* objected to such proposals as 'un-Islamic'.[33] They were also backed up by the conservative clerics of the Council of Guardians, who benefited from the payment of religious dues by traditional merchants. The Council feared that if a government tax were imposed, these payments would be reduced, since tax paid to the 'Islamic state' would almost certainly have been set off against these informal and traditional arrangements.[34] Thus, the merchants were able to maintain a political voice, and although subsequent restrictions were placed on imports, their weight meant that a stop–go attitude was taken to trade policies in this period, which allowed sufficient opportunities for them to reap of hefty profits through the existence of the war economy and black market.[35]

By the mid-1980s, the coincidence of a number of political processes and the socio-economic structure of post-revolutionary Iran accounted for limits to the internal revenues due to a lack of productive industry. The lack of economic growth and profitability restricted the surpluses which could be extracted from industrial enterprise, while the political weight of the influential *bazaari* class within sections of the regime further constrained government ability to raise tax revenue. With restrictions on domestic revenues, the state's source of external revenues – oil rents – would assume greater consequence. Oil revenue, however, fared no better than domestic sources and hardly sufficed to alleviate the government's fiscal burden.

Throughout the 1980s and beyond, oil revenue provided an average of over 60 per cent of the government's total revenue and 90 per cent of Iran's export income. Oil surpluses, circulated through the 'rentier state' and recycled by the purchase of goods and services from international suppliers, provided the Islamic Republic with essential foreign exchange necessary for the conduct of the war. For although the domestic extraction of surpluses provided the state with revenue, almost all of its hard currency was provided through the sale of oil on the international market. The importance of a supply of hard currency during the war is best illustrated by the need for military supplies. The Iranian regime could replenish its dwindling stocks of arms and supplies for the war either by the development of an indigenous military industry or through purchases of equipment from global suppliers.

Though extensive efforts were made towards attaining military self-sufficiency and independence, domestic production could not satisfy all the requirements of the war. Thus, ready access to supplies of arms at the international level was crucial to the ability of the regime to continue its war efforts. The need to finance international expenditure led to the adoption of an aggressive oil export policy, which flew in the face of initially espoused goals of national independence and less reliance on oil revenues. Initially, a combination of US trade sanctions, war damage to oil installations, and the post-revolutionary government's attempt to reduce dependence on oil revenue, led to a fall in the volume of exports and oil revenues in 1980–81. During the third quarter of 1981 Iran was shipping only 1.1 m barrels per day (bpd). When the main oil terminal at Kharg was bombed, foreign reserves fell further. In late 1981 Iran's oil exports had fallen to under 700,000 bpd and reserves were estimated at under $1bn.[36] Under these circumstances, without alternative strategies for the procurement of essential imports, the regime's war policy would have been impaired.

In the first instance, in order to alleviate its economic difficulties, the post-revolutionary government struck a number of deals with the Soviet Union and Eastern Europe, making them major purchasers of Iranian oil in 1981.[37] However, both the need to maintain the policy of 'Neither East nor West' and the inadequacy of these agreements, a proportion of which consisted of barter deals and did not provide for the technological goods required for the war, led to alternative strategies. The regime reacted by severe restrictions on imports, an aggressive marketing campaign and cuts in oil prices.

As the need for foreign exchange revenue escalated, goals of cutting back on production and reducing dependence on oil and thereby on trade with the West were largely abandoned. That oil production was, through this period, nevertheless lower than that of the pre-revolutionary period is arguably more a consequence of the reduction in capacity due to industrial disruption and war damage, along with higher prices which maintained revenues. In August 1982 agreements were reached with a number of mainly European oil companies for oil purchases, and a long-term contract was concluded with Japan.[38] The state-owned National Iranian Oil Company (NIOC) also began to discount oil on the international market, to such an extent that by the beginning of 1983, by undercutting other OPEC exporters by about $4 per barrel, it was able to increase exports to 3 million bpd.[39] When in 1982 the United States resumed purchases of crude from Iran through an intermediary Geneva-based trading company, the 1.8 million barrel transaction was based on a price of $29.5/barrel, compared with $34/barrel for Saudi crude.[40] An agreement with Petrobras, Brazil's national oil company, made the Brazilian role in national reconstruction conditional upon oil purchases which were nevertheless still below the OPEC price.[41] Even during the Gulf 'tanker war' in 1984, by discounting oil by $2–3/barrel to offset insurance premiums the government succeeded in increasing exports from a low of 1.1 million bpd in May to 1.9 million bpd in July.[42]

On this basis, the regime was able to procure foreign exchange from the sale of oil to finance its military offensives.[43] The magnitude of Iranian imports throughout the 1980s was heavily influenced by the availability of foreign exchange, which was almost solely provided through oil exports. In other words, access to essential commodities procured internationally, including war materiel and arms without which the drive to continue the conflict would undoubtedly have been restricted, depended on the availability of oil revenue.

The period 1985 to 1986 saw a drastic fall in both the absolute level of income accrued to the state from oil and the percentage contribution of the petroleum sector to total government revenue. This proportion fell from the former average of around 60 per cent in the first half of the decade to around 40 per cent in 1985/6 and a low of 20 per cent in 1986/7 before recovering slightly to 34 per cent in 1987/8. With increasing shortfalls in the state's access to internal surpluses, the concomitant decline in oil revenues led to further deterioration of the state's fiscal position as the government deficit more than doubled between 1985/6 and 1986/7.

The fall in oil revenues in this period relates both to the export and production capacity of the oil industry and to wider structural factors relating to the world economy and global order, and indicates the precarious autonomy of a state reliant on external rents. The post-revolutionary regime had initially adopted a policy of reducing the Iranian economy's dependence on oil rents. But by late 1982, as a result of political and economic exigencies, including the war-policy, production targets of around 3 million bpd were set; these basically reflected oil production capacity, which had been reduced as a result of disruptions to the industry, reduced oil exploration budgets, a suspension of gas injection projects and war damage. Though Iraq attacked Iran's principal oil export terminal at Kharg Island at the outset of the war, export facilities were adjusted to cope with the damage inflicted. However, reductions in refining capacity, which halved in 1981 from the previous year's level, failed to recover throughout the duration of the war, and from 1982 Iran was no longer self-sufficient in refined oil products, as later indicated by the 1987 agreement with the Soviet Union for the latter's delivery of 2m tonnes of refined products.[44]

The construction of an oil pipeline transporting Iraqi oil through Saudi Arabia to the Red Sea as well as the sale of oil by Saudi Arabia and Kuwait on Iraq's behalf not only made Iranian exports more vulnerable, but seemed also to reduce the risks of retaliation and embolden Iraqi forces in targeting the Iranian petroleum industry. Iraqi attacks on Kharg Island and Gureh Pumping Station in 1985 affected export capacity and forced the establishment of alternative facilities on Sirri, Larak and Lavan islands. In 1986 Iraqi planes began to hit refineries, power stations, petrochemical plants, oil platforms and shipping lines. Between 1984 and 1987, the oil industry experienced negative growth, ostensibly as a result of both war damage and lack of investment. Oil exports fell to 600,000 to 700,000 bpd in the latter half of 1986, reducing the average daily export level for the year to 1.5 million bpd, with adverse consequences for the trade and fiscal balance.[45]

Meanwhile, international developments causing a reduction in the oil price resulted from the structure of the oil industry and wider influences of the world economy, including the hegemonic position of the United States and the role of the US-dollar, although the more immediate cause was the collapse of OPEC's pricing strategy and quota system.

The constraints on domestic surpluses and external rents that became particularly acute from the latter half of the 1980s created difficulties in financing state expenditure, including funding related to the war. The large government deficit that resulted from the concomitant lack of internal and external surpluses was largely met through internal borrowing from the Central Bank, leading to severe inflationary pressures that were directly transmitted to an increasingly economically burdened and dissatisfied population. On the other hand, international pressures and the lack of international support for the Islamic Republic were instrumental in compelling the revolutionary leaders to submit to external military pressure that could no longer be borne in the ailing fiscal circumstances of the state and socio-economic position of the majority of the population.

The end of an era? The important concept of 'maslehat'

By the end of the 1980s, internal and external pressures on the state increasingly pointed to a crisis. This led Khomeini and other state leaders to adopt a more conciliatory approach to the war aims and conditions for peace at the end of the 1980s. Despite pronouncements of readiness to exchange 'blow for blow in any strike' by external forces in the Gulf and claims that it would be 'sweeter ... to be directly at war with such a country as the United States', the leadership was clearly aware of the dangers of an escalating conflict under military and economic constraints.[46] Though the initial response by the leadership to the pressures to end the war was a mobilisation for 'final victory', the failures of this drive led eventually to a downgrading of the stipulated conditions for peace which no longer entailed overthrow of the regime in Baghdad. Thus Rafsanjani, who was appointed Commander-in-Chief in June 1988 and was instrumental in the decision to accept UN Security Council Resolution 598, had already begun to indicate from the previous year that an end to the war could be in sight 'if the world institutions and international organisations were to recognise Saddam as the instigator of the war'.[47] Reference to the necessary overthrow of the Iraqi regime was omitted. The ultimate acceptance of UN Security Council Resolution 598 by the leadership of the Islamic Republic signified a remarkable turning point that we have argued was brought about by the coincidence of domestic and international pressure on the post-revolutionary state.

That the Iranian leadership, and in particular Khomeini himself, finally compromised the maximalist objectives of the Revolution indicates the contradictions of sustaining the Islamic Republic and responding to internal social forces on the one hand and continuing a conflict at the international front on the other. This was an inherent tension often neglected by commentary on this period. In fact, Khomeini's novel concept of Islamic government, introduced some months earlier – whereby *velayat-e-faqih* (absolute vice-regency or rule of the jurisprudent) was assigned primacy over 'all other secondary (religious) injunctions even prayers, fasting and *haj*' – provided the precedent for the political move to end the war, sanctioning the primacy of the Islamic Republic over immediate goals of the Revolution. Khomeini's edict gave *de jure* validity to what had already *de facto* been established by the regime in, for instance, the secret purchase of arms from the Reagan administration.

Khomeini justified his novel proclamations on the Islamic state by recourse to the concept of *maslahat*. Literally meaning 'what is best', *maslahat* has variably been translated as national expediency/interest or the public good.[48] Its significance here is that it assigns the Islamic state's leadership singular precedence to determine the policies appropriate for the eventual perpetuation of the Revolution. The subsequent founding of the *showra-ye tashkhis-e maslahat* (Assembly for the Discernment of *Maslahat*) then gave institutional expression to the leverage of the religious leadership in current control of the state apparatus over and above other centres of power within the political system. Paradoxically, therefore, if the advance of the goals of the Revolution – internal and external – depended on the Islamic state, then the survival of the latter was conferred primacy over and above immediate revolutionary goals. Khomeini and those surrounding him clearly perceived the threat to the Islamic Republic posed by its internal constituencies and expressions of social discontent among the very population which had formed the backbone of the revolutionary movement. The pressures of war added to the plight of the population and inflamed social tensions that threatened to destabilise the structure of the post-revolutionary society. Under these circumstances the revolutionary strategy of the war had to be revised, and this formed the logic behind the adoption of SCR 598. Khomeini gave explicit expression to this when he professed that acceptance of the resolution was 'in the interests of the Revolution and the government' at this juncture.[49]

The end of the first decade of revolution and, more specifically the point at which Khomeini was persuaded that the country could no longer withstand the pressure of war, was a moment of great import in the history of the Islamic Republic. It set the scene for the contradictory policies of the following decades, for from this point the eventual realisation of revolutionary goals was explicitly acknowledged to depend on the survival of the regime. Universalisation of Islamic government remained the ultimate objective, but first the viability of the Islamic regime to compete in the international system from a position of strength had to be ensured. For this, the Islamic Republic had to be fortified. The survival of a revolutionary regime facing domestic and international pressures could only be guaranteed through the safeguarding of national security by establishing a strong national economy, avoiding direct military confrontation and fortifying national security. This was the rationale for the policies adopted by the post-war Rafsanjani governments through the 1990s and, subsequently, by the Khatami governments from 1997.

7 Reform and reaction 1990–2005

The policies of the regime from the 1990s during Hashemi Rafsanjani's presidency focused on strengthening the state through an increase in economic activity and production. This was to be done by providing opportunities for both domestic and international private capital on the one hand, and on the other by eliminating the pressures and burden of military conflict through a policy of improving relations with regional states. In 1997, after the election of the seemingly moderate and reformist Mohammad Khatami, many observers saw the dawn of a new era of greater openness and freedom in Iran. However, the transition from the Rafsanjani to the Khatami presidency was marked more by continuity of policies than change, and this for two underlying reasons. Firstly, the institutional make-up of the state meant that the power structure – particularly the relative power of the spiritual leader and Guardian Council vis-à-vis president and government – limited what could be achieved. Secondly, despite some differences in outlook, the fundamental economic and foreign policies of the two eras were based on a shared contradiction; on the one hand was the need to stabilise the country and improve the state of the economy through reforms and reconciliation with the outside world, while on the other was the principle of never explicitly renouncing the ultimately revolutionary objectives of the Islamic Republic or attempting to change its fundamental structures. Thus, while the presidents, particularly Khatami and his followers, may have had reformist intentions, the reform could only ever be taken so far and no further.

What has been termed a 'tactical alliance' between so-called radicals and moderates, symbolised in the leadership axis formed following Khomeini's death between Khamenei as supreme leader of the Revolution and the respective presidents, is better understood as the shared belief that economic prosperity was needed first to build a strong state before the message of the Revolution could be propagated further – 'revolution first in one country'.

The rationale for the *sazandegi* (economic reconstruction) slogan and policy of the 1990s lay in the need to build a state able to resist domestic and international challenges and act as the political fulcrum for the advancement of the Revolution's ultimate objectives. In the words of Sayyed Mohammad Sadr, director in the 1990s of foreign policy and international relations at the Strategic Studies Centre, affiliated to the Iranian president's office:

the most important strategic aim of the Islamic Revolution is the globalisation of Islam and the Islamic Revolution. ... It follows that all moves and policies in the economic, security, cultural, political and other fields should be in the way of realising this aim. ... Since the Islamic Revolution and the regime is based on Islam, the ultimate aim is export of revolution and the spread of true Islamic thought. *Since export of revolution and globalisation of the Islamic movement is not possible without central backing and permanent support, we should exert all efforts to protect this centre, the Islamic Republic of Iran.*[1]

The impetus for the new policies did not simply come from a 'moderate faction' in the leadership, but was shared by all those who saw this as the only feasible strategy for the ultimate advance of the Revolution. That in this period the faction within the leadership advocating a *continuously revolutionary strategy* was weakened is not to be disputed.[2] But supporters of the new strategy cannot uniformly be designated as the 'moderate wing' of a fragmented leadership. The advocacy by 'hard-liners' such as Ayatollah Ahmad Jannati of policies of reconstruction aimed at transforming the Islamic Republic into a 'power capable of slapping the enemies in the face' serves to illustrate how change was conceived as a means to remove the obstacles to the propagation of the Revolution.[3]

The new government strategy now dictated a programme of reform and modernisation as articulated by Hasan Rowhani, Deputy Speaker and Secretary of the Supreme National Security Council:

The leader of the Islamic movement is Islamic Iran whether we say so or not. ... The eminent leader of the Revolution, his eminence Ayatollah Khamenei ... is the leader of the world of Islam today. ... The guidance of Islamic movements [is] a humanitarian, Islamic, religious and revolutionary duty which our system bears. ... We have to build Iran, strengthen, modernise and develop it. We must establish social justice in this land. Our objective is a modern Iran. If Iran were transformed into a modern developed country it would be a model country for all Muslims.[4]

It is of note that in this period the redistributive social populism and austerity measures of the previous decade were relinquished in the discourse of the leadership in favour of accumulation and promises of 'comfort and a well-deserved lifestyle'.[5] Religious leaders who had painstakingly exonerated spirituality and warned against the vice of material desires now began to preach the importance of wealth and prosperity. Ayatollah Emami-Kashani, spokesman for the influential Council of Guardians, for instance insisted that Islamic society should be rich not only from a spiritual and cultural point of view but also from an *economic point of view*.[6] The new slogans of economic prosperity (*refah-e eqtesadi*) and the goal of turning the Islamic Republic into an 'Islamic Japan' were a far cry from the Khomeinist rejection of economic development a decade earlier.

The reform years

The new strategy for economic development from the 1990s spelt a revision of a number of principles of the Islamic Republic with regard to economic structure and international political and economic relations. Concrete measures were formulated and implemented under the auspices of the first five-year development plan (FFYDP) for 1989/90–1993/4, centring on economic liberalisation aimed at achieving a high growth rate for the economy spurred by increases in production. The programme focused on reductions in state ownership, privatisation and deregulation of large sectors of the economy, encouragement of capital investments, reform of the exchange rate system, and reduction of subsidies on basic consumer goods.

The government abandoned earlier 'alternative strategies' and opted for a policy of capitalist economic growth consistent with that of the majority of semi-industrialised peripheral states.[7] Policies undertaken in the FFYDP conformed to the strategy of 'structural adjustment' (*ta'dil-e eqtesadi*) advocated by the World Bank and International Monetary Fund. As an International Monetary Fund report later summarised, these included:

> decontrolling most domestic prices, raising public utility rates, removing many non-tariff trade barriers, lowering income tax rates, eliminating bank credit ceilings, starting to privatise public enterprises, and liberalising the exchange system [aimed at] rehabilitating the economic infrastructure, transferring the control of economic activities back to the private sector, raising productive capacity, reducing government's role in economic decision making and allowing price mechanisms to determine resource allocation.[8]

Within the bounds of the plan, a privatisation programme for over 400 small and medium-sized state-owned companies was announced. Former Iranian industrialists in exile were called upon to return to Iran and reclaim the property which had been appropriated by the state and nationalised in the aftermath of the Revolution. A stringent vetting process used in the 1992 parliamentary elections eliminated prominent clerics (*majma'-e rowhaniyun-e mobarez*) who opposed these policies. This paved the way for increased liberalisation, including the introduction of a floating exchange rate and the elimination of price controls in the mid-1990s.

While Khatami's landslide election as president in 1997 was seen by many as Iran's entry into a period of fundamental reform in the social and cultural domains, economy policy was marked more by continuity. Although the coalition which brought Khatami to power was broad, he also benefited from the backing of the Servants of Construction, the same pro-market reform and liberalisation group who had supported Rafsanjani and who gained key positions in Khatami's government. As before, the government tried to push through economic reforms. Khatami's five-year plan (2000–05) promoted privatisation and deregulation. There were moves to revive the Tehran stock exchange and for the country to issue its first Eurobond since the Revolution, and in 2002 the government brought forward a law to improve foreign investment. The government also finally established a single floating exchange rate in 2002.

The new economic policies also had an impact on Iran's foreign relations.[9] During the 1990s, the Islamic Republic of Iran attempted to end its international isolation in a bid to encourage the establishment of long-term economic relations and encourage investment in the country. This policy particularly revolved around a *rapprochement* with Western European countries, developing economic relations with Central Asian states and initiating programmes of co-operation with the Arab Gulf states. It was posed by Abbas Maleki, Deputy Foreign Minister, as the major diplomatic challenge of the Islamic Republic in this period:

> Among the myriad of issues that has to be addressed is the need for infrastructural rehabilitation, which necessitates, *inter alia*, the import of technology, and the attraction of foreign investment. The ultimate aim in this context is to stimulate domestic private industries to take their share in the national development scheme and to facilitate the task of 'export-led' growth. Recognising the enormity and sensitivity of this situation, the Iranian foreign policy establishment seeks to base itself on its declared principles and incrementally broaden the range of international contacts that could facilitate the Islamic Republic of Iran's transition through this period of reconstruction.[10]

A change in the external relations of the Islamic Republic was seen as the only way to reduce external hostility and to encourage the flow of capital into the country. Government officials explicitly emphasised the importance of relations and ties with the advanced countries, especially of Western Europe. In March 1993, Alireza Moayeri, presidential advisor on foreign policy issues, noted that Iran had 'good relations with Europe', aimed at 'co-operating with the West collectively' and was 'interested in co-operation with Europe as a body within the framework of the European Community, the united Europe, and in the form of bilateral relations'.[11]

The expansion of relations with Asian states became another mainstay of foreign policy in this period.[12] This took place both within the framework of regional organisations such as the Economic Cooperation Organisation (ECO) and bilateral relations with a number of countries including India, China and South East Asian states.[13] Rafsanjani visited various Asian capitals in 1995. Foreign Minister Ali Akbar Velayati insisted that the foreign policy of the Islamic Republic was based on the principle of expanding its co-operation with neighbouring countries, and noted ECO's potential for achieving 'an ever expanding framework of economic activities amongst the countries of the region'.[14]

These diplomatic attempts were spurred by motives of encouraging economic co-operation and attracting foreign investment as spelt out in the five-year development plans. Thus, alongside the move towards *rapprochement*, incentives were also devised for foreign investment including controversial measures such as the raising of the limit on foreign ownership of industries in joint ventures and providing for the repatriation of profits through the establishment of free trade zones.[15] The new interpretation of the constitutional limits on foreign involvement in the economy was a far cry from the early revolutionary concept.[16] Foreign companies were invited to tender for industrial projects and the authorities explicitly called for help in the development of oil production capacity.[17] Iranian efforts in this domain concentrated largely on attracting foreign oil companies – including US ones – to invest in off-shore oil-exploration projects that accounted for over a tenth of production capacity. Conferences on the oil industry were organised in Tehran. Eleven deals were tendered in 1995, and discussed at an internationally attended conference in Tehran in November 1995.

The issue of foreign credit and borrowing was a thorny one, envisaged as inconsistent with the independence of the Islamic Republic; this was symbolised in the repayment of all foreign debts through the 1980s and abstention from foreign borrowing during the war. This shibboleth was, nevertheless, also thrown open to question by the government. A more conciliatory approach towards multinational financial institutions was subsequently initiated. Links with the World

Bank were re-established.[18] Borrowing needs were then covered through credit lines from a variety of foreign banks and governmental credit agencies. Thus in 1993, Minister of Economics and Financial Affairs Mohsen Nourbakhsh openly admitted that certain international organisations such as the International Monetary Fund and World Bank had approved the economic policies of the Islamic Republic and that the overall credits received from the World Bank amounted to $500–600 million, the equivalent of 4–5 per cent of the country's expenses in 1989–1991.[19] Such an admission would have been impossible a decade earlier. In the following year, the president of the Iran Chamber of Commerce, Industry and Mines, while urging Iran's membership of the General Agreement on Tariffs and Trade (GATT), summed up the essence of the government's policies:

> in today's world capital knows no boundaries and goes where there is a profit. Therefore, we must create conditions than can attract foreign capital. I object to those who say that the attraction of foreign capital means the absorption of foreign culture. ... The *majlis* has permitted direct foreign investment in the country. Now it is up to the government to decide from which country capital must be sought and then sign partnership contracts and import the capital.[20]

The Rafsanjani and subsequent Khatami governments focused increasingly also on maintaining the security of the borders of the Islamic Republic through a policy of 'détente'. If the state was to be strengthened first and foremost, debilitating military conflict like that of the 1980s had to be avoided. This was partly to be achieved through a rapprochement with a number of neighbouring states. These policies began in the Rafsanjani era and were particularly strengthened following the election in 1997 of Khatami, who pursued a foreign policy based on peaceful coexistence with countries in the region and beyond.[21] This strategy ostensibly stemmed from the sense of insecurity of a post-revolutionary state that had experienced the implications of existence in an internationally hostile environment in the form of direct military conflict and the threat of intervention by foreign powers.

The Islamic Republic's regional policies from the 1990s were geared towards the containment of Iraq and reconciliation with neighbouring states.[22] The principle of non-interference in the internal affairs of other states was proclaimed, amounting to a tacit repudiation of the previous engagement in the forceful export of revolution. The opportunity to launch this diplomatic effort on an extensive scale in the region was provided by the Gulf Crisis and War of 1990–91. Adopting a neutral position and effectively supporting the United Nations action, the Islamic Republic signalled to regional states in particular that it would refrain from embarking on adventurist policies that could pose a threat to them. Leaders insisted that export of revolution was confined to the 'the spoken and written word' and did not involve 'interfering in the internal affairs of foreign countries'.[23] Under cover of the Gulf Crisis, controversial foreign policy objectives such as the re-establishment of diplomatic relations with states in the region, including Egypt, Jordan and later even Saudi Arabia, were realised.[24] This background also provides a clue to the constraint displayed by Tehran in its policy toward the Iraqi regime in this period. The *leitmotif* of 'non-interference in the domestic affairs of Iraq' was coined during the Gulf Crisis and War of 1990–91. Foreign policy was largely limited to encouragement of 'unity among the Iraqi opposition' thus effectively supporting a coalition of religious and secular groups.[25] Even when at the end of the Gulf War the Shi'is of southern Iraq rose against the Baghdad regime, assistance from the Islamic Republic was limited.[26]

Iran was depicted as a non-threatening neighbour, keen to establish diplomatic relations within the received international legal framework and with little intention of using force to export revolution in the region. This new-found image rested upon two related dimensions of the Islamic Republic's conception of security. Firstly, the threat of military confrontation with any of the states in the region had to be reduced. Secondly, the presence in the Gulf area of foreign forces in general and US ones in particular, was cause for concern for the regime. Diplomatic and political efforts were therefore also aimed at expelling these forces by creating a forum for security in the Persian Gulf to be ensured by regional states including Iran.

Apprehensions about the US military presence in the region were naturally intensified following the Gulf War of 1991, thereby increasing the Islamic Republic's sense of vulnerability.[27] Warnings were issued against the 'ceaseless efforts of the great powers to establish their hegemony over the Persian Gulf'. 'America's presence in the heart of the Islamic lands' and the use of regional conflicts as 'a pretext to send forces into the region and to justify their presence' were admonished.[28] The Islamic Republic promoted its potentially prominent role in regional security arrangements amongst neighbouring states:

> we proved through the policies we enforced during the past year or so that Iran is not the place for adventurism and that hers is not a runaway revolution so those who look at the events in the region objectively will and can talk of [Iran] as a centre which could have a leading role in the region's security. Iran is a power which can be counted upon.[29]

Officials of the Islamic Republic stressed that an 'imaginary fear from Iran' had been created amongst neighbouring Arab states by external powers, and that these apprehensions were wrong-minded and misguided as the Islamic Republic had every desire to 'co-operate with the Persian Gulf states and to preserve security in the region' and to 'live with [its neighbours] in a peaceful atmosphere'.[30]

The stance taken during the Persian Gulf Crisis of 1990–91 and the freeing of hostages in Lebanon were signs that a move towards better relations could be envisaged. Comments made by US officials, including the president in the context of the 'Bush formula', were interpreted as a positive signal to Iran.[31] Thus, in his inauguration speech in January 1989, Bush made reference to US hostages held in Lebanon, the potential of Iranian intervention and the possibility of US reciprocation to a 'good will' gesture by the Islamic Republic. Subsequent upon the death of Ayatollah Khomeini, President Bush declared that 'as soon as we see some movement away from repression and extremism, we will review our relationship. ... There is a way for a relationship with the United States to improve – and that is a release of the American hostages.'[32] Not long after, there were explicit calls from government sources for the release of hostages held in Lebanon. The *Tehran Times*, a paper close to the president and Foreign Ministry urged 'Muslim forces' to work to 'get the hostages free with no preconditions'.[33] With the freeing of hostages in Lebanon, at least partly due to Iranian pressure, the possibility was held out for an improvement of relations.[34]

The election in 1997 of Khatami as president led to greater attempts at international co-operation. A symbolic culmination of the Islamic Republic's policy of peaceful coexistence came in December 1997 when the Organisation of Islamic Conference Summit was held in Tehran. While on the one hand the meeting was seen as a clear challenge to the United States, its main success was to portray the Islamic Republic as a state keen to co-exist peacefully with its neighbours and not the revolutionary regime of the past.[35] This theme was continued in Khatami's foreign policy over the ensuing years. The president visited various European capitals in 1999 and established normalised relations leading to the signature of trade and investment agreements. Not only did relations with countries in the region and Europe improve, Khatami also made attempts to improve relations with the United States. Famously, in an interview with CNN in 1998, he called for a 'dialogue of civilisations' aimed largely at the United States. Following the terrorist attacks on the United States on 11 September 2001, the Iranian leadership declared support for the war on Afghanistan and, in the following year supported the position that Iraq should abide by UN Resolutions. However, as we shall see in the next chapter, these approaches amounted to little as hostility between Washington and Tehran continued through the decade and beyond.

The conservative backlash

There is little doubt that the Rafsanjani and, particularly, Khatami governments had reformist intentions with regard to the economy and, to an extent, Iran's foreign relations. However, despite some limited improvement in the economy, overall the attempted reforms were marked by failure. At the end of the plan period, well over half of the economy continued to be controlled by the state or the large foundations and few of the reforms were enacted in reality. The economy remained dependent on oil – which continued to account for around half of government revenue and the vast majority of export earnings. Thus economic growth and development remained stunted and Iran's economic fortunes remained dependent on the precarious global price for oil. Despite some attempts at reconciliation, Iran's foreign relations were rocky and by early 2000s marked more than ever by deep hostility with the United States.

Why did the attempted reforms of the 1990s not amount to wholesale change and the normalisation or socialisation of the post-revolutionary regime? Why did they ultimately lead in the mid-2000s to increasing concentration of power in the hands of conservatives, leading to the election in 2005 of a hard-line president who seemed for all intents and purposes to abandon the more conciliatory language of his predecessors and to revert back to the rhetoric of the earlier decade?

There are three related answers to these questions. The first lies largely in the events of the previous decade and the creation of state institutions which concentrated power in the hands of a small elite minority with vested interests in maintaining those institutions and the status quo. Many of the reformist policies were resisted by those who benefited from the role and power of state and para-state institutions, and often had personal ties to the conservative ruling elite. Secondly, the Islamic Republic did not shed its revolutionary credentials and rhetoric. It neither relinquished its status as a revolutionary state in the international system, nor did it make serious attempts at altering the state structure. The ultimate aim of the new economic strategy remained the development of a domestic productive base and strengthening of the economy while, despite this or that piecemeal attempt at institutional change, leaving political institutions and the state structure intact. This meant that the reform process was ultimately contradictory and crisis ridden. Finally, the reform movement had no organisational base. Its success relied on the support of a disaffected public. But as the reforms failed to bring about any real improvements in people's daily lives, they lost credibility. The conservatives and hardliners, on the other hand, could rely on the various revolutionary institutions and military or paramilitary organisations created during the 1980s to rally support.

As the reforms of the 1990s and beyond failed to deliver the promised economic prosperity and as the institutional changes attempted during the Rafsanjani and, particularly, Khatami periods faced increasing opposition by vested interests in the regime, their conservative opponents gained the upper hand. The conservative backlash was marked by the language and rhetoric of the Revolution: appealing to the popular masses through nationalism and anti-Westernism, and rejecting the reforms as un-Islamic, immoral and against the grain of the Revolution. Opposition to the reforms manifested itself both in the economic sphere and in that of foreign relations.

Vested interests within the regime were potentially threatened by political and socio-economic changes to the *status quo*. At the head of these stood the religious leader himself. Khamenei had a prime stake in preserving the *status quo* in a system where he presided over an independent financial base secured by institutional powers and the payment of religious taxes. The leader presides over the various *bonyads*, the Imam Relief Committee and the direct payment of religious taxes not only from the Shi'ite faithful in Iran, but also those abroad who regard him as the source of emulation.[36] The constitutional position of the leader vis-à-vis the president and government moreover, allowed for greater distance from the economic reforms. As the tensions between the reform process and its consequences for the domestic economy and foreign relations of the Islamic Republic became more apparent, clearly revealing the precarious situation of the regime, Khamenei threw his weight against the government's liberalisation plans. Thus, in December 1993 as the budget was being debated, Khamenei's guidelines on national economic policy included 'upholding revolutionary values', including 'social equity' as well as the goal of 'self-sufficiency' and the 'repayment of foreign loans'.[37] The leader also used his constitutional powers to dismiss government-appointed officials. For example he removed Rafsanjani's brother from his powerful position as head of the state-controlled radio and television corporation and replaced him with the hardliner Ali Larijani.

Other institutional bases within the regime, which variously took issue with the policies of the government, included the Council of Guardians and the *majles*. The Council of Guardians – a permanent bastion of conservative clerics that acted in favour of particular social groups and interests – served as an obstacle to the implementation of a number of policies through its exercise of the veto.[38] Both the corporate interests of the semi-public foundations, the *bonyads, and* the private interests of merchant capital were threatened by the formulation of the five-year economic plan. The reform of the exchange rate system and import licensing, as well as the introduction of more systematic state taxation, would affect the opportunities for rent-seeking activities and impinge on the profits of merchant capital which these sectors reaped. While the *bazaar* merchants were in general in favour of liberalisation and privatisation, they attempted to resist the imposition of state taxes and price controls. Managers of the *bonyads,* on the other hand, were loath to loosen their tight grip on the revenues of these conglomerates through privatisation as many of their holdings were bringing in handsome profits, which could often be spent at their discretion. The alliance of merchants and state and corporate managers with clerical elements within the regime, through both patronage networks and respective payment of religious dues, thus functioned, as before, to protect merchant capital against productive capital and industrialisation which stood at the heart of the new economic plan.

A significant proportion of *majles* deputies also had reason to oppose the government policies, whether because of a commitment to the 'true line of the Imam', representation of their deprived constituencies, or motives that squared well with those of the conservative clerics of the Guardian Council. These institutional power centres were also able to mobilise wider support amongst the population. Many conservative clerics, particularly leaders of Friday prayer sermons, vociferously rejected the economic programmes of the Rafsanjani government. Ayatollah Ahmad Jannati, preaching a Friday prayer sermon in Tehran, claimed:

> [economic] problems must be solved. But at what price? Is the price to be [that] economics is replacing revolution – that those passionate revolutionary slogans have gone and such things as money and economy and commerce and the like have arrived? ... Suppose all the country turns into dollars. Well at the most it will become something like America.[39]

The government was accused of deviating from Khomeini's line and thus treading on the sanctities of the Revolution. Ayatollah Mousavi-Ardabili dismissed the people's material demands and instead insisted that the Revolution's objectives went beyond the economic level:

> if today in a miraculous way we become a Japan, can we claim that we have reached our objective? It was not the objective of our Revolution to become like some countries which have a strong economy, a strong currency and a high standard of

living, even though one must admit that those are good things. Instead we aimed to implement the Koran. ... The objective of the Revolution was far superior.

The government's initial official response to such institutional obstacles was to press for changes in the political system of the Islamic Republic. Steps in this direction had already been taken by the constitutional amendments in the immediate aftermath of Khomeini's death in 1989, which conferred the president with greater executive powers. Furthermore, institutional structures of the Islamic Republic were altered to accommodate and implement the new approach.

For example, in order to push through the reformist agenda, the foreign-policy-making apparatus was increasingly centralised and rationalised during the 1990s. The creation of a new Supreme National Security Council and the strengthening of executive power through a process of constitutional amendment contributed to this. A formal foreign policy advisory apparatus was established, the security and defence organisations were amalgamated, and diplomatic channels were increased through greater emphasis on the activities of the foreign ministry.[40] There were also attempts to control the activities of radical clergy within the Ministry of Foreign Affairs. For instance, both Javad Mansuri, Under-secretary for Consular Affairs in the Ministry, and the Director for Arab and African Affairs, Hossein Sheikholeslam, who co-ordinated with the *Pasdaran* in promoting the activities of Iranian embassies and, particularly, the Hezbollah were formally demoted.[41] A similar train of events was also set in motion in the realm of economic policy making through re-structuring of the Plan and Budget Organisation and ministerial appointments.

Nevertheless, clerics opposed to many aspects of the government policy retained a significant number of representatives and a voice in the *majles*.[42] Thus, *majles* Speaker Ali Akbar Nateq Nouri, now leader of the more conservative *jame'eh-e rowhaniyat-e mobarez* (JRM) parliamentary grouping and later presidential candidate, began to refer to the excesses of the 'liberal faction', while Rafsanjani was unsuccessful in obtaining parliamentary approval for the reinstatement of his Finance Minister and architect of the liberalisation policies, Nourbakhsh.[43] Factional voices and institutional obstacles within the regime opposing the government's reforms led to the evolution of an increasingly confused and inconsistent political and economic policy. Progress was plagued by tensions and contradictions that again stood in the way of establishing 'normalised' diplomatic relations or developing coherent economic planning. The regime was thus ensnared in an internal dispute played out in the factional struggles amongst the ruling elite as objections were raised that the core of the Revolution was being hacked out through the pretext of the economy. These setbacks meant that the economic reforms of the decade remained stunted and ultimately unsuccessful.

In the early 1990s, conjunctural factors such as the high oil prices following the Gulf Crisis and War of 1990–1 and the availability of foreign credits had boosted growth. By the middle of the decade, however, a reversal set in,[44] and growth fell far short of projections in the mid-1990s. By 1995, the regime faced an estimated external debt of $30–35 billion and had engaged in repackaging negotiations with its creditors and main trading partners. Under conditions of continued oil-dependence – and the precarious nature of the international market for oil and the low price trends after the Gulf War of 1991 – the prospects for repayment of this debt went hand in hand with the ability to increase oil production capacity. This worked against the commitment to wean the country away from reliance on the oil sector. Furthermore, measures taken to address the balance of payments crisis had a severe impact on the domestic economy as gross domestic expenditure was reduced and went into negative growth by 1993/4.

The pace of foreign investment in the Iranian economy remained slow through the decade. There were few cases of direct investment in industry beyond limited participation in a number of oil-related projects. Foreign involvement was often restricted to financing which, due to the Islamic Republic's good track record and credit rating, had been readily forthcoming in the initial post-war years. However, as debt accumulated and repayments went into arrears due to burgeoning economic problems, the Islamic Republic became a less attractive destination for foreign financial or industrial capital. While it appears that commercial interests prevailed in providing credit lines for imports – Iran remained after all a lucrative market for goods – longer-term commitment to productive projects and industrial development were scarce. The impact on the domestic economy was not insignificant.

A drastic cut was imposed on imports of commodities ranging from consumer items such as cigarettes to industrial goods. Not only was industry, which is heavily dependent on imports for raw materials and parts, adversely affected, but these measures also took their toll on the living conditions of the population.

The promises of the post-war decade of reconstruction of growth regarding improved living standards and prosperity failed to materialise for the majority. Social tensions began to mount. The regime faced a crisis of legitimacy in face of the difficulties encountered in the course of implementing the five year economic plans. The economic liberalisation of the post-war period led to further difficulties as prices of basic goods rose and unemployment increased. The official inflation rate, widely held to be underestimated, driven by the sharp depreciation of the exchange rate, reduction of subsidies and decontrol of prices on certain commodities, increased to 35 per cent in 1994/5 compared with an average of 23 per cent during the 1991/2–1993/4 period; the most pronounced increase was in the food and beverage index and the housing index.[45] In the second quarter of 1994 the price in riyals of vegetable oil, sugar and onions increased by an average of 75 per cent.[46] In March 1995, petrol subsidies were reduced through the imposition of a 100 per cent excise tax.

Price increases clearly had their greatest effect on the poor and those on fixed incomes. Though the overall real wages, salaries and fringe benefits of workers in large manufacturing establishments indicate a small increase, employment in this sector declined during this period. Meanwhile, not only those on fixed incomes such as public sector employees but also other workers in the private sector (e.g. construction workers) saw significant reductions in their real incomes. In the absence of independent trade unions or workers' representation, the minimum wage – in any case rarely observed in small-scale enterprises – was set by a commission chaired by the Minister of Labour. In 1995/6 the minimum wage was raised by only 10 per cent, less than a third of the rate of inflation.[47] Thus the neo-liberal policies of the economic restructuring programme, including the unification of the exchange rate and the elimination of price distortions, gave rise to a number of politically unsustainable social and economic dislocations.[48] The Khatami era fared no better. By 2003, there seemed little prospect of a major improvement in the economy. Job creation lagged behind the increase in the labour force, and true unemployment was running at over 20 per cent and perhaps closer to 30 per cent.[49]

The lack of economic growth and prosperity brought with it popular discontent. As people – mainly the young – expressed their desire for improved living standards and material conditions there was growing demand for numerous goods and services that were dubbed 'Western decadent luxuries' by the ruling elite. The market for videos, music cassettes and compact discs, imported jeans and make-up flourished, though easy access to such commodities was restricted to the privileged few. The growing demands and desires of the Iranian youth for such commodities, under conditions where over one-third of the population is under 14 and over half under 19, posed serious questions for the state and economy.[50]

Growing discontent over living standards persistently spilled over into spontaneous demonstrations. Anti-government protests broke out in a number of cities, including Tehran, in 1990 as food prices increased on a weekly or even daily basis and the housing shortage was exacerbated by increasing rural migration.[51] Riots and demonstrations broke out again in Tehran, Mashad, Arak and Shiraz in 1991–92 in protest against shortages.[52] Workers in Esfahan went on strike in opposition to the addition of two hours to the working day.[53] Another wave of unrest appeared in 1994–95 with the detonation of numerous bombs in Tehran and other cities, assassination attempts on Rafsanjani and other officials, workers' strikes and demonstrations across the country, including Tehran, Zahedan, Qazvin, Tabriz, Mahabad and Eslamshahr.[54]

These destabilising trends had potentially grave consequences for a regime bereft of its earlier populist legitimacy conferred by war and the leadership of Khomeini. In a bid to counter the threat of popular action against the regime, factions within the ruling elite formulated different responses. The main thrust of these policies came from the faction best described by the label of 'traditional right' (*rast-e sonnati*).[55] Pressure both from the conservative deputies of the *majles* and the leader, Ayatollah Khamenei, constituted a 'backlash' against policies of economic liberalisation, arguing instead for re-instituting subsidies on basic goods while also benefiting merchant and trading interests against industry as well as tightening state control.

In the face of both pressure from below and obstacles posed by powerful factions within the ruling elite, the government was forced to reverse some of its policies while at the same time increasing its use of coercive instruments to repress dissent. In his New Year speech of March 1993, therefore, Rafsanjani vowed that his government would maintain its 'supportive policies', such as payment of subsidies for basic goods, electricity and fuels, and would protect basic commodities from being affected by the single parity foreign exchange policy.[56] In the following year Hassan Rowhani, head of the Foreign Policy Commission of the *majles*, reiterated the necessity to 'harness inordinate price hikes' and for the government to 'embark on the pricing of basic goods'.[57] This stand-off on the economy continued into the next decade. The reforms of the Khatami years continued to face obstacles presented by the vested interests in the regime. Khatami also led an attempt at institutional change which would curb the power of the religious elite – especially the Guardian Council. However, the proposals finally brought forward by the government in August 2002 were rejected in 2003 by the very body whose powers they were meant to curtail. The *majles* elections of February 2004 finally signalled the victory of the conservative clerics. In September 2004, conservative MPs backed a bill which gave them a veto over investments with foreign holdings of over 49 per cent. This was more than a symbolic victory. For Khatami it spelled paralysis of the government in the international domain.

Meanwhile, the regime continued to use the instruments of repression against internal dissent both through government-controlled bodies and through militias controlled by key conservative clerics in the state. Khamenei dismissed the notion that the 'honourable and clean people' of Iran might have participated in demonstrations of frustration and dissatisfaction with the regime. Rather, putting these activities down to 'counter-revolutionaries, hooligans and trash', he recommended unflinching confrontation by the security forces, as Rafsanjani encouraged the intelligence forces to be on their guard.[58] *Basij* forces were once more mobilised throughout the country to confront such popular protests and, in a show force of the state against the masses, their battalions staged marches pledging to 'defend the Revolution'.[59] The internal security apparatus continued to be strengthened, and in the wake of the popular protests of 1994–95 the Guardian Council approved the bill on the use of firearms by the security forces, enabling them legally to gun down spontaneous opposition.[60]

Student-led movements in 1999 and again in 2003 resulted in severe repression in which militias such as the Hojjatiyeh organisation took part. The post-2000 period was marked by numerous incidents of protest by reformers that were followed by repression, including waves of arrests as well as occasional unexplained assassinations of opposition members.

Beyond the direct use of force, the regime again fell back on populist rhetoric centred on the conflict with 'global arrogance' and the need to confront the 'Western cultural onslaught' which was allegedly penetrating the country through materialism and consumerism. Ayatollah Jannati, for instance, criticised policies which created discontent among the people as illegitimate:

> why do you export commodities needed by the people and deposit the money in foreign bank or invest it abroad? ... All these unnecessary imports, all these large number of cars which are imported ... they should not be allowed in. ... One way of solving the problem is to curb consumption. Why are they consuming so much? ... The Islamic recommendation is piety in consumption.[61]

The need to confront the 'cultural onslaught of the West' and the 'flood of the Western decadent lifestyle' became the *leitmotif* used by those in the leadership keen to curb popular demands which the economy could ill-provide.[62] The *majles*-approved ban on satellite dishes which came into force in early 1995 served to reinforce this trend of combating 'moral corruption'.[63]

The government was institutionally limited in what it could achieve. Simultaneously, it failed to meet political and economic expectations of the population. Politically, its inability to push forward the reform programme disenchanted those who had seen Khatami as their hope for change. Economically, the Khatami years had failed to improve living conditions for the majority of the population. The reforms had relied for their political organisation on the student movement and Islamic intellectuals. Once these had been disenchanted, it was difficult to find an alternative means of rallying support. The religious conservatives, on the other hand, could rely on a range of revolutionary organisations that they had cultivated during the previous decades: the religious foundations and in particular the paramilitary organisations of the *Pasdaran* and the *basij*. By reverting back to the populist rhetoric of the Revolution, these organisations were better able to rally support. This rhetoric became a major instrument in the hands of internal elements within the regime that stood in opposition to the reform process. With the state apparatus behind them, the conservatives increasingly gained the upper hand. By February 2004, they had a majority in the *majles*. By September 2005, they also had a president in power.

8 Revolutionary foreign policy and international tension

While there were attempts at reform in the second and third decades of the Islamic Republic, these reforms not only faced institutional obstacles internally and externally, but were also caught in the contradictions of a revolutionary state whose policies are marked not only by change but also by continuity. As we saw in the last chapter, the policy of change originated not from truly reformist motives, but from that of creating a stronger Islamic Republic in order better to pursue its ultimately revolutionary objectives in the long term. The attempts at reform, therefore, inevitably clashed continuously with this greater goal. Nowhere was this clearer than in the domain of foreign policy. While on the one hand, the regime tried to display a conciliatory face, the other face of Janus spouted revolutionary rhetoric and supported continuation of revolutionary adventurism.

As we shall see in this chapter, the continuity in the Islamic Republic's international goals, also influenced by internal dispute, resulted in continued external hostility towards the regime, led in the main by Washington. Two aspects of the Islamic Republic's foreign policy goals have, in particular, contributed to this continuing hostility. The first is the language of export of revolution, which has translated into support of Islamic groups and movements in the Middle East and beyond, which include those involved in terrorist activity. The second is the Islamic Republic's military and security strategy and the likely ambition of the development of a nuclear arsenal.

Revolutionary continuity: Islamic universalism

As we have seen, the policies of the Islamic Republic in the economic and external domains changed in the 1990s as a means of preserving and strengthening the Islamic state. However, this policy was conceived by the leadership not as an end but a means to an end. This meant that although reformist policies were pursued, the ultimately revolutionary identity of the state was not questioned. The image of the international system painted by Khomeini continued to prevail as an ideological pivot of the regime: the oppression of the Muslim and non-Muslim masses by the dominant powers, the Islamic Republic as the vanguard of the oppressed and their only path to salvation, the illegitimacy of the status quo, and the necessity to establish an Islamic global order. The Islamic Republic was self-proclaimedly to remain the fulcrum and active agent for the global promotion of the Revolution in accordance with Khomeini's vision of the 'Islamic Revolution' being not limited to the borders of Iran but 'the beginning of the world revolution of Islam'.[1]

The belief of the leadership in the 1990s was that the success of the global struggle spearheaded by the Islamic Republic was predicated on building a strong state able to withstand internal and external pressures. Primacy was given to structural reforms of the state and economy which would enable the ultimate achievement of revolutionary objectives. Herein, however, rested inconsistencies that would serve as the source of perpetual tension within the regime.

These tensions were often expressed in calls within the regime for a continuation of the revolutionary policies of the previous decade and opposition to 'normalisation' of relations with the 'West'. Thus, while government policy focused on attempting to portray a more conciliatory image of the post-revolutionary state, the practice and implementation of 'revolutionary foreign policy' persisted as a result of internal pressures, often backed by semi-independent institutions within the state.

Although the post-Khomeini leadership initiated many reforms, it also endorsed the continued commitment to 'revolutionary Islamic diplomacy' and upheld the status of Iran as the 'axis of Islam'. A primary objective of the Islamic Republic would be to build a 'powerful capital of the Muslim world'.[2] The legitimacy of the Islamic metropolis was then sanctioned by its alleged role in the confrontation with 'global arrogance' (*estekbar-e jahani*) as well as the promotion of the Islamic Republic as the centre of the international activities of the struggling masses and the encouragement of Islamic movements.

Khomeini's image of the international system had pivoted around two principal axes: firstly that the international system was constituted by dominant powers on the one hand and dominated states on the other, and secondly, that the Islamic Republic was an alternative model which would conform to or compromise with 'Neither East nor West'. The endemic confrontation of the Islamic Republic with 'imperialism of East and West' was asserted and reasserted. The main thrust of this policy had, from its inception, been tilted towards conflict with the United States and persisted as an axis of revolutionary rhetoric in the post-Khomeini period. The United States continued to be denounced by the new leader, Khamenei, as a 'usurping bullying colonialist and aggressive entity [whose] intentions are still hostile'.[3] On the eve of the tenth anniversary of the storming of the US embassy in Tehran, which was declared by the Foreign Ministry a 'national day for the struggle against world arrogance spearheaded by the world-devouring United States', he reiterated and justified the pivotal function of the hostility of the Islamic Republic towards the United States:

the interpretation and meaning of arrogance is a Koranic one. ...
The nature of arrogance is such that we must have constant
confrontation with it and not seasonal or tactical ones. This is
the basis of the Revolution and so far as there is a revolution
such a situation will persist. ... Arrogance and dominance are
reflected in all the Western regimes and those who are subject to
them. ... America is more arrogant than all the others.[4]

Numerous allusions by the leadership to the 'criminal nature of
America' frustrated any potential rapprochement as 'those who spoke
of the possibility of a compromise between the Islamic Republic of Iran
and the United States' were denounced as 'ignorant of the nature of
Western arrogance'.[5] The establishment of ties between Iran and the
United States was deemed impossible, as the United States was
perceived to be persistently hostile towards the Iranian nation.[6] This
vehement antipathy towards the United States is, as we have discussed
previously, partly to be understood in terms of the antecedent history
of relations in the pre and post-revolutionary periods, but also as an act
of self-endorsement by a regime that gains legitimacy from its
purported role in confronting global imperialism. With the end of the
war, and having failed to create a 'just society' or provide for the material well-being of the population, the populist appeal of the Revolution
had clearly declined. This elevated the importance of the 'anti-imperialist' rhetoric of the regime. That this rhetoric was devoid of
meaningful content in the analysis of imperialism and the structure of
the international system was nothing new. Its novelty came with the
more explicit move to the cultural sphere as the Islamic Republic was
increasingly presented as the bastion of resistance to the 'cultural
onslaught' of the West.

Meanwhile, the leadership was very quick to grasp the opportunity
in the wake of the revolutions in Eastern Europe to present Islam and
the model of the Islamic Republic as the only alternative to the
exploitative global capitalist system. What had previously been
presented as the 'Third Way' between the capitalist West and the Soviet
system was now reformulated as the only alternative to capitalism.
Concomitant with the popular upheavals in Eastern Europe, Rafsanjani stressed – contrary to pronouncements in the West of the 'victory
of capitalism' in face of the 'defeat of Marxism' – that the Islamic
Republic remained as the bearer of the torch of resistance against the
hegemony of the West:[7]

Now that Marxism has disintegrated Muslim revolutionaries
are the standard bearers in the struggle against imperialism and
against the sovereignty and domination of capitalism. ... Today

Islam is the only pivot which can attract justice seekers of the world around itself.[8]

Other leaders were even more explicit if also cruder in presenting an image of an undifferentiated 'Islam' as embodying a universal and all-encompassing ideology of resistance. Ayatollah Mousavi-Ardebili's Friday sermon shortly after the Eastern European revolutions is a typical example:

> Marxism-Leninism has gone. What should it be replaced with? Islamic logic. Islamic philosophy. Islamic policy. Islamic education. Islamic economics. Everything Islamic.[9]

As the disintegration of the Soviet Empire branded 'really existing social-ism' with the mark of a failed ideology, the leaders of the Islamic Repub-lic drew upon this conjunctural collapse to confirm the role of Islam as the 'only strong trench, platform and hope for justice-seeking people' in standing up to 'the entire world materialist power and the dangerous empire of the West'.[10] The demise of 'Marxism' would hasten the dawn of global Islamic resistance as Islamic movements showed a more and more active presence on the scene. Detached from their specific political and socio-economic circumstances, the rise and proliferation of Islamic movements were attributed to the 'global Islamic revival' and 'Islamic renaissance' under the leadership of the Islamic Republic, thereby adding credence to its rhetoric.[11] The Islamic Republic was presented as the model which other Muslim and oppressed nations would follow in their opposition to 'imperialism' and 'global arrogance':

> if Muslims, true followers of Islam anywhere in the world seek deliverance, if they want to repel the dominant and power of the Great Satan ... they have no other way but to follow the path the Imam laid down for the Iranian nation.[12]

> Islamic Iran, the base of the new movement of the world of Islam, *ummah al-Qurah* of the world of Islam, today is proud to note that the path they have chosen led by the late Imam, thank God is an evolu-tionary path and the eyes of the world Muslims are focused here and look to the exalted leadership of the Revolution [i.e. Khamenei].[13]

Naturally, the 'Islamic Revolution' in Iran was to take the credit for lead-ing the Islamic revival that had arisen to counter the 'West' in Palestine and Lebanon, Sudan, Algeria, Tunisia, Egypt, Bosnia and elsewhere[14] – a portrayal fed by mirror-images in the Western academies and media of the 'clash of civilisations' or cultures.[15]

In order actively to promote its global leadership role, the Islamic Republic fortified the prevailing institutional and organisational means for disseminating propaganda and created new ones. The issue of global unity continued to be stressed in the political agenda of the regime and various forums were realised to encourage consensus and unanimity, under the leadership of the Islamic Republic, amongst the various sects and movements within the Islamic world.

Embassies and cultural attaches were entrusted with the task of 'passing the message of Islam and the Revolution abroad ... [in] areas which have always remained outside the realm of our propaganda'.[16] The external service of the Islamic Republic of Iran Broadcasting Corporation, operating under the supervision of the three governmental branches, provided a medium for propagation of the voice of the Islamic Republic across the continents. Targeting most specifically the Middle East, Africa and Asia, but also other parts of the world, by the mid-1990s, it was broadcasting in Arabic, Armenian, Azerbaijani, Bengali, Bosnian, Dari, English, French, German, Hausa, Malay, Pashtu, Russian, Spanish, Swahili, Turkish, Turkmen and Urdu.[17] Two years later Albanian, Azeri, Italian, Tajiki, Kazakh and Kurdish had been added to this list.[18]

The Islamic Propaganda Organisation (*sazman-e tablighat-e eslami*), founded in 1981, remained active through the following decade under the leadership of Ayatollah Ahmad Jannati. A further organisation of Islamic Message Propagation was set up in April 1989, concerned with 'spreading Shi'a Islam, fighting against Western capitalism and Eastern communism'.[19] Free videos and books in various languages were distributed throughout Islamic societies worldwide, and by 1992 propaganda activities included backing Islamic societies abroad, distribution of publications at an international level including the printing and dissemination of the Koran, and the staging of international conferences.[20] Other organisations such as the Qom-based Imam Hosein Foundation distributed Islamic literature across the globe free of charge. The Islamic Thought Foundation was by the end of the decade publishing at least 24 publications (magazines) in Arabic, English, French, Hausa, Hindi, Spanish, Swahili, Turkish and Urdu on various social, cultural and political issues.[21]

The Ministry of Islamic Culture and Guidance (*vezarat-e farhang va ershad-e Islami*) served as a further channel of international propaganda. The existing departments of Hajj Affairs and International Affairs were supplemented with Tourism and Pilgrimage Affairs, and Directorate Generals for Foreign Press and Media, Foreign Publicity and Planning Co-ordination, Asia and the Subcontinent, Arab and African Countries, Europe and America.[22] Partially organised by this Ministry, the *hajj* continued to serve as a political platform, as indicated by the importance of the issue of organisation of the Iranian pilgrims and the choice of who would lead them.[23] The messages of Khamenei to the pilgrims, distributed in various languages, urged Muslim unity and solidarity (*ettehad va yeganegi-ye moslemin*) and the centrality of the confrontation with the imperialist powers (*qodrathaye estekbari*) .[24]

These media repeatedly emphasised the importance of the unity of the Islamic world and cautioned against the isolation of Iran's (Shi'i) Islamic Revolution from the rest of the world's Muslims.[25] In order further to advance this cause, organisations aimed at the promotion of Islamic unity and the formulation of a unified political strategy were established. These were attempts to escape the 'Shi'i ghetto' in which the Islamic Republic had boxed itself and to reach out to the wider Muslim community of believers.[26] An Assembly for Inter-Islamic Understanding (*majma'-e taqrib-e mazaheb-e Islami*), whose secretary-general was appointed directly by the leader, and the International Assembly of the Ahl ul-Bayt were established in 1990 to bring the various Muslim sects closer together.[27]

Representatives of Islamic organisations were invited to the country at every opportunity. In September 1990, for instance, those present in Tehran included Hasan al-Turabi of Sudan's National Islamic Front, Qazi Hussain Ahmad of Pakistan's Islamic Assembly, Rachid al-Gannouchi of Tunisia's Islamic Trend Movement, Yasin abd al-Aziz of Yemen's Muslim Brotherhood, Ibrahim Ghushah of Hamas, and representatives from Egypt, Algeria and Jordan. In the following year during Unity Week (*hafte-ye vahdat*) at the First session of the Supreme Council of the Assembly for Affinity among Islamic Sects[28] Khamenei reiterated and emphasised the role of the Islamic Republic of Iran as 'the global base of Islam [embracing] all those who long for materialisation of this aspiration and those who are ready to take practical steps in this connection'.[29] Muslims worldwide were encouraged to participate in these international conferences hosted by the Islamic Republic, and calls for papers on various aspects of Islamic thought, unity and political issues appeared in its foreign publications, encouraging Muslims worldwide to attend.[30] With the principal aim of creating a global Islamic movement under the leadership of the Islamic Republic, the activities of the international conferences and organisations continued to be expanded in subsequent years, as signalled by the establishment of affiliate associations such as a Women's International Office of the Ahl-ul Bayt World Assembly.[31]

The revolutionary credentials of the Islamic Republic as the centre of the global Islamic movement were affirmed not only in propaganda and rhetorical proclamations, but also in the active encouragement of Islamic movements. When the radical policy of direct export of revolution was abandoned in the 1990s, foreign policy was to maintain 'an active idealistic presence in the world'.[32] This entailed support for Islamic movements and the establishment of institutional and organisational means for the propagation of the message of the Revolution abroad. Though concrete evidence for the support of Islamic movements by the Islamic Republic is difficult to obtain, at least a number of cases can be singled out, including the moral and material support of Islamic opposition groups and co-operation with new Islamic governments professing allegiance to the Islamic Republic.

The clearest manifestation of 'active engagement' in Islamic movements and the continuity of revolutionary foreign policy was with regard to the Lebanese and Palestinian cases and opposition to the Arab–Israeli peace process following the Gulf War of 1991. Rafsanjani, seen by many as a 'moderate', was very explicit on this issue when he not only declared support for armed struggle of the Palestinian people to be the only option, but also appeared to endorse terrorism and random violence as part of this struggle.[33] Soon after assuming the leadership, Ayatollah Khamenei issued a message of support for the 'Islamic uprising of the Palestinian nation', declaring it a 'duty of all Muslims' to help them in their struggle.[34] Despite suggestions that the level of material assistance given to Palestinian and Lebanese groups declined compared with the previous decade, partly due to limits on revenues and partly as a result of the weakening of the radical factions in favour of more direct methods of exporting the Revolution, channels of contact were maintained so that at no time was there a complete cessation of support to these groups. Furthermore, there is evidence to suggest that from the end of 1991 and the launch of the Arab–Israeli peace process, training and support infrastructure were expanded. In addition facilities were provided for the support not only of radical Shiite elements but also of Sunni Islamists.[35] Prominent officials in Tehran frequently received leaders of the Popular Front for the Liberation of Palestine-General Command (PFLP-GC), Hamas and the Lebanese Hezbollah. Tehran pledged to provide resources for the 'continuation of the sacred defence against the regime occupying Quds [Israel]' and underlined the continued centrality of 'today Iran, tomorrow Palestine' as principles of the Revolution.[36] The *majles* ratified a law on the 'support for the Islamic Revolution of the People of Palestine', and following the establishment of a corresponding committee, funds were allocated for this purpose.[37]

In opposition to the peace process, an International Conference in Support of the Islamic Revolution of the Palestinians took place in Tehran in October 1991. In its final declaration, strong backing of the 'struggle of the Palestinian people for the total liberation of the occupied lands, elimination of the Zionist existence and establishment of an independent Palestinian state' was declared. Furthermore, armed struggle was affirmed as the legitimate right of the people of the territories. Islamic countries were called upon to establish permanent military units forming the 'Al-Quds Liberation Army' – centred on the *Pasdaran* – and a fund to be administered from the Secretariat in Tehran for the support of the Intifadah.[38] In 2001, speaking at a conference in Tehran in support of the Palestinian Intifadah which included delegates from radical Islamic groups such as Hamas and Islamic Jihad as well as Hezbollah, Khamenei called for the Palestinians to 'follow the example of Hezbollah' in order to force Israel to withdraw and for the armed resistance against Israel to continue.[39]

The Islamic Republic also took an increasing interest in developing ties with a significant number of African countries that came to be targeted for the promotion of revolution. An official seminar on Africa held in May 1991 concluded that practical ways for co-operation aimed at 'defending the rights of the oppressed people of Africa' needed to be devised and *majles* Speaker Nateq Nouri urged that the revitalisation of Islam in the African Continent should be among the prime objectives of Iranian foreign policy.[40] Subsequent activities of the Islamic Republic and nurturing of relations confirm its practical engagement in this region.[41]

The only state, however, which saw the rise to power of an Islamic government was Sudan. This was an opportunity for the Islamic Republic to demonstrate a continued commitment to political Islam.[42] In 1991 President Rafsanjani visited the country, together with heads of the Iranian intelligence services and the Revolutionary Guards. The Sudanese National Islamic Front, led by Hassan al-Turabi, the de facto head of government, then became a recipient of aid and assistance from the Islamic Republic.[43] Talks and agreements following a visit of a Sudanese military delegation to Tehran ensued.[44] An estimated 800–2000 Iranian Revolutionary Guards were stationed in Sudan by early 1992, some of whom have been engaged as military advisers to their counterparts in the regular Sudanese army. Additionally, weapons valued at around $300 million, including ammunition, machine-guns, anti-aircraft batteries and Chinese-made Silkworm missiles, were provided by the Iranian government. In November 1993 a high-level Sudanese delegation was received by President Hashemi Rafsanjani and a commitment to friendship between the two 'brother Islamic nations' was reaffirmed by both sides.[45]

In Central Asia too, in the aftermath of the breakdown of the Soviet Union, the Islamic Republic opened embassies in the new republics of Azerbaijan, Turkmenistan and Tajikistan in 1991. In Afghanistan also, Iran remained an important player both prior and subsequent to the withdrawal of Soviet forces.[46] In this period Iranian aid to its mainly

Shi'ite clients was increased.[47] In order to encourage unity amongst these groups a conference was staged in Tehran in March 1990 to develop a common political and military strategy and form an alliance now called *Hizb-i Wahdat*.[48] The Islamic Republic played a role in the formation of the Mojahedin coalition government and its subsequent concerns have been to prevent the establishment of the Taliban, seen as a base of Saudi and US influence against Iran, by providing assistance to the anti-Taliban coalition.[49] Further afield, Iranian assistance to the Bosnian Muslims included not only moral and rhetorical gestures, but also the shipment of material supplies, including weapons. There is some evidence that the Islamic Republic provided support to extremist groups in Algeria, Morocco, Tunisia and Egypt.[50]

Iran's alleged support of extremist and terrorist groups in the Middle East and beyond has received much coverage in recent years. While evidence for direct support is sometimes difficult to establish, the motives for such assistance are much clearer in the light of the different pressures within the regime. The Islamic state continued, as we have shown, to rest on the notion of a challenge to the prevailing international and regional order and maintained export of revolution as its long-term objective. While during the 1990s and the early part of the following decade the regime attempted to present a conciliatory face to other countries, many revolutionary activities abroad continued covertly or as unofficial policy.

Military and security strategy

The Islamic Republic has meanwhile also attempted to replenish its military arsenal and capability, which was much depleted at the end of the Iran–Iraq war. This was, indeed, the other arm of the regime's policy of securing the borders of the Iranian state which in part had translated, as we saw in the last chapter, into rapprochement and reconciliation with regional states. The experience of war in the 1980s had indicated that a capability to withstand considerable external pressure would be required for the survival of the regime. Widespread international hostility and resistance to the universal message of the Revolution illustrated the need for security arrangements that would safeguard the borders of the Islamic Republic. This policy embodied two aspects. On the one hand, the geo-political borders of the state had to be secured through diplomatic initiatives aimed largely at regional states, while a programme of rearmament and strengthening of military capability was followed. The two arms of this policy have, however, appeared to be incompatible, as regional and international concerns about Iran's nuclear capabilities in the 1990s and through the next decade indicate.

As the regime attempted to assure its neighbours that it had no designs for aggrandisement in the region, the other arm of Iran's strategy for security remained the development of its defence establishment and military capability. Although Iranian military expenditure declined as a proportion of GDP in the aftermath of the war with Iraq, a more concerted build-up of arms began in the early 1990s. In 1992 Iranian air-force, ground-force and missile capabilities were still inferior to those of neighbouring Iraq.[51] Its weapons procurement programme was at least partly an attempt to bridge this gap, and consisted of both a diversification of foreign arms supplies and the development of indigenous military industries. Iran's military expenditure increased from around $2 billion in 1992 to $2.5 billion in 1993 and over $3.5 billion in 1994 (in constant 1995 prices).[52] Its arms acquisitions included purchases of MiG and SU fighter aircraft, T-72 tanks and submarines from Russia, F-7 fighters from China and Scud missiles from North Korea. On the home front efforts were concentrated on restructuring the armed forces and increasing their preparedness and professionalism.[53] Moreover, industrial efforts were concentrated on the development of an indigenous military industry. There was widespread dissemination of news concerning the 'remarkable successes' in this field and pioneering achievements in military industries. These included the first Iranian-built warship, indigenous repair of F-14 bombers, manufacture of defence equipment with 90 per cent of parts made in Iran, the first Iranian-made tank, and Iranian-made rocket fuel and off-shore platforms. The publicity given to these achievements was undoubtedly partly for domestic consumption, but also intended to project the image of strength and defensive capability and deter potential military threats.[54]

The onset of the US-led 'war against terror' following 11 September 2001 resulted in the war in Afghanistan and the stationing of NATO troops on Iran's eastern border, and in 2003 in the US occupation of Iraq on Iran's western border. This exacerbated the regime's concerns regarding security and undoubtedly led to the acceleration of plans to boost Iran's defence capabilities. President Khatami's pledge in September 2003 to 'increase Iran's military strength' was only one of numerous statements by the regime on this issue.[55]

It is also in this context that the controversy in recent years over Iran's nuclear programmes capability and potential development of nuclear weapons needs to be considered. Iran professes to have entirely peaceful nuclear intentions. However, there can be little doubt that the development of nuclear capability fits well into the regime's military and security strategy. In other words, the nuclear programme in Iran also needs to be seen as part of the strategy of creating a strong Islamic Republic able not only to defend itself but also to establish itself as a regional power and project itself as a successful post-revolutionary model. Thus, in the early 1990s, the regime began to step up measures to develop nuclear energy with the assistance of Russia. A decade later, Iran had developed significant capability, which IAEA inspectors in 2003 reported as being 'extremely advanced'. By 2006, Iran was in a position to announce the successful enrichment of uranium – an event which unsurprisingly caused great alarm in Washington and other Western capitals and led to a situation of great tension.

International tension

The persistence of what may be called a revolutionary foreign policy by the Iranian regime has resulted in continued international tension, in particular with respective administrations in Washington which have perpetuated the image of the Islamic Republic as a revolutionary ('rogue') state in the international system. There have been three distinct phases in Washington's policies towards the Islamic Republic since the 1990s, coinciding with the change in administrations from Bush to Clinton to Bush Jr. If during the first two periods, White House officials signalled a potential thaw in attitudes toward the Islamic Republic, the US Department of State and Congress remained concerned about Iranian involvement in terrorist activities, opposition to the Arab–Israeli peace process and the Ta'if Agreement, and procurement of weapons of mass destruction. With the election of George W. Bush there was, at least until 2006, greater unity across the administration and Congress regarding Iran policy.

In the early 1990s, international terrorist activities were probably the 'single biggest obstacle to normalisation of relations'.[56] This view was reinforced by the influence of the pro-Israel lobby in Congress in the form of the Israeli Public Affairs Committee.[57] Keen Congressional interest in Iran's nuclear intentions was evidenced by nine hearings between 1989 and 1992 on this matter. Efforts by Iran to acquire nuclear weapons were regarded as contrary to US national security interests, leading to the Bush administration to urge restraint from world nuclear suppliers for nuclear exports to Iran.[58] All these pressures resulted in strengthening of prohibitive legislation with respect to Iran. In 1991 The Foreign Operations, Export Financing and Related Programs Appropriation Act came into force; under this act the Secretary of Treasury instructs the US director of each international financial institution to 'vote against any loan or other use of funds of the respective institution to or for a country for which the Secretary of State has determined that the country supports international terrorism'. The institutions, of course, include the World Bank and IMF, in which the United States, by virtue of its quotas, has greatest voting power.[59]

The inauguration of the Clinton administration spelt an end to equivocation in Washington by coming down strongly in favour of a staunchly uncompromising position with respect to the Islamic Republic. As Gary Sick has argued, although there was some prevarication in public confirmation of the policy, a strategy of 'containment' of Iran was devised in Washington in order to counter Iranian attempts to re-establish a 'Persian sphere of influence' in former Soviet republics to the north, oppose the Arab–Israeli peace process, support anti-Israeli terrorist groups and support Islamic fundamentalism throughout the Muslim world. What later came to be known as the policy of 'dual containment' – meant to deal simultaneously with both Iraq and Iran – aimed at containing Iran and changing the behaviour of the Islamic Republic in a number of areas: support for international terrorism, support for Hamas and opposition to the Arab–Israeli peace process, subversion through support of Islamic movements, domination of Persian Gulf, and prospective acquisition of weapons of mass destruction.[60] Secretary of State Warren Christopher asserted that the administration 'thinks that Iran is an international outlaw ... and [is] trying to persuade other nations of the world ... to treat Iran as an outlaw'.[61] The administration launched a series of measures aimed at putting economic pressure on the Islamic Republic in order to change its international behaviour. This policy was clearly spelt out in November 1995 by Peter Tarnoff, Undersecretary of State for Political Affairs:

Our problems with Iran are based on our concerns about specific Iranian policies which we judge to be unacceptable to law-abiding nations. Our goal is to convince the leadership in Tehran to abandon these policies and to abide by international norms. ... First, we concentrated on blocking the transfer to Iran of dangerous goods and technologies. ... Second, by pressuring Iran's economy we seek to limit the government's finances and thereby constrict Tehran's ability to fund rogue activities. We launched the initiative to block Iran's access to the international capital its economy needs.[62]

The Iran–Iraq Arms Non-Proliferation Act of 1992 provided for sanctions against persons or countries that transfer to Iran or Iraq goods or technology contributing to the acquisition of certain weapons. Economic sanctions against Iran were extended. In May 1995, the Clinton administration banned all United States trade with and investment in Iran including the purchase of Iranian oil by US companies abroad. This order prohibited the export from the United States to Iran of goods, technology or services; the re-export of such goods from third countries; new

US investments in Iran; and financing, investment and trade by US subsidiaries. It also continued the 1987 prohibition on the import into the United States of Iranian goods.[63] As a result, the US oil company, Conoco, was forced to abandon a deal with the National Iranian Oil Company and further deals with Iran by any US company were prohibited. This executive action was followed by a Congressional Bill passed in 1996 as the 'Iran and Libya Sanctions Act of 1996' imposing sanctions on any person or company investing more than $40m towards the enhancement of Iran's ability to develop petroleum resources. In August 1997 a further Executive Order was issued by Clinton which confirmed and extended the sanctions.

The administration in Washington also attempted to put pressure on other allied states to follow suit in respect of policy towards Iran.[64] These efforts included messages to diplomatic partners calling on them to review their ties with Iran, and pressure on allies at various international meetings, including the G-7 summit held in Halifax in 1995.[65] According to Peter Tarnoff, Undersecretary of State for Political Affairs, the administration was 'working aggressively' to urge other governments to join a multilateral embargo on Iran.[66]

Other states remained, nonetheless, more reluctant to sever ties with the Islamic Republic, due largely to commercial interests though also to differing conceptions of the Islamic Republic.[67] A number of European and Japanese companies concluded contracts for projects in Iran. France's ETPM secured an agreement to rebuild the Kharg offshore oil terminal in March 1990, while the contract for a new refinery at the port of Bandar Abbas was awarded to an Italian/Japanese consortium.[68] France's Societe Generale concluded a $2.2 billion financing package in 1990, and a number of French banks extended further credits in 1991. The German state export insurance agency, Hermes, lifted a DM 500 million ceiling on medium-term cover for credits, subsequent to which Deutsche Bank led a syndicate of German banks in providing credit for the Bandar Khomeini petrochemical complex. The Italian medium-term credit agency, Mediocredito Centrale, agreed to a $1 billion credit line in 1991 for a number of services and industrial projects. Japan's Petroleum Exploration Company entered a $1.6 billion joint venture investment in an offshore oil field venture with NIOC.[69] European and Japanese companies also engaged in debt rescheduling programmes for the short-term debt, which went into arrears from 1993.[70]

Nevertheless, the impact of the US sanctions on the Iranian economy and foreign economic relations was not negligible. Firstly, the US embargo on Iran led to a dramatic devaluation of the riyal, aggravating domestic inflation and creating problems for the economy, which we shall consider in more detail in the next section. Moreover, in light of the US pressure, allied countries did in fact review their policies towards Iran, causing impacts on a number of specific projects. In 1991 following discussions with US officials, the German Foreign Ministry blocked the completion of two nuclear reactors in Bushehr by the subsidiary of Siemens, KWU.[71] India also assured the United States that US concerns would be taken into account in its proposal to sell a research reactor to Iran in the same year, while in 1992 Argentina blocked a shipment of nuclear equipment to Iran. The Japanese government responded to US call by halting further official loans towards a hydroelectric dam project in 1995. Furthermore, the countries of the European Union found further reason to approach the issue of ties with the Islamic Republic with some equivocation, not only due to the precarious nature of investments and the lack of a stable legal and political environment in Iran, but also as a result of political uncertainties arising from the continuities in revolutionary policies.[72] The repercussions of incidents such as the Rushdie Affair and terrorist activities, including the assassination of Iranian exiled opposition leaders, took their toll on the attitude of the European Union member states to the Islamic Republic.

The final turn in US–Iranian relations came with the inauguration of George W. Bush. Iran was classified as part of the so-called 'axis of evil' and a key state sponsor of international terrorism. This, coupled with suspicions with regard to Iran's nuclear ambitions, has driven US hostility to Iran in recent years. Although the 'war on terror' had some inconsistent consequences for Iran's international relations, for example resulting in some Iranian co-operation in Afghanistan, it led to the presence of US forces in two of Iran's neighbours, leading to increased fears in the country of the resurgence of US regional imperialism and its consequences for the Islamic Republic. As Washington increasingly focused on the prospect of regime change in Iran, both in rhetoric and through the funding of various opposition groups, tensions between Tehran and Washington escalated.

The most recent act in the drama of US–Iranian post-revolutionary relations came with the Iranian presidential election of 2005. President Ahmadinejad ratcheted up the rhetoric against US imperialism and against Israel and made a firm commitment to the further development of Iran's nuclear programme. The United States, in response, has increasingly focused its attempts on crafting a response. In March 2006, Nicholas Burns, US Undersecretary of State for Political Affairs, summarised the administration's position:

> The Iranian leadership is actively working against all that the United States and our allies desire for the region. ... No country stands more resolutely opposed to our hope for peace and

freedom in the Middle East than Iran. ... Iran's leadership directly threatens vital American interests. ... Crafting an effective response to this Iranian threat is as important as any challenge America faces in the world today.[73]

This language and policy in Washington, however, has again easily played into the hands of the Iranian leadership who, by drawing on the early populist rhetoric of the Revolution are able to rally support. The more Iran is seen as a challenge to US interests in the region, the more can the leadership present the Islamic Republic as the centre of resistance against US domination of the region and the more can they draw on the deep-seated and deep-rooted nationalist sentiment of the Iranian population for support. This lesson, of the central tension of the existence of an anti-systemic revolutionary state in the international system is perhaps the hardest of all to learn. Part of the legitimacy of a revolutionary state with a long history of foreign intervention rests on its anti-systemic credentials, and the greater the tension with the dominant global power, the better can the leadership rally internal support driven by a national-populist revolutionary discourse.

9 Conclusion

Fred Halliday says of revolutionary states that 'the fact that they introduce truces, abandon internationalist rhetoric and participate in diplomacy does not [mean that they] have been "socialised"'.[1] This book has shown that this is no less true of the Islamic Republic.

Confrontation and challenge to the existing global order has been a common feature of many modern social revolutions. In the Iranian case, a history of foreign intervention and imperialism, the domestic and international forces complicit in changing the socio-economic structure of society, and the attendant upheavals that the expansion and development of capitalism has entailed, all help to explain why this was so.

International processes were central to the emergence of the revolutionary movement in Iran, both in giving rise to its objective circumstances and in influencing the subjective formation of the Revolution's participants. The outbreak of the Iranian Revolution had an international context and dimension and cannot be analysed in abstraction from this. The anti-systemic rhetoric of the Revolution and confrontation of the post-revolutionary state with the international system has historical roots and cannot be reduced to unexplained 'rogue' or 'renegade' behaviour rooted in essentialised cultural or religious attributes. The socioeconomic transformation of Iran in the decades preceding the Revolution was carried out in the context of the uneven global development of capitalism and against the backdrop of US influence. The expansion and development of capitalism in Iran was mediated by the geopolitical institutions of the international system. State-led and imperially supported capitalist development were at the root of the changes that shaped the social basis of the revolutionary forces.

The subjective formation of the participants in the Revolution was influenced both by a history of intervention of great powers and by the specific international conjuncture. The historical experience of foreign involvement in Iran buttressed the prevailing global worldview of revolutionaries, who saw the root cause of the problems of their societies in imperialism and dependency. The articulation of these concepts, combined with religion in Iran, constituted the populist politics of the Revolution and regime: Khomeinism. In particular, it reinforced the hostility of the new post-revolutionary regime to the international status quo.

The Iranian Revolution, much like other contemporary populist movements, tended to direct its rhetoric against imperialism, foreign capitalism and the economic and political configuration of the international system. This ideological disposition lies in historical experience. The West in general and the United States in particular were seen as adversaries precisely due to the historical experience of intervention and interference by these powers. The anti-imperialism, anti-Westernism or anti-Americanism of the Revolution stemmed from very real historical processes. The manifestation of this disposition in post-revolutionary policy had a correspondingly real material impact on interests vested in the regional and global status quo, leading to international response and confrontation.

The Iranian Revolution challenged the international status quo, thus producing the reaction of regional and global powers. It threatened interests vested in the status quo and resulted in actions to contain and limit its impact. The Iranian Revolution led to the appropriation and nationalisation of foreign capital and popular attacks on private property. It threatened to remove an important area from the capitalist sphere while bringing instability to the strategically vital region of the Persian Gulf. Iran's withdrawal from CENTO and hostility to Israel altered the United States' regional alliances and strategic consensus in the Middle East through the fall of a major ally. The political culmination came with the storming of the US embassy in Tehran. Regionally, its immediate consequences were an alternation in the regional strategic balance, post-revolutionary war and changes to the domestic politics of states in the region. Globally, it contributed to changes in strategy and policy, in particular of the United States.

Successive administrations in Washington were faced with the Iranian challenge after 1979. The attempts to alter the political configuration of Iran led to a range of often contradictory policies, from forming contacts with more 'moderate' sections of the Iranian elite to overthrowing the regime. The equivocation in Washington and failure of its Iran policy have shown the far-reaching implications of social revolution in a state with the collective experience of intervention and involvement of imperial power. As a result, the United States has been unable to regain a foothold or influence in Iran. The persistent tensions of US policy lasted well beyond the immediate post-revolutionary aftermath as the Clinton administration struggled with the inconsistencies of its 'dual containment' policy and the Bush administration's belligerence has led to even greater anti-US rhetoric in Tehran.

The Iranian Revolution also made an enduring impact on the regional balance of power and the political constellation of the Middle East. While the policy of exporting the Revolution gained no significant success in literal terms of the emergence of a parallel Islamic Republic in the region, there is little doubt that in the context of uneven international development, increasing US influence in the region and the stark social inequalities reproduced by the prevailing international order, the Revolution fired the imagination of anti-systemic activists regionally and beyond. While the exact model of the Islamic state may not have been reproduced elsewhere, the Revolution stood for many as a movement against the oppression and injustice of the global order. It showed, above all, that it was possible to use Islamic discourse against the prevailing global order in the contemporary world to create change.

Elites in power in neighbouring countries were starkly aware of this reality. The perils of the Iranian Revolution included an immediate threat both to their political power and to the broader global social power of extraction and exploitation which their political position conserved. With the complicity of the United States and other Western powers, regional responses to the Revolution ranged from the assistance of the Iranian exiled opposition, economic sanctions and political isolation to outright military invasion in 1980 by neighbouring Iraq. Beyond these responses, though, the Iranian Revolution had a more fundamental impact on the domestic policy and organisation of states in the region. It led to greater allegiance to and recognition of Islam, thereby legitimising Islam's central place in the political discourse of the region. The previously firmly secular leaders of states like Iraq and Egypt began to rely on Islamic symbolism and terminology in their political discourse. Moreover, the images of a homogeneous Islamic resurgence, which the Iranian leadership itself propagated, were used – often successfully – by these nationalist leaders to discredit as Iranian-backed what were in fact often home-grown internal movements of dissent against undemocratic regimes. Thus, while Islamic movements began to flourish in the region, in part inspired by the success of the Iranian Revolution, few – with the singular exception perhaps of the Hezbollah in Lebanon – actually came to pledge allegiance to the Islamic Republic or accept its position as vanguard and leader of a global Islamic movement.

The Islamic Republic's external relations and existence in a global context conversely had a decisive impact on the formation of the post-revolutionary state. The centralisation of state power and concentration of the means of administration, production and coercion is to be seen in the context of external pressures and the coercive policies of status quo states. Orthodox paradigms – in the disciplines of international relations and historical sociology – have posited the strengthening of the state following a successful social revolution. What is often missing from analyses though, is how this process relates to and is influenced by the existence of the revolutionary state within a hostile global order.

War and international hostility facilitated the development of both the coercive apparatus of the state and state control of the means of surplus extraction in the aftermath of the Iranian Revolution. On the one hand, external conflict was used as a justification for the suppression of internal dissent. On the other hand, power was centralised through ownership of or command over the means of administration, production and distribution. The centralisation and strengthening of the state in the aftermath of revolutionary change must be theorised in an international context of hostility, conflict and intervention. It is neither the result of some unexplained 'rogue behaviour' nor a transhistorical structural outcome of revolution. It needs to be set in the context of the threat to material interests posed by specific revolutions to the prevailing global order. Revolutionary states have been put under systemic pressure for challenging the international status quo and its prevailing order, and this pressure – both economic and political – has contributed to internal political developments that have resulted in the making of coercive state instruments.

Moreover, continued existence in a global order which the revolutionary state ultimately challenges is a long-lasting inconsistent process which eludes simplistic theories of 'socialisation' of revolutionary states. As we have seen, revolutionary policies were temporarily revised under the Islamic Republic in its second decade as it became clear that the conjuncture of external and internal pressures were leading to state crisis. This was not, though, a gradual process of 'socialisation' or 'normalisation', but a practical strategy of survival. Both for ideological and institutional reasons, a commitment to the universalist and radical aims of the Revolution endured. This duality in policy and behaviour of the revolutionary state is the key to the continuing contradictions of the revolutionary state almost three decades after its inception. Strategies of change and reform attempted in the 1990s and early part of the following decade questioned the revolutionary credentials and, therefore, legitimacy of the state. There remained a contradiction between the ultimate revolutionary goals from which the regime's leaders drew their legitimacy and the means adopted to attain those ends. On the other hand, however, pursuit of radical universalist revolutionary goals and the rejection of the international status quo, as espoused by Iran's current leadership in 2005, spells continued international pressure and hostility from the dominant powers.

Here lies an irony. The best hope of a change of regime in Iran towards greater openness and democracy is an indigenous movement for change from within, resulting from the dissatisfaction of the population with the economic and political failures of the government. However, the more pressure and hostility there is from external powers, in particular the United States, the better able is the regime to rally support drawing on national-populist sentiment and to manage or suppress internal dissent and opposition; and the easier it is for the regime to persuade the population that it is through national strength – including the symbolically increasingly important possession of nuclear power – that the country will be able to resist chaos and instability of the kind seen on its eastern and western borders in Afghanistan and Iraq. This contradiction will remain the thorn in the side of successive US Administrations as long as they continue to exercise imperialist power in the region.

The solution to this predicament is still to be played out in contemporary Iran and will depend heavily on the decision of the United States and its allies whether to act with force against Iran.

Notes

1. The Iranian Revolution in international context

1. For an exposition of the conspiratorial myth, see Ervand Abrahamian, *Khomeinism: Essays on the Islamic Republic* (London: Tauris,
   1993). The 'myth of confrontation' is discussed in Fred Halliday,
   Islam and the Myth of Confrontation (London: Tauris, 1996).
2. Samuel Huntington, 'The Clash of Civilisations?', *Foreign Affairs*,
   72:3 (Summer 1993) and *The Clash of Civilisations and the Remaking
   of World Order* (New York: Simon and Schuster, 1996). The notion
   of a 'clash of civilisations' was adopted by the Orientalist Bernard
   Lewis prior to Huntington's article. See Bernard Lewis, 'The Roots
   of Muslim Rage', *The Atlantic Monthly* (September 1990), pp. 47–60.
3. Huntington, *Clash of Civilizations* (1996), pp. 109–10.
4. *Ibid.*, p. 216.
5. John Esposito (ed.) *Political Islam* (London: Lynne Rienner, 1997);
   John Esposito, *The Islamic Threat: Myth or Reality* (Oxford: Oxford
   University Press, 1995); James Piscatori (ed.) *Islam in the Political
   Process* (Cambridge: Cambridge University Press, 1983);
   Mohammad Ayoob (ed.) *The Politics of Islamic Reassertion* (London:
   Croom Helm, 1981).
6. Esposito, *Islamic Threat*, p. 14.
7. '"The Sixth Great Power": Revolutions and the International
   System' in Fred Halliday, *Rethinking International Relations*
   (London: Macmillan, 1994), p. 134.
8. Nikki Keddie (ed.) *Debating Revolutions* (New York: New York
   University, 1995); John Foran (ed.) *Theorizing Revolutions* (London:
   Routledge, 1997) are good historical and sociological analyses.
9. Maryam Panah, 'Social Revolutions: The Elusive Emergence of an
   Agenda in International Relations', *Review of International Studies*
   (2002), 28; pp. 271–91.
10. On capitalism, see Robert Brenner, 'The Social Basis of Economic
    Development' in John Roemer (ed.) *Analytical Marxism* (Cambridge:
    Cambridge University Press, 1986), pp. 23–53. For a working of the
    Brenner thesis from an IR perspective, see Benno Teschke, *The Myth
    of 1648: Class, Geopolitics and the Making of Modern International Rela-
    tions* (London: Verso, 2003), pp. 262–8.
11. On the expansion of capitalism, see Karl Marx, *Capital: Volume One*
    (Harmondsworth: Penguin, 1976). On uneven and combined

development, see Leon Trotsky, *The History of the Russian Revolution* (London, Gollancz, 1933).

12. Justin Rosenberg, *Empire of Civil Society* (London: Verso, 1994), p. 129.

13. On Weberian and Marxist conceptions of the state, see Derek Sayer, *Capitalism and Modernity: An Excursus on Marx and Weber* (London: Routledge, 1991). See also Kees van der Pijl, *Transnational Classes and International Relations* (London, Routledge, 1998).

14. A classic analysis of this historical specific formation of social classes is E.P. Thompson, *The Making of the English Working-Class* (London: Victor Gollancz, 1963).

15. G. Rude, 'Ideology and Popular Protest' in Harvey Kaye, *The Face of the Crowd: Studies in Revolution, Ideology and Popular Protest. Selected Essays of George Rude* (New Haven: Harvester Wheatsheaf, 1988), p 197.

16. Panah, 'Social Revolutions'.

17. Immanuel Wallerstein, *The Capitalist World Economy* (Paris: Cambridge University Press, 1979), pp. 68–9.

18. *Ibid.*, p. 74.

19. Fred Block, 'The Ruling Class Does not Rule: Notes on the Marxist Theory of the State', *Socialist Review* (May/June 1977), pp. 6–28.

20. Sami Zubaida, *Islam, the People and the State* (London: Tauris, 1993), pp. 26–32.

21. Letters and declarations issued by the principal Shi'i clergy in Iran over the two decades prior to the Revolution attest to this. See *Asnad-e Enqelab-e Eslami* [Documents of the Islamic Revolution] (Tehran: Markaz-e Asnad-e Enqelab-e Eslami, 1374 [1995]).

22. Misagh Parsa, *Social Origins of the Iranian Revolution* (Rutgers University Press, 1989); Ervand Abrahamian, *Iran Between Two Revolutions* (New Jersey: Princeton, 1982).

23. Ervand Abrahamian, *Iran Between Two Revolutions*, p. 427.

24. Bashiriyeh, Hossein, *The State and Revolution in Iran* (London: Croom Helm, 1984); Farideh Farhi, *States and Urban-Based Revolutions* (Urbana: University of Illinois Press, 1990); Theda Skocpol, 'Rentier State and Shi'i Islam', *Theory and Society* (1982), pp. 265–83.

2. The Iranian Revolution

1. See Nikki Keddie, *Roots of Revolution: An Interpretive History of Modern Iran* (New Haven: Yale, 1981), pp. 79–112. See also Wilfrid Knapp, '1921–1941: The Period of Riza Shah' in Hossein Amir-sadeghi (ed.) *Twentieth Century Iran* (London: Heinemann, 1977).

2. Keddie, *Roots of Revolution*, pp. 113–41.

3. Val Moghadam, 'Making History But Not of Their Own Choosing: Workers and the Labour Movement in Iran' in Ellis Jay Goldberg (ed.) *The Social History of Labour in the Middle East* (Colorado: Westview, 1996). See also Sepehr Zabih, *The Communist Movement of Iran* (Berkeley: University of California Press, 1966), pp. 109–10.

4. *Ibid.*, p. 113.

5. James A. Bill, *The Eagle and the Lion: The Tragedy of American–Iranian Relations* (New Haven and London: Yale, 1988), p. 78.

6. *Ibid.*, p. 86.

7. Nikki Keddie, *Iran: Religion, Politics and Society* (London: Frank Cass, 1980), pp. 219–25.

8. Keddie, *Roots of Revolution*, pp. 146–8; Bill, *Eagle and the Lion*, p. 114.

9. Fred Halliday, *Iran: Dictatorship and Development* (Harmondsworth: Penguin, pb. 1979), pp. 78–90. See also Harald Irnberger, *Savak oder der Folterfreund des Westens* (Hamburg: Rowohlt, 1977), pp. 23–5.

10. Bill, *Eagle and the Lion*, p. 119.

11. Mark Gasierowski, *US Foreign Policy and the Shah: Building a Client State in Iran* (Ithaca and London: Cornell University Press, 199), p. 112 Table 6.

12. Quoted in C. Vaziri, *Le Petrole et le Pouvoir en Iran* (Lausanne: Piantanida, 1978).

13. Bill, *Eagle and the Lion*, p. 200.

14. Various views on the nature of socio-economic development in pre-revolutionary Iran can be found in: Halliday, *Iran: Dictatorship and Development*; Robert Looney, *The Economic Development of Iran* (New York: Praeger, 1973); Abrahamian, *Iran Between Two Revolutions*.

15. Maxine Rodinson, *Islam and Capitalism* (Harmondsworth: Penguin, pb. 1974), p. 129.

16. Eric Hooglund, *Land and Revolution in Iran 1960–80* (Austin: University of Texas Press, 1982); Afsaneh Najmabadi, *Land Reform and Social Change in Iran* (Salt Lake City: University of Utah Press, 1987).

17. Halliday, *Iran: Dictatorship and Development*, p. 103.

18. James F. Petras and Robert LaPorte, *Cultivating Revolution: The United States and Agrarian Reform in Latin America* (New York: Vintage, pb. 1971).

19. Halliday, *Iran: Dictatorship and Development*, p. 134–5.

20. Bill, *The Eagle and the Lion*, p. 131–2.

21. Marvin Zonis, *The Political Elite of Iran* (New Jersey: Princeton, 1971).

22. Keddie, *Iran: Religion, Politics and Society*, p. 197.

23. Keith McLachlan, 'The Iranian Economy 1960–1976' in Hossein Amirsadeghi (ed.) *Twentieth Century Iran*, p. 133.
24. Halliday, *Iran: Dictatorship and Development*, pp. 149–50.
25. Mohammad Reza Pahlavi, 'Westernisation: Our Welcome Ordeal' in *Mission for My Country* (London: Hutchinson, 1961), pp. 132–60, *passim*.
26. Keith McLachlan, 'The Iranian Economy 1960–1976' in Hossein Amirsadeghi (ed.) *Twentieth Century Iran*, pp. 129–70.
27. Keddie, *Iran: Religion, Politics and Society*, p. 197. For an overview of Iran's foreign relations in this period, see Halliday, *Iran: Dictatorship and Development*, pp. 249–84.
28. *Ibid.*, p. 261–2.
29. Halliday, *Iran: Dictatorship and Development*, p. 38.
30. This section of the dominant class is referred to as the 'bureaucratic bourgeoisie' by Bizhan Jazani, *Capitalism and Revolution in Iran* (London: Zed, 1980), p. 85. Halliday refers to this component of the capitalist class the 'upper stratum of state employees'.
31. McLachlan, 'The Iranian Economy 1960–1976' p. 152.
32. Vaziri, *Le Petrole et le Pouvoir*, pp. 227–36.
33. Jazani, *Capitalism and Revolution in Iran*, p. 87.
34. For a systematic study of the 'urban marginals' or 'sub-proletariat' see Asef Bayat, *Street Politics: Poor People's Movements in Iran* (New York: Columbia University Press, 1998). This sector is also emphasised by Masoud Kamali, *Revolutionary Iran: Civil Society and State in the Modernisation Process* (Aldershot: Ashgate, 1998).
35. Kamali, op cit., p. 176.
36. Bayat, *Street Politics*, pp. 23–33.
37. Kamali, *Revolutionary Iran*, pp. 196–203.
38. Bayat, *Street Politics*, p. 56.
39. For a detailed discussion of the working class, see Asef Bayat, *Workers and Revolution in Iran: A Third World Experience of Workers' Control* (London: Zed, 1987). See also Halliday, *Iran: Dictatorship and Development*, pp. 173–210; Jazani, *Capitalism and Revolution in Iran*, pp. 125–31.
40. Bayat, *Workers and Revolution*, pp. 45–65.
41. For a history of workers' collective action, see Moghadam, 'Making History But Not of Their Own Choosing'; see also Halliday, *Iran: Dictatorship and Development*, pp. 197–202.
42. Parsa, *Social Origins of the Iranian Revolution*, p. 118, Michael Fisher, 'Persian Society: Transformation and Strain' in Hossein Amirsadeghi (ed.) *Twentieth Century Iran*, pp. 171–96.
43. For a detailed account of clergy–state relations in this period, see

Shahrough Akhavi, *Religion and Politics in Contemporary Iran: Clergy–State Relations in the Pahlavi Period* (Albany: SUNY, 1980), pp. 117–58.

44. Jazani, *Capitalism and Revolution in Iran*, p. 135.

45. Akhavi, *Religion and Politics*, pp. 132–4. This land was distributed to high-ranking military officers, state officials and other individuals, including a number of famous singers.

46. *Ibid.*, p. 141.

47. Richard Cottam, *Nationalism in Iran* (Pittsburgh: University of Pittsburgh Press, 1979), p. 344.

48. Fred Halliday, *Rethinking International Relations*, pp. 170–80.

49. Forrest Colburn, *The Vogue of Revolution in Poor Countries* (Princeton, N.J.: Princeton University Press, 1995). See also, Halliday, *Rethinking International Relations*, especially p. 133 and pp. 141–2. On 'novelty' and revolution, see Hannah Arendt, *On Revolution* (London: Penguin, 1965), pp. 46–8.

50. Colburn, *Vogue of Revolution*, pp. 5–6.

51. Eric Hobsbawm, *Age of Extremes: The Short Twentieth Century* (London: Abacus, 1994), pp. 436–7.

52. Arendt, *On Revolution*, p. 22.

53. Hobsbawm, *Age of Extremes*, pp. 350–2.

54. *Ibid.*, pp. 354–6.

55. For a good summary of 'dependency theory', see A. Brewer, *Marxist Theories of Imperialism* (London and New York: Routledge, 1990), Chapter 8. See also B. Hettne, 'Dependency Theory' in Tom Bottomore (ed.) *A Dictionary of Marxist Thought* (Oxford: Blackwell, 1995).

56. Val Moghadam 'The Left and Revolution' in H. Amirahmadi and M. Parvin (eds) *Post-Revolutionary Iran* (Boulder and London: Westview, 1988), pp. 25–6.

57. Keddie estimates their numbers as exceeding one hundred thousand at a time. See *Roots of Revolution*, p. 235.

58. See Zabih, *The Communist Movement of Iran*, p. 200.

59. Hamid Dabashi, *Theology of Discontent: The Ideological Foundation of the Islamic Republic of Iran* (London: New York University Press, 1993), pp. 39–101.

60. Jalal Al-e Ahmad, *Gharbzadegi* (Tehran: Ravagh, 1341 [1962]), p. 29.

61. Nikki Keddie, 'Islamic Revival as Third Worldism' in N. Keddie (ed.) *Iran and the Muslim World: Resistance and Revolution* (New York: New York University Press, 1995), pp. 212–19.

62. Maxine Rodinson, *Marxism and the Muslim World* (London: Zed, 1979).

63. Houchang Chehabi, *Iranian Politics and Religious Modernism* (Ithaca: Cornell, 1990), pp. 214–18.

64. Hashemi Rafsanjani, *Dowran-e mobarezeh: khaterat, tasvirha, asnad, gahshumar* (Tehran: Daftar-e nashr-e ma'aref enqelab, 1374 [1995]), pp. 239–58.

65. Ruhollah Khomeini, *Islam and Revolution: Writings and Declarations,* translated by Hamid Algar (London: KPI, 1985), pp. 181–8.

66. Seyyed Mahmoud Taleqani, *Islam and Ownership,* translated by Ahmad Jabbari and Farhang Rajaee (Kentucky: Mazda, 1983). For one analysis of Taleqani's work and role, see Mangol Bayat, 'Mahmud Taleghani and the Iranian Revolution' in Martin Kramer, *Shi'ism, Resistance, Revolution* (Boulder: Westview, 1987), pp. 67–93.

67. Yann Richard, *Shi'ite Islam* (Oxford, Blackwell, 1995), p. 194.

68. These themes appear in Ali Shariati's essay *Che Bayad Kard* and 1972 lectures on Islamology, *Islamshenasi* .

69. Hamid Dabashi, *Theology of Discontent,* pp. 102–45.

70. Ervand Abrahamian, 'Khomeini: Fundamentalist or Populist?', *New Left Review,* No.186, 1991, p. 109.

71. Kenrick Abbot, 'Ayatullah Khumayni's Quest for a Just Society', *Orient,* 36:2 (1995), p. 254.

72. Zubaida, *Islam, the People and the State,* pp. 13–20.

73. Ervand Abrahamian, 'Khomeini: Fundamentalist or Populist', pp. 112–13.

74. *Ibid.,* p. 110.

75. Akhavi, *Religion and Politics in Contemporary Iran,* p. 150.

76. In his memoirs, Rafsanjani, then one of Khomeini's followers and students recounts discussions with Khomeini during his exile on the question of revolution and activism. See Rafsanjani, *Dowran-e Mobarezeh.*

77. Khomeini, *Islam and Revolution,* pp. 209–11.

78. Azar Tabari, 'The Role of the Clergy in Modern Iranian Politics' in N. Keddie (ed.) *Religion and Politics in Iran,* pp. 47–72.

79. Mehrzad Boroujerdi, *Iranian Intellectuals and the West: The Tormented Triumph of Nativism* (New York: Syracruse, 1996), pp. 80–1.

80. Parsa, *Social Origins of the Iranian Revolution,* p. 114.

81. Shaul Bakhash, *Reign of the Ayatollahs* (London, Unwin, 1985).

3. Populism and the Revolution

1. Margaret Canovan, 'Populism' in *The Social Science Encyclopaedia* (London: Routledge, 1996).

2. See for example A. Walicki, *The Controversy over Capitalism: Studies*

in the Social Philosophy of the Russian Populists (Oxford: OUP, 1969); Carlos Moscoso Perea, *El Populismo en America Latina* (Madrid: Centro de Estudios Constitucionales, 1990); David Rock (ed.) *Argentina in the Twentieth Century* (London: University of Pittsburgh 1975); Gavin Kitching, *Development and Underdevelopment in Historical Perspective: Populism, Nationalism and Industrialisation* (London: Routledge, 1989); Ernest Gellner and Ghita Ionescu (eds) *Populism: Its Meaning and National Characteristics* (London: Macmillan, 1969); Gino Germani, *Authoritarianism, Fascism and National Populism*, New Brunswick: Transaction, 1978).

3. Ernesto Laclau, *Politics and Ideology in Marxist Theory: Capitalism–Fascism–Populism* (London: Verso, 1977), pp. 143–98.

4. *Ibid.*, p. 175.

5. Kitching, *Development and Underdevelopment*, pp. 19–22.

6. Hamza Alavi, 'Populism' in Tom Bottomore (ed.) *A Dictionary of Marxist Thought* (Oxford: Blackwell, 1991), p. 432.

7. See for example Ervand Abrahamian, *Khomeinism: Essays on the Islamic Republic* (London: I.B. Tauris, 1993); Fred Halliday, 'The Iranian Revolution: Uneven Development and Religious Populism' in Fred Halliday and Hamza Alavi (eds) *State and Ideology in the Middle East and Pakistan* (New York: Monthly Review Press, 1988), pp. 31–63; Val Moghadam, 'The Revolution and the Regime: Populism, Islam and the State in Iran', *Social Compass*, 36:4 (1989), pp. 415–50.

8. Asef Bayat, 'Labour and Democracy' in Amirahmadi and Parvin, *Post-Revolutionary Iran*; Asef Bayat, *Workers and Revolution*; Saeed Rahnema 'Work Councils in Iran', *Economics and Industrial Democracy*, 13, pp. 69–94 (1992). For a brief account, see Shaul Bakhash, *Reign of the Ayatollahs*, pp. 176–7; Moaddel, 'Class Struggles' p. 324.

9. Rahnema, 'Work Councils'; Moaddel, 'Class Struggles'; Bayat, 'Labour and Democracy'.

10. *Kayhan*, 25 Bahman 1357 (15 February 1979), *Kayhan* 27 Bahman 1357 (17 February 1979).

11. Rahnema, 'Work Councils in Iran', pp. 72–3 and 85.

12. Bayat, *Street Politics*, pp. 109–31.

13. Mehrdad Haghayeghi, 'Agrarian Reform Problems in Post-Revolutionary Iran' *Middle East Studies*, 26 (1990), p. 36. See also Bakhash, *Reign of the Ayatollahs*, pp. 197–201, and Moaddel, 'Class Struggles'.

14. *Kayhan*, 30 Bahman 1357 (20 February 1979).

15. See Eliz Sanasarian, *The Women's Rights Movement in Iran* (New York: Praeger, 1982); Farah Azari, 'The Post-Revolutionary Women's Movement in Iran' in Farah Azari (ed.) *Women of Iran: The*

Conflict with Fundamentalist Islam (London: Ithaca, 1983); Guity Nashat 'Women in the Ideology of the Islamic Republic' in Guity Nashat (ed.) *Women and Revolution in Iran* (Boulder: Westview, 1983). Haideh Moghissi, *Populism and Feminism in Iran: Women's Struggle in a Male-Defined Revolutionary Movement* (London and Basingstoke: Macmillan, 1994); Mahnaz Afkhami 'Women in Post-Revolutionary Iran: A Feminist Perspective' in Mahnaz Afkhami and Erika Friedl (eds) *In the Eye of the Storm* (London: Tauris, 1994).

16. Afkhami, 'Women in Post-Revolutionary Iran', p. 12.

17. *Kayhan*, 16 Esfand 1357 (March 1979). See also Azari 'The Post-Revolutionary women's Movement in Iran' pp. 194–5; Sanasarian, *The Women's Rights Movement in Iran* p. 125.

18. See Richard Cottam, 'Nationalism and Islamic Revolution in Iran', *Canadian Review of Studies in Nationalism*, 9:2 (1982); Fred Halliday, 'Iranian Foreign Policy since 1979' in Juan Cole and Nikki Keddie (eds) *Shi'ism and Social Protest*, pp. 88–107.

19. Ruhollah Khomeini, *Sahifeh-e Nur*, Volume 10, pp. 57–8, 4 Aban 1358 (October 1979), It must be noted that Khomeini's early speeches indicate a use of the 'East' in the sense of the 'Orient' and refer to the need for the latter to free itself from the domination of the West. Later this meaning becomes less frequent as the rhetoric of independence from 'East and West' – the two superpower blocs – comes to prevail.

20. Abrahamian, *Khomeinism*, pp. 111–31. Halliday, 'The Iranian Revolution and Great Power Politics' in Keddie and Gasiorowski (eds) *Neither East Nor West (New Haven, Yale University Press, 1990)*, p. 248.

21. British Broadcasting Corporation, *Summary of World Broadcasts (Middle East)* – hereafter BBC SWB ME – 7215/A/9, 22 December 1982.

22. Cottam, 'Nationalism and Islamic Revolution in Iran'; Halliday, 'Iranian Foreign Policy since 1979' in Cole and Keddie (eds) *Shi'ism and Social Protest*, pp. 88–107.

23. Khomeini, *Sahifeh-e Nur*, Volume 13, p. 195, 1359 [1980].

24. Zubaida, *Islam the People and the State*, p. 33.

25. For specific reference to the role of these issues in the discourse of the Revolution, see Shaul Bakhash, 'Islam and Social Justice in Iran' in Martin Kramer (ed.) *Shi'ism, Resistance and Revolution* (Boulder: Westview, 1987), pp. 95–116.

26. Abrahamian, 'Khomeini: Fundamentalist or Populist', pp. 112–13.

27. See for instance *mataleb va mowzu'at va rahnemudha-ye eqtesadi dar bayanat-e Imam Khomeini* [Economic issues, matters and guidance in the speeches of Imam Khomeini] (Tehran: Moaseseh-e motale'at va pazhoheshha-ye bazargani, 1370 [1991]).

28. These included Seyyed Mahmood Taleqani, *Islam and Ownership*; Abolhasan Bani-Sadr, *Eqtesad-e towhidi* (1979).

29. Khomeini, *Sahifeh-e Nur*, Volume 10, p. 128, 1358 [1979].

30. Houchang Chehabi, *Iranian Politics and Religious Modernism* (Ithaca: Cornell, 1990), pp. 214 and 245.

31. Bahman Nirumand and Keywan Daddjou, *Mit Gott für die Macht: Eine politische Biographie des Ayatollah Khomeini* (Hamburg: Rowohlt, 1987), p. 221.

32. *Kayhan*, 15 Esfand 1357 (March 1979), *Kayhan*, 30 Ordibehesht 1358 (May 1979).

33. Halliday, 'The Iranian Revolution' p. 248. Nikki Keddie notes that Muslim students groups abroad associated themselves with the National Front particularly in France and venerated both Mosaddeq and Khomeini, *Roots of Revolution*, p 236.

34. Parsa, *Social Origins*, pp. 120–1.

35. Phil Marshall, *Revolution and Counter Revolution* (London: Bookmarks, 1988), p. 49. See also Parsa, *Social Origins*, p. 144; Moaddel 'Class Struggles', p. 323.

36. Moghadam, 'The Left and Revolution', pp. 27–8.

37. James Petras, 'Reflections on the Iranian Revolution' in *Capitalist and Socialist Crises of the Late Twentieth Century* (Rowman and Allanhead, 1983), p. 291.

38. The background to this organisation can be found in Ervand Abrahamian, *Radical Islam: The Iranian Mojahedin* (London: Tauris, 1989). Although Abrahamian provides an excellent account of the ideas and policies of the Mojahedin leadership as well as the backgrounds of members, his research makes no mention of the impact of international factors on the group, in particular, their sources of inspiration or resources.

39. Massoud Rajavi, Mojahedin leader, in *Kayhan* 7 Esfand 1357 (February 1979).

40. *Kayhan*, 21 Bahman 1357 (11 February 1979).

41. *Kayhan*, 25 Bahman 1937 (15 February 1979).

42. Abrahamian, *Radical Islam*, pp. 189–97.

43. An excellent analysis of the Tudeh Party strategy and influences is given by Maziar Behrooz, *The Iranian Communist Movement 1953–1983: Why Did the Left Fail?* (PhD Thesis, UCLA, 1994).

44. *Ibid. pp.* 340–54. See also Moghadam, 'The Iranian Left', p. 34; Sami Zubaida, *Islam The People and The State*, p. 73. Richard Cottam gives an alternative more 'pragmatic' explanation for the Tudeh strategy. See 'US and Soviet Responses to Islamic Political Militancy' in Keddie and Gasiorowski (eds) *Neither East Nor West*, p. 278.

45. *Nameh-e Mardom,* 25 May 1980 cited in Behrooz, *Iranian Communist Movement,* pp. 351–2.

46. *Kayhan,* 21 Esfand 1357 (March 1979).

47. *Kar* 90, 23 December 1980, cited by Behrooz, *Iranian Communist Movement,* p. 316.

48. Khomeini, *Sahifeh-e Nur,* Volume 9, pp. 10–11, 10 Shahrivar 1358 (August 1979).

49. Khomeini, *Sahifeh-e Nur,* Volume 9, p. 60, 17 Shahrivar 1358 (September 1979).

50. See 'American Plan for the Occupation of the Persian Gulf', *Kayhan,* 19 Khordad 1358 (June 1979); 'Shah is Planning a Coup d'Etat', *Kayhan,* 5 Tir 1358 (June 1979), 'Shah's conspiracy against Iran', *Kayhan,* 7 Mordad 1358 (July 1979), 'American, Israeli, Egyptian conspiracy for the overthrow of the Iranian regime', *Kayhan,* 5 Mehr 1358 (September 1979).

51. *Kayhan,* 30 Bahman 1357 (20 February 1979); *Kayhan,* 2 Esfand 1357 (22 February 1979); *Kayhan,* 23 Esfand 1357 (March 1979).

52. *Kayhan,* 24 Esfand 1357 (March 1979).

53. *Kayhan,* 31 Ordibehesht 1358, 1 Khordad 1358, 2 Khordad 1358 (May 1979).

54. Khomeini, *Sahifeh-e Nur,* Volume 10, p. 238, 6 Azar 1358 (November 1979).

55. Gary Sick, *All Fall Down: America's Fateful Encounter with Iran* (London: I.B. Tauris, 1985) pp. 148–9 and 227–9; James Bill, *The Eagle and the Lion,* p. 290.

56. *Kayhan,* 1 Khordad 1358 (May 1979).

57. Maziar Behrooz, 'Trends in the Foreign Policy of the Islamic Republic', in Keddie and Gasiorowski (eds) *Neither East Nor West* pp. 16–20.

58. *Kayhan,* 12 Aban 1358 (3 November 1979).

59. *Kayhan,* 13 Aban 1358 (4 November 1979).

60. *Kayhan,* 14 Aban 1358 (5 November 1979).

61. It appears that news of the Bazargan–Brzezinski meeting was transmitted to the Islamic Republic Party by the Tudeh Party. This is corroborated by Chehabi's claim that the Tudeh's Algerian comrades were probably the originators of this message. H. E. Chehabi, *Iranian Politics,* p. 272.

62. Russell Leigh Moses, *Freeing the Hostages: Reconsidering US–Iranian Negotiations and Soviet Policy 1979–81* (Pittsburgh: University of Pittsburgh Press, 1996), pp. 80–2.

63. Sick, *All Fall Down,* p. 191.

64. Keddie, *Roots of Revolution,* p. 262.

65. Khomeini, *Sahifeh-e Nur,* Volume 10, p. 242, 7 Azar 1358 (November 1979).

66. Khomeini, *Sahifeh-e Nur*, Volume 10, pp. 259–60, 15 Azar 1358 (December 1979).
67. *Kayhan*, 16 Khordad 1358 (June 1979).
68. BBC SWB ME/6407/A/10, 29 April 1980.
69. *Kayhan*, 26 Khordad 358 (June 1979).
70. Farah Azari, 'Post-revolutionary Women's Movement', p. 211.
71. Guity Nashat, 'Women in the Ideology of the Islamic Republic', pp. 97–9, 119; Azari, 'Post-Revolutionary Women's Movement', p. 207.
72. Cited by Nashat, 'Women in the Ideology of the Islamic Republic', p. 121.
73. *Ibid.*, pp. 153–69.
74. Azari, 'Post-Revolutionary Women's Movement', 205.
75. Quoted in Nashat, p. 179.
76. Khomeini, *Sahifeh-e Nur*, Volume 10, p. 42, 2 Aban 1358 (October 1979).
77. Khomeini, *Sahifeh-e Nur*, Volume 12, p. 65, 10 Ordibehesht 1359 (April 1980).
78. Khomeini, *Sahifeh-e Nur*, Volume 8, p. 230, 17 Mordad 1358 (August 1979).
79. Khomeini, *Sahifeh-e Nur*, Volume 9, pp. 218–19, 5 Mehr 1358 (September 1979).
80. Khomeini, *Sahifeh-e Nur*, Volume 9, p. 245, 10 Mehr 1358 (October 1979).
81. Moaddel, 'Class Struggles', p. 327.
82. *Kayhan*, 17 Ordibehesht 1358 (May 1979).
83. Khomeini, *Sahifeh-e Nur*, Volume 10, p. 59, 4 Aban 1358 (October 1979).
84. On the programmes of the radical faction, see Manouchehr Parvin and Majid Taghavi, 'Land Tenure Under the Monarchy and under the Islamic Republic' in Amirahmadi and Parvin (eds) *Post-Revolutionary Iran*. See also Haghayeghi, 'Agrarian Reform'.
85. See the incident of the murder in April 1979 of four Fedai leaders cited by Azari, *Women of Iran*, p. 199.
86. For the activities of landowners against the radical policies of the government, see Haghayeghi, 'Agrarian Reform', pp. 40–3; Moaddel, 'Class Struggles', p. 326; Bakhash, *Reign of the Ayatollahs*, pp. 203–6.
87. Khomeini, *Sahifeh-e Nur*, Volume 10, pp. 135–8, 14 Aban 1358 (November 1979).
88. Parvin and Taghavi, 'Land Tenure', p. 176.
89. Bayat, *Street Politics*, p. 126.
90. *Ibid.*, p. 127.
91. *Ibid.*, p. 67.

92. Khomeini, *Sahifeh-e Nur*, Volume 10, p. 141, 14 Aban 1358 (November 1979).

93. See *Kayhan*, 19 Farvardin 1359, *Kayhan*, 23 Farvardin 1359, *Kayhan* 25 Farvardin 1359 (April 1980).

94. BBC SWB ME/6406/A/8, 28 April 1980.

95. BBC SWB ME/6480/A/6, 25 July 1980.

96. For broadcasts of the 'National Voice of Iran' in this period, see BBC SWB ME, various.

97. BBC SWB ME/6323/A/7, 19 January 1980.

98. BBC SWB ME/6488/A/2, 4 August 1980.

99. *Kayhan*, 27 Bahman 1358 (February 1980).

100. See for example Hojjatoleslam Ali Khamenei's Friday prayer sermon, *Kayhan*, 9 Farvardin 1359 (March 1980).

101. *Kayhan*, various.

102. Islamic Republic Party statement in BBC SWB ME/6817/A/7, 2 September 1981.

103. See list of broadcasts of 'The Voice of the Islamic Republic of Iran' radio in various languages in *Imam* (November 1980).

104. For more details on the *Pasdaran*, see Chapter 5.

105. This text appears as 'The text of the constitution and information organisation of the Mehdi Hashemi Group', as a document appendixed to the political memoirs of the Information Minister Reyshahri, published after this group was repressed by the government following their revelation of the secret negotiations with the United States. Mohammad Reyshahri, *Khaterat-e Siasi*: (Tehran, 1369 [1990]), pp. 149–53.

106. For a list of these conferences, see Wilfried Buchta, *Die Iranische Schia und die Islamische Einheit: 1979–1996* (PhD Thesis, Rheinis-chen-Friedrich-Wilhelms University, Cologne, 1996), p. 65.

107. BBC SWB ME/7563/A/4, 10 February 1984.

108. See resolutions of Tehran Rally in BBC SWB ME/6690/A/10, 3 April 1981; *Pasdaran* declaration of support for the Irish struggle BBC SWB ME/6713/A/8, 2 May 1981; Ali Khamenei voicing support for Afro-Americans BBC SWB ME/7810/A/5, 26 November 1984.

109. For a historical background of these organisations and the perceptions of Iranian involvement, see Hanna Batatu, 'Shi'i Organisations in Iraq: Al-Dawah al-Islamiyah and al-Mujahdin' in Cole and Keddie, *Shi'ism and Social Protest*, pp. 179–200.

110. *Kayhan*, 12 Aban 1358 (November 1979).

111. *Kayhan*, 24 Azar 1358 (December 1979).

112. *Kayhan*, 19 Farvardin 1359 (April 1980).

113. BBC SWB ME/6338/A/8, 6 February 1980.
114. Batatu, 'Shi'i Organisations', p. 590; Chibli Mallat, 'Religious militancy in Contemporary Iraq', *Third World Quarterly*, 10:2 (1988).
115. Joyce N. Wiley, *The Islamic Movement of Iraqi Shi'is* (London: Lynne Rienner, 1992), p. 53.
116. For the full text of this statement, see *Ibid.*, Appendix 4.
117. *Kayhan*, 30 Farvardin 1359 (April 1980).
118. BBC SWB ME/6403/A/8, 24 April 1980.
119. For instances of declared mutual support and Yasser Arafat's presence in Tehran, see *Kayhan*, 30 Bahman 1357 (20 February 1979), *Kayhan*, 2 Esfand 1357 (22 February 1979), *Kayhan*, 23 Esfand 1357 (March 1979).
120. BBC SWB ME/7030/A/3 19 May 1982.
121. For a background to the rise of the radical Islamic movement in Lebanon and the impact of the Iranian Revolution, see Magnus Ranstorp, *Hizb'allah in Lebanon: The Politics of the Western Hostage Crisis* (Basingstoke and London: Macmillan, 1997), pp. 25–59.
122. Jalaleddin Madani, *Iran-e islami dar barabar-e sahyunism* (Tehran, 1362 [1983]).
123. *Ashna'i ba bonyad-e shahid-e enqelab-e islami* [Introduction to the Islamic Republic Martyrs Foundation] (Tehran, 1365 [1986]), pp. 40–80.
124. BBC SWB ME/6381/A/11, 27 March 1980.
125. Joseph Kostiner, 'Shi'i Unrest in the Gulf' in Martin Kramer (ed.) *Shi'ism, Resistance and Revolution* (Boulder: Westview, 1987), pp. 173–86.
126. *Ibid.*, pp. 178–9.
127. BBC SWB ME/6357/A/7, 28 February 1980, SWB ME/6465/A/7, 8 July 1980.
128. BBC SWB ME/6381/A/11, 27 March 1980.
129. Olivier Roy, *Islam and Resistance in Afghanistan* (Cambridge: Cambridge University Press, 1990), p. 52.
130. *Ibid.*, pp. 139–44. See also Asta Olesen, *Islam and Politics in Afghanistan* (Richmond: Curzon Press, 1995), p. 285.

4. International containment of the Islamic Republic

1. James Bill, *The Eagle and the Lion: The Tragedy of American-Iranian Relations* (New Haven and London: Yale University Press, 1988), pp. 276–93; Gary Sick, *All Fall Down: America's Fateful Encounter with Iran* (London: I.B. Tauris, 1985).
2. US Library of Congress, Congressional Research Service, 'Petroleum Imports from the Persian Gulf', Issue Brief 79046 (20

February 1980); US Library of Congress, Congressional Research Service, 'An Economic Embargo of Iran', Report No.80-4E (13 December 1979).

3. Gary Sick (National Security Council staff member for the region during the hostage crisis), 'Military Options and Constraints' in Warren Christopher et al. (eds) *American Hostages in Iran: The Conduct of a Crisis* (New Haven and London: Council on Foreign Relations/Yale University Press, 1985), pp. 144–72.

4. This formed part of the NSC guidelines devised on November 6, which were not intended as declaratory policy but as policy boundaries for Carter advisers in developing US strategy. See Sick, 'Military Options', pp. 146–7.

5. *Ibid.*, p. 168.

6. This was a major topic for discussion during Secretary of State Cyrus Vance's visit to the UK, France, Italy and FRG prior to the NATO meeting in December. See US Library of Congress, Congressional Research Service, 'An Economic Embargo of Iran', Report No.80-4E (13 December 1979).

7. See *The Declassified Documents Quarterly Catalogue*, Volume 23 (1997), No. 0208. US Library of Congress, Congressional Research Service, 'Iran: Confrontation with the US', Issue Brief No. 79118 (27 February 1980 – updated).

8. One instance was the concern of the Schmidt government in Germany as noted by Zbigniew Brzezinski in his 21 January 1980 memo to Carter. See *Declassified Documents Quarterly Catalogue*, Volume 22 (1996), No. 2864.

9. See 'draft cable to allies' telegram to Bonn, London, Paris, Rome, Tokyo and Ottowa from Washington dated 25 March 1980. The *Declassified Documents Quarterly Catalogue*, Volume 23 (1997), No. 2872.

10. Sick, 'Military Option', p. 153.

11. US Library of Congress, Congressional Research Service, The Iran Hostage Crisis: A Chronology of Daily Developments (1981) and United States Economic Sanctions imposed against specific foreign countries 1979 to present (1988); *The Declassified Documents Quarterly Catalogue*, Volume 23 (1997), No. 2584.

12. Dilip Hiro, *Iran Under the Ayatollahs* (London: Routledge, 1987), pp. 323–4, for German British Italian and French relations.

13. See US Library of Congress, Congressional Research Service, Number 207 and 208 and US Library of Congress, Congressional Research Service, Number 256.

14. This is due largely to the selectivity in declassification of documents. For example US diplomatic strategy towards Iran during

the hostage crisis is set out in a non-dated document declassified in 1997. However, pages 5 through 12 of this document are completely sanitised. See *The Declassified Documents Quarterly Catalogue*, Volume 23 (1997), Number 2585.

15. Bakhash, *Reign of the Ayatollahs*, pp. 149, pp. 175–7.

16. Mahvash Alerassool, *Freezing Assets: The USA and the Most Effective Economic Sanction* (London: Macmillan, 1993), p. 185.

17. *Ibid.* p. 26 and pp. 36–7.

18. Roy Assersohn, *The Biggest Deal* (London: Methuen, 1982), pp. 197–214.

19. 'US-Iran dispute over hostage funds deepens', *Financial Times*, 29 October 1982; 'US cautious on hopes of Iran assets deal,' *Financial Times*, 30 December 1986. Alerassool estimated that of the total $14bn assets Iran was able to recover only a total of $4bn, see *Freezing Assets*.

20. Barry Rubin, *Cauldron of Turmoil* (New York: HBJ, 1992), p. 58.

21. See memorandum dated 13 March 1980, *The Declassified Documents Quarterly Catalogue*, Volume 22 (1996), No.2895.

22. Quoted in Rubin, *Cauldron of Turmoil*, p. 58.

23. Gary Hufbauer, Jefferey Schott and Kimberely Elliott, *Economic Sanctions Reconsidered: Supplemental Case Histories, Case 80–2, US vs. Iraq* (Washington: Institute for International Economics, 1990), pp. 524–7.

24. See US Library of Congress, Congressional Research Service, 'An Economic Embargo of Iran', Report No.80-4E, 13 December 1979.

25. US Library of Congress, Congressional Research Service, 'Iraq: An overview of current issues and policies', Brief 80214 (1 December 1980, original dated 16 May 1980). See also US Library of Congress, Congressional Research Service, 'Iran: Confrontation with the US', Issue Brief 79118 (5 December 1980 – updated).

26. Amazia Baram, 'The Impact of Khomeini's Revolution on the Shi'i Movement of Iraq' in David Menashri (ed.) *The Iranian Revolution and the Muslim World* (Boulder and San Francisco: Westview, 1990); Hanna Batatu, 'Iraq's Underground Shi'i Movements: Characteristics, Causes and prospects', *Middle East Journal*, 35 (Autumn 1981), pp. 578–94; Michael Hudson, 'The Islamic Factor in Syrian and Iraqi Politics' in James Piscatori, *Islam in the Political Process* (Cambridge: Cambridge University Press, 1983), pp. 73–97; Chibli Mallat, 'Religious Militancy in Contemporary Iraq', *Third World Quarterly*, 10:2 (April 1988), pp. 699–729.

27. Joyce Wiley, *The Islamic Movement of Iraqi Shi'is* (London: Lynne Rienner, 1992), p. 58.

28. Mehrdad Khonsari, *The National Movement of the Iranian Resistance 1979–1991: The Role of a Banned Opposition Movement in International Politics* (PhD Thesis, LSE, June 1995).

29. *Ibid.*, p. 138.

30. W. Thom Workman, *The Social Origins of the Iran–Iraq War* (London: Lynne Rienner, 1994), pp. 87–113.

31. On the purges in the army, see William F. Hickman, *Ravaged and Reborn: The Iranian Army* (Washington: Brookings Institution, 1982), pp. 8–18.

32. Andrew T. Parasiliti, 'Iraq's Military Containment of Iran', *Journal of South Asian and Middle Eastern Studies*, 13:1 (1989), pp. 128–45.

33. Ruhollah Ramazani, 'Shi'ism in the Persian Gulf' in J. Cole and N. Keddie (eds) *Shi'ism and Social Protest* (New Haven and London: Yale University Press, 1986), pp. 30–54.

34. Estimated Shi'i populations in the Gulf states are: Iraq 60 per cent, Bahrain 70 per cent, Kuwait 24 per cent, UAE 18 per cent, Qatar 16 per cent, Saudi Arabia 8 per cent, Oman 4 per cent. See Shahram Chubin and Charles Tripp, *Iran and Iraq at War* (London: Tauris, 1988), p. 275.

35. Jacob Goldberg, 'The Shi'i Minority in Saudi Arabia' in Cole and Keddie, *Shi'ism and Social Protest*, pp. 230–46.

36. Shahram Chubin and Charles Tripp, *Iran–Saudi Arabia Relations and Regional Order*, Adelphi Paper 304 (London: IISS, 1996), p. 16.

37. See James P. Piscatori, 'Ideological Politics in Saudi Arabia' in James Piscatori (ed.) *Islam in the Political Process* (Cambridge: Cambridge University Press, 1983) especially pp. 63–7.

38. In 1986 Ramazani estimated the Shi'i to constitute 40–60 per cent of the oil workers while Goldberg equated them with 7000 of ARAMCO's Saudi workers (35 per cent of total workforce). See Ramazani, 'Shi'ism', p. 45 and Goldberg, 'Shi'i Minority', p. 242.

39. Quoted in Joseph A. Kechichian, 'The Gulf Cooperation Council: Containing the Iranian Revolution', *Journal of South Asian and Middle Eastern Studies*, 13:1 (1989), pp. 146–65.

40. Ramazani, 'Shi'ism', pp. 48–52.

41. 'The shadow of Khomeini', *Financial Times*, 14 December 1983, 'Iranian threats revive Saudi insecurity', *Financial Times*, 4 August 1987.

42. Erik Peterson, *The Gulf Cooperation Council: Search for Unity in a Dynamic Region* (Boulder and London: Westview, 1988), pp. 76–9.

43. Chubin and Tripp (eds) *Iran and Iraq*, p. 163.

44. Peterson, *Gulf Cooperation Council*, pp. 82–3.

45. Gerd Nonneman, *Iraq, The Gulf States and the War: A Changing Relationship 1980–1986 and Beyond* (London: Ithaca, 1986), p. 37.

46. Chubin and Tripp (eds) *Iran and Iraq*, p. 165.
47. Peterson, *Gulf Cooperation Council*, pp. 123–4.
48. Nonneman, *Iraq*, pp. 85–92.
49. Ramazani, 'Shi'ism', p. 43.
50. 'Iraq Asks for $7bn as Oil Exports Decline', *Financial Times*, 31 January 1983; US Library of Congress, Congressional Research Service, 'The Iran–Iraq War', Issue Brief No. 88060 (15 July 1988).
51. 'Saudis in $6bn Oil Deal With Iraq', *Financial Times*, 9 February 1983, 'Saudis to Aid France with $2bn Deposit', *Financial Times*, 8 December 1982.
52. Congressional Research Service, 'The Iran–Iraq War', Issue Brief No. 88060, 15 July 1988.
53. Nonneman, *Iraq*, pp. 102–7.
54. 'Saudi Cash Tempts Iran's Only Ally', *Financial Times*, 23 July 1987.
55. Dilip Hiro, *The Longest War* (London: Grafton, 1989), p. 159.
56. Bassam Tibi, 'The Iranian Revolution and the Arabs: The Quest for Islamic Identity and the Search for an Islamic System of Government', *Arab Studies Quarterly*, 8:1, pp. 29–44. See also Johannes Jansen, 'Echoes of the Iranian Revolution in the Writings of Egyptian Muslims' in David Menashri (ed.) *The Iranian Revolution and the Muslim World* (Boulder and San Francisco: Westview, 1990).
57. Nader Entessar, 'The Lion and the Sphinx: Iranian Egyptian Relations in Perspective' in Hooshang Amirahmadi and Nader Entessar, *Iran and the Arab World* (London: Macmillan, 1993), pp. 161–79.
58. Eric Hooglund, 'The Policy of the Reagan Administration toward Iran' in Keddie and Gasiorowski (eds) *Neither East Nor West*; Steven Emerson deals with the Arab-centrist tendency in *The American House of Saud: The Secret Petrodollar Connection* (New York: Franklin Watts, 1985).
59. Fred Halliday, 'The Iranian Revolution and Great Power Politics: Components of the First Decade' in Keddie and Gasiorowski (eds) *Neither East Nor West*, pp. 255–6.
60. United States Department of State, Bureau of Public Affairs, Statement by George Shultz, Current Policy No.899: Iran and US Policy (Washington, D.C.: GPO, 1986).
61. In 1985 a National Intelligence Council memo warned of Soviet inroads after Khomeini. Concerns regarding scenarios for Soviet invasion especially in the case of an Iranian victory in the war or post-Khomeini instability continued to be voiced in mid-1987. See US Library of Congress, Congressional Research Service, 'Soviet policy towards Iran and the strategic balance in South West Asia' (19 June 1987).

62. *Ibid.*
63. See US National Security Archive, *The Chronology: The Documented Day-by-day Account of the Secret Military Assistance to Iran and the Contras.* A brief analysis is given by James A. Bill, 'The US Overture to Iran: 1985–1986' in Keddie and Gasiorowski (eds) *Neither East Nor West.*
64. US Library of Congress, Congressional Research Service, 'The Iran Iraq War: Implications and Options for the United States' (17 January 1983).
65. Speech to the Foreign Policy Association, New York, quoted by Chubin and Tripp (eds) *Iran and Iraq*, p. 208.
66. US Library of Congress, Congressional Research Service 'US–Iraq Relations' (30 July 1986).
67. For a detailed account of American, but also British, involvement in the war and arming and support of Iraq, see Alan Friedman, *Spider's Web: Bush, Saddam, Thatcher and the Decade of Deceit* (London: Faber, 1993). See also Mark Phythian, *Arming Iraq: How the US and Britain Secretly Built Saddam's War Machine* (Boston: Northeastern University Press, 1997).
68. Rubin suggests that Iraqi courting of Washington was achieved through Kuwaiti and Saudi lobbying, *Cauldron of Turmoil*, pp. 80–2.
69. Though Washington maintained the notion of neutrality in the war, the Baghdad regime admitted direct American assistance. See 'US Manned AWACs Providing Help to Iraq', *Financial Times*, 12 May 1984. See also 'Iraq Seeks International Help to End War', *Guardian*, 14 May 1984.
70. United States, Department of State, Bureau of Public Affairs, *Current Policy No.324: Dangerous Illusions and Real Choices on AWACS* (Washington D.C.: GPO, 5 October 1981).
71. Hiro, *Longest War*, p. 160.
72. US Library of Congress, Congressional Research Service, 'US–Iraq Relations' (30 July 1986).
73. Geoffrey Kemp, *Forever Enemies? American Policy and the Islamic Republic of Iran* (Washington: Carnegie, 1994), pp. 105–6.
74. Mehrdad Khonsari, 'National Movement of Iranian Resistance', pp. 205–6.
75. 'Survey: Arab Banking and Finance', *Financial Times*, 3 October 1983.
76. 'More Oil for Goods Deals', *Financial Times*, 1 April 1985.
77. This dispute was finally resolved in 1986 after an attempt to normalise relations due to French attempts to secure the release of hostages in Lebanon. See 'France and Iran Make Progress in $1bn Loan Row', *Financial Times*, 30 October 1986.

78. Although the Islamic Republic does not publish data regarding foreign debt, UK Minister of State for Foreign and Commonwealth Affairs David Mellor gave evidence to the Foreign Affairs Committee on 15 June 1988 of these remaining debts. See House of Commons, 'The Iran Iraq Conflict' (1988).

79. Anthony Sampson, *The Arms Bazaar* (Sevenoaks: Coronet, 1988) p. 348.

80. For an interesting analysis of the impact on Egypt, see Asef Bayat, 'Revolutionary Iran and Egypt' in Nikki Keddie and Rudi Matthee (eds) *Iran and the Surrounding World* (Washington: University of Washington Press, 2002).

81. Wilfried Buchta, 'The Failed Pan-Islamic Programme' in Nikki Keddie and Rudi Matthee (eds) *Iran and the Surrounding World* (Washington: University of Washington Press, 2002).

82. For the 'Orientalist' account of Islamic movements, see Bernard Lewis, 'The Roots of Muslim Rage', *Atlantic Monthly* (September 1990). See also Huntington, *Clash of Civilisations*.

83. See the various essays in John Esposito, *Political Islam* and *The Iranian Revolution: Its Global Impact*.

84. Joyce Wiley, *The Islamic Movement of Iraqi Shi'as* (Boulder: Lynne Rienner, 1992), p. 143.

85. Mamoun Fandy, 'From Confrontation to Creative Resistance: The Shi'as Oppositional Discourse in Saudi Arabia', *Critique* (Fall 1996), pp. 3–27.

86. Olivier Roy, *The Failure of Political Islam*, translated by Carol Volk (Cambridge, Mass.: Harvard, 1994).

87. Vali Nasr, 'The Iranian Revolution and Changes in Islamism in Pakistan, India and Afghanistan' argues that the impact of the Iranian Revolution in South Asia was to lead to worsening sectarian divisions.

88. For a list of the different Islamist parties in the Afghan resistance, see Asta Oleson, *Islam and Politics in Afghanistan* (Richmond: Curzon, 1995), pp. 284–5.

89. For the influence of international actors in Afghan politics, see Roy, *Islam and Resistance*, pp. 228–34.

90. Hanna Batatu, 'Iraq's Underground Shi'a Movements', *Middle East Journal*, 35 (Autumn 1981), p. 593.

91. Wiley, *Islamic Movement*, pp. 60–1.

92. Andrew Parasaliti, 'Iraq's Military Containment of Iran', *Journal of South Asian and Middle Eastern Studies*, 13:1 (1989).

93. Wiley, *Islamic Movement*, p. 63.

94. BBC SWB ME/8497/A/6 20 February 1987. See also Rafsanjani's

calls for the expansion of the activities of SAIRI, BBC SWB ME/85333/A/9 3 April 1987.
95. Wiley, *Islamic Movement*, p. 63.

5. Populism, war and the state

1. 'Holy alliance' is used in this context by Eric Rouleau, 'The War and the Struggle for the State', *Middle East Report* (July/August 1981), pp. 3–8.
2. BBC SWB ME/6637/A/1,2, 31 January 1981.
3. BBC SWB ME/7233/A/6, 17 January 1982.
4. See also *Ministry of Islamic Guidance, Views on War: A Selection of Articles from International Press Concerning the Iraq–Iran War* (Tehran, 1982).
5. See *Imam* (November 1981), p. 14.; William Quandt, 'Reactions of the Arab Gulf States' in Ali E. Hillal-Dessouki, *The Iran–Iraq War: Issues of Conflict* (Princeton University, 1981).
6. See Rafsanjani's speeches BBC SWB ME/7205/A/1, 10 December 1982, and BBC SWB ME/7228/A/10, 11 January 1983.
7. Iranian Foreign Ministry BBC SWB ME/7580/A/7, 1 March 1984.
8. BBC SWB ME/7270/A/2, 1 March 1983.
9. Islamic Republic News Agency revelation of documents to show US deliveries of chemical weapons in January, BBC SWB ME/7687/A/6, 5 July 1984. British arms sales are discussed in BBC SWB ME/7555/A/2, 1 February 1984; BBC SWB ME/7625/A/8, 24 April 1984; BBC SWB ME/7729/A/8, 23 August 1984; BBC SWB ME/8062/A/2, 21 September 1985. Condemnation of regional states BBC SWB ME/7812/A/1, 28 November 1984.
10. BBC SWB ME/7422/A/9, 26 August 1983.
11. *Jomhuri-ye Eslami*, 2 September 1985; BBC SWB ME/8047/A/1; 4 September 1985; BBC SWB ME/8201/A/7, 7 March 1986; 8387/A/2, 11 October 1986.
12. BBC SWB ME/7643/A/1.
13. *Islamic Revolution's Guards Corps: A Glance at Two Years of War* (Tehran: Political office, 1982), p. 20, p. 133.
14. *Imam*, November 1980, p. 15.
15. Foreign Minister Velayati criticised the Security Council for unilateral decisions in favour of Iraq. BBC SWB 7765/A/11, 4 October 1984. Further criticism of Security Council: BBC SWB 8187/A/5, 19 February 1986; Foreign Ministry statement BBC SWB 8194/A/5, 27 February 1986; Foreign Ministry criticism of UN Resolution BBC SWB 8387/A/1, 11 October 1986.

16. BBC SWB ME/6669/A/7, 10 March 1981.
17. *Islamic Revolution's Guards Corps: A Glance at Two Years of War* , p. 131, pp. 142–3.
18. *Ibid.*, pp. 37–9.
19. *Ibid.*, p. 21.
20. BBC SWB ME/7035/A/6, 25 May 1982.
21. BBC SWB ME/7059/A/7, 23 June 1982.
22. Arabic commentary BBC SWB ME/7120/A/3, 2 September 1982. See also BBC SWB ME/7074/A/2,10 July 1982.
23. Khomeini, *Sahifeh-e Nur*, Volume 13, p. 201, 22 Aban 1359 (November 1980).
24. BBC SWB ME/7358/A/6, 13 June 1983,.
25. BBC SWB ME/7079/A/10, 16 July 1982.
26. BBC SWB ME/6538/A/3, 2 October 1980.
27. BBC SWB ME/7157/A/3, 15 October 1982.
28. BBC SWB ME/7299/A/9, 5 April 1983.
29. BBC SWB 7347/A/3, 31 May 1983. See also BBC SWB ME/7408/A/7, 10 August 1983, ME/7414/A/9, 17 August 1983.
30. BBC SWB 7666/A/5, 11 June 1984.
31. BBC SWB 8562/A/11, 8 May 1987.
32. BBC SWB 8458/A/13, 6 January 1987.
33. Circular of Ministry of Education and Training BBC SWB 8542/A/11, 14 April 1987.
34. Asghar Schirazi, *Islamic Development Policy: The Agrarian Question in Iran* (London: Lynne Rienner, 1993), pp. 147–61.
35. BBC SWB 8285/A/2, 14 June 1986.
36. Schirazi, *Islamic Development Policy*, p. 159.
37. BBC SWB ME/8199/A/14, 5 March 1986.
38. BBC SWB 8205/A/4, 12 March 1986; 0014/A/3, 1 December 1987.
39. BBC SWB 8066/A/4, 26 September 1985; 8225/A/7, 5 April 1986.
40. BBC SWB 8293/A/6, 24 June 1986; 8322/A/6, 28 July 1986.
41. See Prime Minister Musavi's statement BBC SWB ME/8227/A/7, 8 April 1986, and circulars issued regarding the assignment of government personnel BBC SWB 8296/A/3, 27 June 1986; BBC SWB 8297/A/4, 28 June 1986.
42. This was passed on 1 Khordad 1364 (May 1985). See *Edarah-e koll-e ravabet-e omumi-ye sazamn-e omur-e edari va estekhdami-ye keshvar. majmu'ah qavanin va moqararat-e nazer bar karkonan-e dowlat dar ertebat ba jang-e tahmili va hefz-e dastavardha-ye enqelab* (Tehran, 1367 [1988]), p. 46.
43. Order issued 17 Mehr 1364 (October 1985). *Ibid.*, p. 48.
44. Order issued 4 Esfand 1364 (February 1986). *Ibid.*, p. 53.

45. BBC SWB ME/8552/A/12 27, April 1987.
46. Prime Minister Rajai 6617/A/9, 8 January 1981.
47. BBC SWB ME/7214/A/7, 21 December 1982.
48. BBC SWB ME/7257/A/8, 14 February 1983.
49. Montazeri for instance had various accounts earmarked for dona- tions to fronts, religious dues and helping liberation movements. See BBC SWB ME/8115/A/8, 22 November 1985.
50. 'Regime that Rests on Religion', *Financial Times*, 14 February 1986.
51. BBC SWB 7248/A/10, 3 February 1983. A personal donation of $568,000 by Ayatollah Montazeri was publicised in 1984; see BBC SWB 7687/A/7, 5 July 1984..
52. BBC SWB ME/6638/A/3, 2 February 1981.
53. BBC SWB ME/6849/A/6, 9 October 1981.
54. BBC SWB ME/6667/A/5, 7 March 1981.
55. Prime Minister Rajai, BBC SWB ME/6669/A/8, 10 March 1981. BBC SWB ME/6803/A/8, 17 August 1981.
56. BBC SWB ME/7113/A/5, 25 August 1982.
57. BBC SWB ME/7421/A/6, 25 August 1983.
58. BBC SWB ME/7945/A/4, 8 May 1985.
59. BBC SWB ME/7825/A/1, 13 December 1984.
60. Prime Minister Mousavi, BBC SWB ME/7677/A/2, 23 June 1984.
61. Ali Ashtiani, 'The War and the Islamic State Apparatus in Iran', *Khamsin* 12 (September 1984).
62. BBC SWB 8546/A/9, 20 April 1987.
63. Khomeini, *Sahifeh-e Nur*, Volume 12 p. 94, 1 Mehr 1359 (September 1980).
64. BBC SWB ME/6548/A/5, 14 October 1980.
65. Khomeini, *Sahifeh-e Nur*, Volume 14, p. 128–9, 25 Esfand 1359 (March 1981).
66. BBC SWB ME/6696/A/11, 10 April 1981.
67. BBC SWB ME/6588/A/9, 29 November 1980.
68. BBC SWB ME/6718/A/12, 8 May 1981.
69. BBC SWB ME/6726/A/3, 18 May 1981.
70. BBC SWB ME/6744/A/7, 9 June 1981.
71. For a detailed account of the use of the media in the Revolution, see Annabelle Srebreny-Mohammadi and Ali Mohammadi, *Small Media, Big Revolution: Communication, Culture and the Iranian Revo- lution* (Minneapolis: University of Minnesota, 1994), pp. 139–88.
72. BBC SWB ME/7330/A/2, 11 May 1983. Also see Minister of Infor- mation Reyshahri reports BBC SWB 8044/A/6, 31 August 1985; BBC SWB ME/8349/A/5, 28 August 1986.
73. BBC SWB 7874/A/5, 13 February 1985.

74. National Voice of Iran issued warnings against an imminent coup: BBC SWB ME/6342/A/4.
75. BBC SWB ME/6347/A/5, 16 February 1980. See Khamenei BBC SWB ME/6353/A/4, 23 February 1980.
76. For a good detailed analysis of the evolution of the *Pasdaran* and *basij*, see Nikola B. Schahgaldian, *The Iranian Military Under the Islamic Republic* (RAND, March 1987). See also Kenneth Katzman, *The Warriors of Islam: Iran's Revolutionary Guard* (Boulder: Westview Press, 1993).
77. BBC SWB ME/6868/A/11, 31 October 1981.
78. See Nader Entessar, in Amirahmadi and Parvin, *Post-Revolutionary Iran*, p. 66; and Schahgaldian, *Iranian Military*, p. 69.
79. The intelligence unit was later merged with the Ministry of Information established in 1984. BBC SWB ME/7219/A/6, 31 December 1982; ME/7184/A/3, 16 November 1982; ME/7242/A/10, 27 January 1983; allocation of funds ME/7474/A/8, 26 October 1983. While prior to this the defence minister had been responsible for the control, recruitment and deployment of the *Pasdaran*, the establishment of a '*Pasdaran* Ministry' consolidated the development of the two parallel military institutions.
80. Schahgaldian, *The Iranian Military*, pp. 74–5.
81. *Ibid.*, p. 95.
82. Hooshang Naserzadeh, *majmu'ah qavanin-e niruha-ye mosallah-e jomhuri-ye islami-ye Iran* (Tehran: Khorshid, 1372 [1993]), p. 65.
83. BBC SWB 8565/A/7, 12 May 1987.
84. Naserzadeh, *majmu'ah qavanin*.
85. See also Chapter 6.
86. BBC SWB ME/0043/A/7, 8 January 1988.
87. Kamran Mofid, *The Economic Consequences of the Gulf War* (London: Routledge, 1990), p. 34. See also Hooshang Amirahmadi, *Revolution and Economic Transition: The Iranian Experience* (New York: State University of New York Press, 1990). Both authors tend to calculate the economic costs of the war without attributing these to political decisions of the post-revolutionary leaders.
88. Islamic Republic of Iran, Plan and Budget Organisation, *The First 5–year Economic, Social and Cultural Macro Development Plan of the Islamic Republic of Iran, 1362–1366 (1983/4–1987/8)*. Dated 31 Shahrivar 1362 (31 August 1982). For an evaluation, see Kamran Mofid, *Development Planning in Iran: from Monarchy to Islamic Republic* (Wisbech: Middle East and North African Studies Press, 1987), pp. 205–22.
89. BBC SWB/ME/7113/A/1, 25 August 1982.

90. BBC SWB W1368/A1/5, 10 December 1985.
91. For instance, the *majles'*s final amendment to the 1987 budget allocated an additional $3.6bn to the war and increased the foreign exchange allocation from $2bn to $2.8. BBC SWB 8522/A/1, 21 March 1987.
92. See Keith Krause, *Arms and the State* (Cambridge: Cambridge University Press, 1992), pp. 152–81.
93. BBC SWB ME/7690/A/5, 25 May 1985. For a list of ministries with war affairs sections by December 1986, see CIA, Directorate of Intelligence, *Directory of Iranian Officials*.
94. BBC SWB 8414/A/8, 12 November 1986. See also BBC SWB ME/8373/A/5, 25 September 1986 on the development of the defence industry and comments by Minister for Heavy Industries Behzad Nabavi, BBC SWB ME/8658/A/8, 28 August 1987.
95. BBC SWB 7305/A/4, 12 April 1983;d 7289/A/5, 23 May 1983.
96. BBC SWB 7556/A/5, 2 February 1984.
97. BBC SWB ME/6953/A/1, 13 February 1982; 7325/A/4, 6 June 1983.
98. BBC SWB ME/8424/A/6, 24 November 1986.
99. BBC SWB 8181/A/2, 12 February 1986.
100. BBC SWB ME/7733/A/1, 28 August 1984.
101. BBC SWB 7945/A/4, 8 May 1985. See also BBC SWB 7874/A/5, 13 February 1985.
102. The Protection and Development of Iranian Industries Act Official Gazette No.10031, 9 Mordad 1358 in *A Digest of Laws and Regulations Volume II*, tr. Masoudozzafar (Tehran: Pars Associates, 1980), pp. 23–6.
103. Amuzegar estimates an increase in the number of public sector employees from 1.6m in the pre-revolutionary period to 4.7m by 1990/1. See Jahangir Amuzegar, *Iran's Economy under the Islamic Republic* (London: I.B. Tauris, 1993), p. 86.
104. Reza Ghaffari 'The Economic Consequences of Islamic Fundamentalism in Iran', *Capital and Class*, 56 (1995).
105. BBC SWB 6690/A/10, 3 April 1981.
106. BBC SWB 8275/A/2, 3 June 1986 and BBC SWB ME/8343/A/12, 21 August 1986.
107. President Ali Khamenei's speech, BBC SWB 8437/A/8, 9 December 1986.
108. For a comprehensive account of working conditions, managerial practices and workers, see Bayat, *Workers and Revolution*.
109. For a list of these foundations, see CIA, Directorate of Intelligence, *Directory of Iranian Officials*, December 1986 and November 1988. Though state owned, these semi-private corporations are treated as part of the private sector in the macroeconomic accounts of Iran.

110. BBC SWB 7396/A/7, 27 July 1983.
111. BBC SWB ME/8071/A, 2 October 1985.
112. Bonyad-e Shahid, *Ashna'i ba bonyad-e shahid-e enqelab-e eslami* (Tehran: Bonyad-e Shahid, 1365 [1986]).
113. 'Survey of Iran: A Focus on the Bonyad Mostazafin Group of Companies', *Financial Times*, 1 April 1985.
114. International Monetary Fund, *Islamic Republic of Iran: Recent Economic Developments*, p. 46.
115. Reported donation of *bonyad-e mostazafin*, BBC SWB ME/8138/A/4, 19 December 1985. See also Behdad 'Winners and Losers', note 27.
116. 'Regime that Rests on Religion', *Financial Times*, 14 February 1986.
117. *Encyclopaedia Iranica, Volume One*, p. 360.

6. State crisis and change

1. For a similar classification of views of the post-war period, see Henner Fürtig, *Liberalisierung als Herausforderung: wie stabil ist die Islamische Republik Iran?* (Berlin: Verl.Das Arabishe Buch, 1996), p. 5.
2. Fariba Adelkhah, Jean-Francois Bayart and Olivier Roy, *Thermidor en Iran* (Bruxelles: Espace, 1993); Anoushirevan Ehteshami, *After Khomeini: The Iranian Second Republic* (London: Routledge, 1995); Jahangir Amuzegar, *Iran's Economy under the Islamic Republic* (London: I.B. Tauris, 1993).
3. Ray Takeyh, 'Iran at a Crossroads', *Middle East Journal*, 57:1 (Winter 2003), pp. 42–56.
4. Kenneth Pollack and R. Takeyh, 'Taking on Tehran', *Foreign Affairs* (March/April 2005), pp. 20–34.
5. For examples of explanation of the shift in factional terms, see Sussan Siavoshi, 'Factionalism and Iranian Politics: The Post-Khomeini Experience', *Iranian Studies*, 25:3&4 (1992), pp. 27–50; Ali Banuazizi, 'Political Factionalism and Societal Resistance', *Middle East Report*, 24:6 (1994), pp. 2–8; Hossein Seifzadeh, 'The Landscape of Factional Politics and its future in Iran', *Middle East Journal*, 57:1 (2003).
6. Yassaman Saadatmand, 'State Capitalism: Theory and Application Case of Iran', *Critique* (Fall 1993), p. 59.
7. Fred Block, 'The Ruling Class Does Not Rule: Notes on the Marxist Theory of the State', *Socialist Review*, 33 (May–June 1977), pp. 6–28
8. The argument that under emergency conditions such as war, 'state managers have the opportunity to expand their own power' has been made by Block, *Ibid.*

9. *Ibid.*, p. 34.
10. *Ibid.*, p. 37.
11. *Ibid.*
12. Awareness of this is indicated by Rafsanjani's weekly lessons in economics. See *Financial Times*, 'Survey of Iran: Keen to Leave the Cold', 8 February 1993.
13. On the notion of an Islamic economics, see Hamid Hosseini, 'From Homo Economicus to Homo Islamicus: The Universality of Economic Science Reconsidered' in Cyrus Bina and Hamid Zangeneh (eds) *Modern Capitalism and Islamic Ideology in Iran* (London: Macmillan, 1992).
14. Block, 'The Ruling Class Does not Rule', p. 36.
15. Karshenas and Pesaran contrast the 'managed war economy' with centrally planned ones of Eastern Europe. 'Economic Reform and the Reconstruction of the Iranian Economy', *Middle East Journal*, 49:1 (1995), p. 97.
16. See also Saadatmand, 'State Capitalism', p. 75.
17. Firouzeh Khalatbari, 'The Tehran Stock Exchange and Privatisation of Public Enterprises in Iran' in Coville, *l'Economie de l'Iran Islamique* (Tehran: Institut Francais de Recherche en Iran, 1994), p. 186.
18. See Foreign Minister Velayati's lecture at a seminar on international affairs indicating the need to assimilate international events quickly and draw necessary conclusions and strategies. BBC SWB ME/665/A/2, 18 January 1990.
19. Michel Camedessus, president of the International Monetary Institute, warned of the risk of 'more marginalisation of countries that fail to integrate themselves into the global economy', *Financial Times*, 8 March 1995.
20. See speech by President Rafsanjani, BBC SWB ME/778/A/6, 31 May 1990.
21. Block, 'The Ruling Class Does Not Rule', pp. 40–1.
22. Saadatmand, 'State Capitalism', p. 71.
23. Sohrab Behdad, 'Production and Employment in Iran: Involution and Deindustrialisation Theses' in Thierry Coville, *L'Economie de l'Iran*, p. 107.
24. See for example the editorial in *Jomhuri-ye Islami*, organ of the IRP, calling for 'immediate measures' by the government, BBC SWB ME/8048/A/5, 5 September 1985.
25. BBC SWB ME/8058/A/3, 17 September 1985. The employment of absentee conscripts was made an imprisonable offence in 1986. BBC SWB ME/8156/A/10, 14 January 1986. The population was

further called upon to report such cases to the Revolutionary Guard or the Basij, BBC SWB ME/8326/A/6, 1 August 1986.

26. Examples of various bomb incidents that were reported by the media can be found on BBC SWB ME/8012/A/3, 25 July 1985; BBC SWB ME/8031/A/7, 16 August 1985(Radio Iran); BBC SWB ME/8054/A/6, 12 September 1985; BBC SWB ME/8056/A/4, 14 September 1985; BBC SWB ME/8061/A/11, 20 September 1985; BBC SWB ME/8108/A/2, 8 November 1985; BBC SWB ME/8131/A/4, 11 December 1985; BBC SWB ME/8187/A/5, 19 February 1986; BBC SWB ME/8256/A/7, 12 May 1986. Mourning ceremonies after the death of Shariatmadari became protests against the regime (reported by Radio Iran and Voice of the Liberation of Iran BBC SWB ME/8227/A/10, 8 April 1986; also BBC SWB ME/8232/A/,7 14 April 1986). Anti-war demonstration in Shiraz (Free Voice of Iran BBC SWB ME/8327/A/3, 2 August 1986. Demonstrations in Tehran, Tabriz, Mashad, Hamadan in April 1987.

27. For the doctor's strike incident, see BBC SWB ME/8321/A/12, 26 July 1986.

28. M. Hashem Pesaran, 'The Iranian Foreign Exchange policy and the Black Market for Dollars', *International Journal of Middle East Studies*, 24 (1992), pp. 101–25.

29. *Middle East Economic Digest*, 13 January 1995. See also Eliyahu Kanovsky, *Iran's Economic Morass* (Washington: Institute for Near East Policy, 1997).

30. See Behdad, 'Winners and Losers of the Iranian Revolution', *International Journal of Middle East Studies*, 21 (1989); Wolfgang Lautenschlager, 'The Effects an Overvalued Exchange Rate on the Iranian Economy: 1979–1984', *International Journal of Middle Eastern Studies*, 18 (1986).

31. 'Food Shortages Cool Iran's Revolutionary Ardour', *Financial Times*, 10 March 1982.

32. On the benefits to the merchants and the profits of merchant capital, see Reza Ghaffari 'The Economic Consequences of Islamic Fundamentalism in Iran', *Capital and Class*, 56 (1995).

33. For taxation figures, see 'Government Tax Revenues' in Islamic Republic of Iran, Central Bank, *Economic Report and Balance Sheet*, various years.

34. 'High Taxation Proves Minefield', *Financial Times*, 1 April 1985.

35. For government trade policy and indications of various pressures and contradictions, see BBC SWB ME/Weekly Economic Report W1298/A1/2, 31 July 1984.

36. Hiro, *Iran under the Ayatollahs*, p. 206; Bakhash, *Reign of the Ayatollahs*, pp. 230–1.

37. See 'Iran's Trade shows shift to Soviet bloc', *Financial Times*, 10 March 1982.
38. These companies included SIRIP, IMICO, OGOKO, Espanola and Tetrophon (Belgium). See BBC SWB W1196/A1/2, 3 August 1982; BBC SWB W1245/A1/3 19 July 1983.
39. 'Fragile Iran's Oil Bonanza Comes Under Threat', *Financial Times*, 28 January 1983.
40. 'US Resumes Purchases of Crude Oil from Iran', *Financial Times*, 27 April 1982.
41. 'Brazil Drops Iraq in Favour of Iran', *Financial Times*, 17 May 1983.
42. 'Iran's Economy: Bathing in Oil Keeps it in Shape', *The Economist*, 8 September 1984.
43. In 1985 an estimated $300 million/month of revenue was earmarked for the war, rising to $500 million during a military offensive. See 'Survey of Iran', *Financial Times*, 1 April 1985.
44. Mofid, *Economic Consequences of the Gulf War*, p. 124.
45. Amuzegar, *Iran's Economy*, pp. 234–5.
46. See Musavi and Rafsanjani's respective comments in BBC SWB ME/8572/A/7, 27 March 1987; BBC SWB ME/8547/A/6, 21 April 1987.
47. BBC SWB ME/8494/A/5, 17 February 1987.
48. See respectively Homa Omid, *Islam and the Post-revolutionary State in Iran* (New York: St Martin's, 1994), pp. 143–4, and Oliver Roy, *Failure of Political Islam*, p. 15.
49. *Echo of Islam*, Jul/Aug 1988; See also Ramazani, 'Iran's Resistance', p. 51.

7. Reform and reaction 1990–2005

1. 'The highest strategic aim of the I.R.Iran', *Echo of Islam* (October 1992), p. 10. Emphasis added.
2. Rainer Hermann, 'Von der Wirtschafts- zur Legitimationskrise: Die Ära Khamenei/Rafsanjani in der Islamischen Republik Iran', *Orient*, 35:4 (1994), pp. 541–64. Hermann identifies three ideological tendencies or factions (*Strömungen*) one of which is that of the 'left revolutionary theologians'.
3. BBC SWB ME/1539/A/6, 16 November 1992. Jannati's Friday prayer sermon.
4. BBC SWB ME/2379/MED/1, 2 June 1995.
5. Khamenei, BBC SWB ME/967/A/17, 11 January 1991.
6. BBC SWB ME/680/A/1, 5 February 1990.
7. Ehteshami, *After Khomeini*, pp. 100–25. See also Amuzegar, *Iran's Economy*; Karshenas and Pesaran, 'Economic Reform'; Ghasimi, 'The

Iranian Economy after the Revolution', *International Journal of Middle East Studies*, 24, pp. 599–614 (1992) for various appraisals of the plan.

8. International Monetary Fund (IMF), *Islamic Republic of Iran.*

9. Anoushiravan Ehteshami, 'Iran's International Posture after the Fall of Baghdad', *Middle East Journal*, 58:2 (Spring 2004).

10. Abbas Maleki, 'Myth and Reality of the New World Order: Challenges to Iranian Foreign Policy', *Iranian Journal of International Affairs*, 5:2 (Summer 1993).

11. *Islamic Republic News Agency*, 3 March 1993.

12. Morteza Sarmadi, 'Foreign Policy of the Islamic Republic of Iran in the Asian Region', *Pakistan Horizon*, 49:2 (April 1996), pp. 19–22.

13. The Economic Cooperation Organization (ECO), is an intergovernmental regional organization established in 1985 by Iran, Pakistan and Turkey for the purpose of promoting economic, technical and cultural co-operation among the Member States

14. *Iran News*, 11 January 1995.

15. IMF, *Islamic Republic of Iran*, pp. 16–17.

16. Article 81 of the Constitution reads: 'the granting of any concessions and privileges to foreigners for establishing companies and institutions in the field of trade, industry, agriculture, mines and services is absolutely prohibited.'

17. Velayati and Nourbakhsh at International Conference in Isfahan. See 'Iran Calls for Technical Help with Oil Industry', *Financial Times*, 28 May 1991.

18. 'Iran Seeks More Economic Co-operation', *Financial Times*, 30 May 1991; 'West Scrambles for Share of Iranian Market', *Financial Times*, 4 December 1991.

19. *Islamic Republic News Agency*, 20 May 1993.

20. *Iran News*, 27 November 1994.

21. See the articles by Roshandel, Rouleau and Hooglund in Eric Hooglund (ed.) *Twenty Years of Islamic Revolution: Political and Social Transition in Iran since 1979* (Syracruse, 2002).

22. For the lessons learnt from the war, see Shahram Chubin, *Iran's National Security Policy: Capabilities, Intentions and Impact* (Washington: Carnegie, 1994) especially pp. 17–28. For details of policies in the region, see R.K. Ramazani, 'Iran's Foreign Policy: Both North and South', *Middle East Journal*, 46:3 (Summer 1992), pp. 393–412; John Calabrese, *Revolutionary Horizons* (London, St Martins, 1994), pp. 45–74.

23. See speech by Ayatullah Emami-Kashani, BBC SWB ME/1058/A/10, 29 April 1991.

24. See Shaul Bakhash, 'Iranian Politics since the Gulf War' in Robert

B. Satloff (ed) *The Politics of Change in the Middle East* (Boulder: Westview, 1993), pp. 63–84.

25. BBC SWB ME/1019/A/5, 13 March 1991. See also SAIRI statements BBC SWB ME/411/A/4, 17 March 1989 and BBC SWB ME/521/A/3, 29 July 1989.

26. A number of religious leaders called for such assistance at this point. Ayatollah Meshkini Friday Qom BBC SWB ME/1029/A/14, 25 March 1991. See Ayatollah Meshkini's Friday Prayer sermon in Qom BBC SWB ME/1023/A/18, 18 March 1991. Ayatollah Khamenei's calls for the Iraqi nation to 'finish the job' which it had started', BBC SWB ME/1040/A/14, 8 April 1991. For the limited nature of this assistance, see Bakhash, 'Iranian Politics Since the Gulf War' in Satloff, *Politics of Change*, p. 65.

27. See also Adam Tarock, 'Iran's Foreign Policy Since the Gulf War', *Australian Journal of International Affairs*, 48:2 (November 1994), pp. 267–81.

28. See address by Ali Akbar Hashemi-Rafsanjani, President of the Islamic Republic of Iran, tr. J.Goodarzi, *Middle East Journal*, 44:3 (Summer 1990), pp. 459–66. See also for example Mousavi Ardebili, BBC SWB ME/1076/A/5, 20 May 1991, Friday prayers.

29. See Rafsanjani's speech in BBC SWB ME/1124/A/7, 15 July 1991.

30. Alireza Moayeri, Presidential Advisor on Iran's foreign policy issues, *Islamic Republic News Agency*, 3 March 1993.

31. Gary Sick, 'The United States and Iran: Truth and Consequences', *Contention*, 5:2 (Winter 1996), pp. 59–78, p. 61.

32. 'Iran after Khomeini: US and Britain Put Pressure on Khamenei', *Financial Times*, 6 June 1989.

33. See *Financial Times*, 23 February 1990, p. 4.

34. 'US–Iran Relations Ease after Further Hostage Release', *Financial Times*, 1 May 1990.

35. See for example the pro-government Egyptian daily *Al Akhbar*, "Iran: From Revolution to Statehood", 8 December 1997.

36. On this latter point, see Ayatollah Yazdi's comments, in the context of the issue of *marja'iyyat*, on the necessary payment of taxes to the 'guardian jurisconsult'; BBC SWB ME/2176/MED/2, 12 December 1994. For details of the role of *bonyads,* see Chapter 5.

37. BBC SWB 1878/MED/4, 22 December 1993.

38. See for example the rejection of the bill on Free Trade Zones (*Financial Times*), BBC SWB ME/1728/A/5, 30 June 1993.

39. Ayatollah Jannati's comments, BBC SWB/ME 1377/A/8, 11 May 1992.

40. Calabrese, *Revolutionary Horizons*, p. 25.

41. Magnus Ranstorp, 'Hizbollah's Command Leadership: Its Structure, Decision-Making and Relationship with Iranian Clergy and Institutions', *Terrorism and Political Violence*, 6:3 (Autumn 1994), pp. 303–39.

42. For an analysis of this election and campaign, see Farzin Sarabi, 'The Post-Khomeini Era in Iran: The Elections of the Fourth Islamic Majlis', *Middle East Journal*, 48:1 (Winter 1994), pp. 89–107. See also Hermann, 'Von der Wirtschafts- zur Legitimationskrise'.

43. 'Iranian MPs crack whip at Rafsanjani', *Financial Times*, 17 August 1993.

44. For a comprehensive analysis of the economy and sectoral trends of the Islamic Republic, see Amuzegar, *Iran's Economy*.

45. International Monetary Fund (IMF), *Islamic Republic of Iran*, pp. 15–16. Non-governmental estimates of inflation have been up to double the figures quoted.

46. Economist Intelligence Unit, *Country Report 'Iran'* (Second Quarter 1994), p. 18.

47. IMF, *Islamic Republic of Iran* (1995).

48. On the impact of the removal of the subsidies on the poor, see Karshenas and Pesaran, 'Economic Reform'.

49. *The Economist*, 19 January 2003.

50. According to census data, of the total population of 60 million in 1996/7 over 23 million were under 14 years of age. See IMF, *Islamic Republic of Iran* (1998), Table 21

51. 'Protests Breaking Out in Iran's Cities', *Financial Times*, 23 February 1990; 'Iran's Revolution Stuck in Neutral', *Financial Times*, 5 June 1990.

52. BBC SWB ME/1221/A/3, 5 November 1991; BBC SWB ME/1401/A/2, 8 June 1992.

53. BBC SWB 1221/A/3, 5 November 1991; BBC SWB 1400/A/1, 6 June 1992.

54. BBC SWB 1913/MED/4, 4 February 1994; Transport workers strike in Shiraz, BBC SWB 1968/MED/10, 11 April 1994; Clashes in Qazvin, BBC SWB 2066/MED/11, 5 August 1994; BBC SWB 2067/MED/8, 6 August 1994; demonstration in Tabriz, BBC SWB 2094/MED/6, 7 September 1994; unrest in Mahabad BBC SWB 2213/MED/10, 28 January 1995; Unrest in Elsamshahr, BBC SWB 2270/MED/9, 5 April 1995.

55. For an analysis of Iran's factions in this period and their division into the 'traditional right', 'modern right' and 'religious left' see Wilfried Buchta, 'Irans fraktionierte Führungselite und die fünften iranischen Parlamentswahlen', *KAS Auslands-Informationen*, 8 (1996), pp. 50–78.

56. *Islamic Republic News Agency*, 20 March 1993.
57. *Iran News*, 27 October 1994.
58. BBC SWB ME/1405/A/3, 12 June 1992; SWB ME/1407/A/10, 15 June 1992.
59. BBC SWB ME/1412/A/7, 20 June 1992; SWB ME/1420/A/6, 30 June 1992.
60. BBC SWB 2206/MED/1, 20 January 1995.
61. BBC SWB 2134/MED/17, 24 October 1994.
62. Khamenei referred to this as a decadent lifestyle of 'prostitution lust and hedonism', BBC SWB 1972/MED/11, 15 April 1994.
63. BBC SWB 2194/MED/1, 6 January 1995, for passing of bill by *majles*; Emami-Kashani BBC SWB 2202/MED/4, 16 January 1995.

8. Revolutionary foreign policy and international tension

1. Quoted in 'Imam and the foreign policy of the Islamic government', *Echo of Islam*, 1990, Year 9, No.86, p. 28.
2. Khamenei's speech, BBC SWB ME/543/A/1, 24 August 1989 and BBC SWB ME/588/A/2 ,16 October 1989; Yazdi Deputy Foreign Minister, Larijani quoted in *Echo of Islam*, May 1989, No.70, p. 8.
3. Khamenei's speech 562/A/1, 15 September 1989.
4. For Foreign Ministry statement, see BBC SWB ME/605/A/2, 4 November 1989; Khamenei 604/A/1, 3 November 1989; See also Jannati for confirmation of the priority given to the struggle against America, BBC SWB ME/604/A/3, 3 November 1989.
5. Association of Combatant Clerics statement BBC SWB ME/546/A/4, 28 August 1989.
6. Ahmad Khomeini, BBC SWB ME/1055/A/6, 25 April 1991 and Khamenei, BBC SWB ME/1062/A/9, 3 May 1991.
7. BBC SWB ME/618/A/2, 20 November 1989.
8. BBC SWB ME/650/A/4, 30 December 1989.
9. BBC SWB ME/674/A/1, 29 January 1990.
10. BBC SWB ME/1181/A/3, 19 September 1991.
11. Ayatollah Yazdi referred to the 'Global Islamic revival' in his Friday prayer sermon, BBC SWB/793/A/5, 18 June 1990.
12. BBC SWB ME/1399/A/1, 5 June 1992.
13. BBC SWB ME/1295/A/5, 4 February 1992.
14. Rafsanjani in BBC SWB ME/1643/A/5, 22 March 1993. See also BBC SWB ME/615/A/3, 16 November 1989; BBC SWB ME/1269/A/3, 4 January 1992; Khamenei praises the Islamic movement in Algeria, BBC SWB ME/1113/A/6, 2 July 1991. Also Rafsanjani BBC SWB ME/792/A/4, 16 June 1990; Velayati, BBC SWB ME/990/A/20, 7 February 1991.

15. Huntington, *Clash of Civilisations*.
16. Rafsanjani addressing cultural attaches, BBC SWB ME/1057/A/6, 27 April 1991.
17. See schedule of broadcasts, *Echo of Islam*, 134, August 1995 (Appendix VIII).
18. See broadcasting schedule, Islamic Republic Broadcasting, November to May, *Mahjubah*, Vol.17, No.3, March 1998, p. 52.
19. See Farhang Jahanpoor, *Directory of Iranian Officials* (Caversham: BBC Monitoring, 1992). This organisation, also headed by Ahmad Jannati, was supervised by a deputy chief, Hojjatoleslam Mohammad Ali Taskhiri.
20. See BBC SWB ME/983/A/18, 30 January 1991; BBC SWB ME/1416/A/3, 25 June 1992 for details of propaganda activities.
21. See 'Annual Subscription Rate of International Magazines of Islamic Thought Foundation' in *Echo of Islam*, October 1996, No.148. (Appendix IX).
22. See Jahanpoor, *Directory*. The earliest information about these sections dates from January to February 1990.
23. See Rafsanjani's comments regarding Hajj, BBC SWB ME/1079/A/6, 23 May 1991. See Khamenei's instructions following appointment of Hojjatoleslam Reyshahri to lead the Iranian pilgrims, BBC SWB ME/1058/A/8, 29 April 1991.
24. *Payam-e rahbar-e mo'azam-e enqelab* 1372 h (Tehran: IPO, 1993) This message was distributed to pilgrims in Farsi, Arabic, Urdu, English and French.
25. BBC SWB ME/648/A/2, 28 December 1989, Rafsanjani and Khamenei to Sunni leaders.
26. Olivier Roy, *The Failure of Political Islam*, translated by Carol Volk (Cambridge, Mass: Harvard, 1994), p. 184.
27. See Jahanpoor, *Directory*. For detailed exposition of these organisations, their activities, resources and structures, see Buchta, *Die Iranische Schia*.
28. This is denoted by Jahanpour as Council for the Unification of Islamic Denominations and appears under the Assembly for Inter-Islamic Understanding entry.
29. BBC SWB ME/A/4, 24 September 1991.
30. Examples of calls for papers are for the Seventh International Islamic Unity Conference held in Tehran in August 1994 in *Echo of Islam*, June 1994 and call for papers for Ahl al-Bayt World Assembly Fifth Conference in *Echo of Islam*, November 1995 (Appendix X).
31. See the proposed plans of this office in 'Second meeting of General

Assembly of Ahl-ul Bayt' in the women's publication, *Mahjubah*, 17:3, March 1998, pp. 53–4.

32. Rafsanjani, BBC SWB ME/1643/A/5, 22 March 1993.

33. Rafsanjani, BBC SWB ME/453/A/1, 8 May 1989.

34. BBC SWB ME/739/A/3, 16 April 1990.

35. See Richard H. Schultz Jr. 'Iranian Covert Aggression: Support for Radical Political Islamists Conducting Internal Subversion Against States in the Middle East/Southwest Asia Region', *Terrorism and Political Violence*, 6:3 (Autumn 1994), pp. 281–302.

36. See Velayati, BBC SWB ME/790/A/5, 14 June 1990. See also BBC SWB ME/546/A/5, 28 August 1989; BBC SWB ME/788/A/5, 12 June 1990. Rafsanjani's BBC SWB ME/897/A/8, 17 October 1990; declaration by Mohsen Rezai, Commander-in-Chief of IRGC, expressing readiness for jihad alongside Palestinians, BBC SWB ME/897/A/8, 17 October 1990; Khamenei's reiteration of 'helping the people and combatants of Palestine as a religious duty', BBC SWB ME/1025/A/8, 20 March 1991. See also Velayati, BBC SWB ME/1033/A/9, 29 March 1991.

37. BBC SWB ME/908/A/10, 30 October 1990. In January 1991 2 billion rial credit and $20m were put at the disposal of this committee for the support of the 'Islamic Revolution of Palestine', BBC SWB ME/983/A/18, 30 January 1991.

38. See 'Landmark Conference on Palestine', *Echo of Islam*, December 1991, pp. 19–21.

39. BBC News Report, 24 April 2001.

40. BBC SWB ME/1685/A/4, 11 May 1991. For the detailed discussions of this seminar, see Daftar-e motale'at-e siyasi, *majmu'eh maqalat-e seminar-e afriqa* [Collection of Papers of the Seminar on Africa] (Tehran, 1372).

41. See Gambian foreign minister's visit, BBC SWB ME/1045/A/12, 13 April 1991; relations with Nigeria, BBC SWB 1055/A/4, 25 April 1991; with Sierra Leone, BBC SWB ME 1056/A/8, 26 April 1991; Mozambique, BBC SWB ME/1114/A/4, 3 July 1991; Senegal, BBC SWB ME/1134/A/8, 26 July 1991.

42. See Peter Woodward, 'Islam in Sudan' in Esposito, *Political Islam*, p. 111.

43. BBC SWB ME/1259/A/2, 19 December 1991, on Rafsanjani's visit. For Iran's involvement in Sudan, see also Mohammad-Reza Djalili, 'Iran: vers un nouveau rôle régional?', *Problèmes politiques et sociaux*, No.720 (Geneve: Institut universitaire de haute études internationale, 1994), p. 36; Samuel M. Makinda, 'Iran, Sudan and Islam', *The World Today* (June 1993), pp. 108–11.

44. BBC SWB ME/1419/A/7, 29 June 1992.

45. BBC SWB 1847/MED/1, 16 November 1993.

46. See Rasul B. Rais, 'Afghanistan and Regional Security after the Cold War', *Problems of Communism*, May–June 1992, pp. 82–94; Hafizullah Emadi, 'Exporting Iran's Revolution: The Radicalisation of the Shiite Movement in Afghanistan', *Middle Eastern Studies*, 31:1, January 1995, pp. 1–12.

47. 'Holy War within Afghanistan's Battlefields', *Financial Times*, 7 June 1989. Shi'i groups in Afghanistan: *Shuraye ettefaq-e Islami, Harekat-e Eslami, Sazman-e Mujahedin-e Mostazafin, Sazamn-e Al-nasr, Sepah-e Pasdaran, Hizballah, Hizb-e Wahdat.* See Hafizullah Emadi, 'Exporting Iran's Revolution: The Radicalisation of the Shiite Movement in Afghanistan', *Middle Eastern Studies*, 31:1, January 1995, pp. 1–12. On the various shi'ite groups in Afghanistan, see Asta Olesen, *Islam and Politics in Afghanistan* (Richmond: Curzon, 1995), pp. 291–2.

48. 'Afghan Shi'i Conference Opens with Messages from Rafsanjani and Velayati', BBC SWB, 16 March 1990.

49. Zalmay Khalilzad, 'Anarchy in Afghanistan', *Journal of International Affairs*, 51:1, Summer 1997, pp. 37–56.

50. Anthony Cordesman, *Iran and Iraq: The Threat from the Northern Gulf* (Boulder: Westview, 1994), p. 34.

51. US Library of Congress, Congressional Research Service, Brief 92-620-F 1992-13:0328.

52. See Appendix VII. SIPRI, Military Expenditure Database, *Iran, Military expenditure 1988–97.*

53. For details of these programmes, see Chubin, *Iran's National Security Policy*, pp. 17–28.

54. See BBC SWB ME/1560/A/3, 10 December 1992; BBC SWB ME/1653/A/9, 2 April 1992; BBC SWB ME/1728/A/6, 30 June 1993; BBC SWB ME/1974/MED/12, 18 April 1994;.

55. BBC News Report, Monday 22 September 2003.

56. See US Congress Joint Committee Print. Country Reports on Human Rights Practices for 1990. Report Submitted to the Committee on Foreign Affairs, House of Representatives, Committee on Foreign Relations, Senate by the Department of State (Washington: GPO, 1990), p. 1400. See also US Library of Congress, Congressional Research Service, 'US–Iran Relations following the Death of Ayatollah Khomeini', 1990–9:0001.

57. Sick, 'United States and Iran', pp. 59–78.

58. US Library of Congress, Congressional Research Service, Issue Brief Number 92076, October 5, 1992.

59. Geoffrey Kemp, *Forever Enemies*, p. 3.
60. Sick, 'United States and Iran', pp. 59–78. p. 66.
61. Kemp, *Forever Enemies*, p. 3.
62. Statement by Peter Tarnoff, Under Secretary of State for Political Affairs before the House International Relations Committee, Washington D.C., November 9, 1995, United States Information Agency.
63. United States Executive Order 12959 (60 Fed. Reg. 24757, May 9, 1995), United States Information Agency (Appendix VI).
64. Some of the differences between Washington and European counterparts with respect to policy regarding Iran are mentioned in Olivier Roy, 'Faut-il diaboliser l'Iran?', *Politique Internationale*, 78 (1997/8).
65. Statement before the House International Relations Committee, Subcommittee on International Economic Policy and Trade, Washington D.C., May 2, 1995, United States Information Agency.
66. Statement by Peter Tarnoff, Under Secretary of State for Political Affairs, before the House International Relations Committee, Washington D.C., November 9, 1995, United States Information Agency.
67. 'Europe shuns US action against Iran', *Financial Times*, 3 May 1995; 'EU seeks improved relations with Iran', *Financial Times*, 23 June 1995.
68. 'Iran in No Position to Fill Oil Supply Gap: The Struggle to Rebuild a War-damaged Industry', *Financial Times*, 30 August 1990.
69. *Financial Times*, 4 December 1991.
70. 'Tokyo Tries to Defend Policy towards Iran', *Financial Times*, 3 May 1994.
71. US Library of Congress, Congressional Research Service, Issue Brief Number 92076, October 5, 1992.
72. See Fred Halliday, 'An Elusive Normalisation: Western Europe and the Iranian Revolution', *Middle East Journal*, 48:2, Spring 1994, pp. 309–26.
73. US State Department, Opening Statement before the House International Relations Committee, March 8, 2006.

9. Conclusion

1. Halliday, *Rethinking International Relations*, p. 138.

Index